*One Act*

# One Act

### Eleven Short Plays
### of the Modern Theatre

---

### Edited by Samuel Moon

Grove Press, Inc.   New York

First Black Cat Edition 1965
17    16    15    14
ISBN: 0-394-17105-5
Grove Press ISBN: 0-8021-4144-7
Library of Congress Catalog Card Number:

Manufactured in the United States of America

Distributed by Random House, Inc., New York

GROVE PRESS, INC., 196 West Houston Street, New York, N.Y. 10014

# CONTENTS

# Introduction

The vigor and intensity promised by a good one-act have always excited my anticipation as I have watched the curtain rise on a new one or turned its pages for the first time. This vigor comes partly from the demands of the one-act form itself for economy of means and narrowness of focus, but it does not come automatically. If the focus is narrow, it must also be deep; the playwright must have something real to say—something human and at the same time personal. If he has, his short play will be strong from the sense of big things under pressure. This feeling of power confined I cannot resist in a one-act, and the hope of finding it dies hard. The plays in this book are here because they have richly rewarded that hope. I have found them all to be narrow, deep, and strong.

None of these plays exhibit the groping of immature writers or the mechanical writing necessitated by arbitrary limitations on casting, subject matter, and seriousness of purpose. With two exceptions, they come from men who had already achieved great stature as dramatists when they wrote them. One of these exceptions, Thornton Wilder's *Pullman Car Hiawatha*, though it antedates *Our Town* and *The Skin of Our Teeth*, was written by an already accomplished novelist. The other, Tennessee Williams' *27 Wagons Full of Cotton*, like his early work in general, seems to me superior to his more recent plays. *27 Wagons* is much stronger than *Baby Doll*, the film Williams later based upon it. The bawdy joke that provides the framework of the action in both the play and the film is transformed in *27 Wagons* into an absorbing glimpse of human greed, cruelty, and depravity, for the joke is conceived by Vicarro, and we see it as a product of his sense of humor, a part of his character. But in *Baby Doll* the joke is not transformed; it is the point of the film, and we are asked to share it with Vicarro. Williams in his one-act illustrates what all the others in this book have found in the one-act form—a personal way to show some human truth.

The one-act is extremely flexible and rich in potentialities; it is an art form precisely because it enables an extremely sensitive and complex expression of human variety. If my first hope for this book is that it will demonstrate the depth and power of the one-act, my second is that the variety of the plays will show how variously the concept of "the one-act play" may be filled out and stretched.

In length, for example, the one-act is something less than a full evening's theatre, but these plays range from a few minutes' playing time to over an hour, as in *Miss Julie* or *A Memory of Two Mondays*—and not necessarily to the disadvantage of the shorter plays, for Yeats has superbly condensed the entire tragic action of *Purgatory* into seven pages of verse.

There is no closet drama, no radio or television drama included here; all the plays combine the language of dialogue with the living action of the theatre. Yet they represent a variety of styles ranging from the verse of Yeats and MacLeish, who do almost everything with words, setting their own stage as Shakespeare did, to the extremely visual theatre style of Ionesco. Yeats raises language to the full height of its power; Ionesco dramatizes the collapse of language, exercising his keen visual imagination, using the spectacle of the theatre with brilliant simplicity and originality.

Anouilh's *Cecile* may seem at first glance to be little more than a delightful exercise in style—the style of a Molière farce. But although Anouilh's dark view of reality is least apparent in his *pièces brillantes,* of which this is an example, it is nevertheless still there, inconspicuous below the surface, but lending a deepening shadow to the play. Its wit and comedy are not mere froth; they are the laughter that covers a darkness. Cecile will marry a young fool without money; Araminthe, a girl of real intelligence and beauty, must support herself as governess and will marry another fool for his modest income. Fools and puppy lovers are always funny, but Araminthe is a real woman with a real problem. We laugh at the others, but we laugh with her. Her wit is her courage, and she wears it lightly, while the play lasts.

There are plays here that stretch the typical dramatic structure of the one-act. The action of a "well-made" one-act moves without interruption to a single climax, in contrast to the climactic movement within each act of a longer play. For this reason, some would prefer to call *Miss Julie* a two-act play. Yet Strindberg explicitly wished to avoid the interruption of attention and the violation of a naturalistic unity of time caused by a curtain break into two acts. In *A Memory of Two Mondays*, Arthur Miller has similarly bridged the two separate phases of his action with a lyrical passage, and Anouilh's *Cecile* sharply divides into two actions, each with its own climactic movement.

In *The Man With the Flower in His Mouth*, Pirandello wrote a one-act whose structure will be very familiar to readers of the modern short story. He does not lead us through the beginning, middle, and end of a conflict, but is intent on defining the conflict only. His focus is on the immediate inner struggle of his "man with the flower in his mouth." This character is a familiar Pirandello figure: his strength is in his subtle intellectual imagination, in his effort to endure the knowledge of his imminent death by projecting himself into the roles or "masks" of others; but this effort is painfully disrupted by his awareness of his wife hovering in the background, sympathetically assuming his role, his suffering, wanting to share it with him.

Many of the plays included here, though not all, are moving and strong chiefly because of the impact of their characters. Saroyan's *Hello Out There* is so swiftly powerful, I think, because the Young Man is absolutely spontaneous, gentle, and free in spirit; when the mob arrive, their hypocrisy and violence are doubly outrageous by contrast. O'Casey is another whose characters are superbly alive. In *Bedtime Story*, he drops the lusty gusty Angela into a world of hypocritical respectability, and she sweeps through its moralizing, poeticizing, and playing at lovemaking like proud life itself, leaving it in utter confusion. What a bloodless game Schnitzler's Anatol pursues when we see it from the perspective of this "Anatol burlesque"!

Thornton Wilder stretches the possibilities of the one-act

in *Pullman Car Hiawatha* by his innovations in staging and by his remarkable achievement in the logical development of an abstract theme. Wilder himself has said that his Stage Manager is a "hang-over from a novelist technique," representing the omniscient author's point of view, but Wilder seems in this play rather less a novelist than an essayist, or perhaps, as Francis Fergusson has said, an allegorist. He neither pursues a plot nor explores character, but peoples his stage with figures representing the towns and fields, the hours and planets, and the kaleidoscope of individuals that surround this pullman car and its dying woman. Together they make a harmony to which the woman belongs, and it is this religious idea above all that Wilder seeks to display.

Archibald MacLeish's play, *This Music Crept by Me Upon the Waters*, like *Pullman Car Hiawatha*, is at the "frontier of drama" in Miss Ellis-Fermor's sense, because it attempts to dramatize what is essentially non-dramatic, a religious, mystical experience. MacLeish is concerned here, as he has frequently been, with man's alienation from nature. This Caribbean island, like Prospero's enchanted isle, is a paradise for those who can find it—the natives, and at this moment of moonrise, some of the whites, especially Elizabeth and Peter. They experience an awakening into the absolute present, a feeling of harmony with the natural process that is without thought or knowledge, but they are called back from their glimpse of the timeless moment by their human distractions and responsibilities. Oliver, Chuck, and Keogh, on the other hand, all in their own way, live in the world of history and the future, remember and wait, unable to bear the vacancy of idleness, and find that "Happiness is difficult." Much of the power of *This Music* lies in the honest complexity of the two views it brings into conflict, in the striking theatricality of its successive and contrasting moods of waiting, fulfillment, confusion, peace, and alarm. These and the power of its poetry succeed in embodying an extremely elusive idea.

A favorite device in the drama of ideas for developing the full range of variations on a theme is a large and various cast of characters. In *Pullman Car Hiawatha* the characters are very briefly sketched; in *This Music Crept by Me Upon the Waters* they are somewhat more fully drawn. In *A Memory of Two Mondays*, Arthur Miller gives us a cross-section of the people trapped in the paralyzing routine of unskilled labor in a warehouse, and one boy who is not caught in its paralysis but leaves it for something better. His purpose, like that of MacLeish and Wilder, is primarily to explore an idea. "I hoped to define for myself the value of hope," Miller writes of the play, "why it must arise, as well as the heroism of those who know, at least, how to endure its absence." Here, as he has said of some of his other plays, he is concerned with the "moral awareness" of his characters, their degree of consciousness, and the freedom and strength they can find within them to exercise their will. His characters show a varying awareness of their plight, ranging from innocence to experience, from good to evil, from helpless victim to self-willed hero. This is a depression play written in retrospect; gone is the doctrinaire approach so familiar in plays of the thirties, and in its place is a fuller appreciation of the complexities of human reality.

Ionesco uses the distortions of expressionism and the symbols of surrealism in a drama which is existentialist in outlook. His world is a nightmare world in which the individuality, freedom, and growth that he values are stifled at every turn by a devitalizing, dehumanizing absurdity. The human condition is one in which language fails to communicate, degenerates from cliché to nonsense, and ultimately is paralyzed; in which people are interchangeable or are reduced to mere furniture; in which inert matter, the furniture of the world, overwhelms us. Unlike some existentialist writing, however, Ionesco's plays achieve a victory over this desperation by means of their humor, for the absurd is after all both nightmare and comedy.

The one-act play is not popular on Broadway. Although several of the plays in this volume have had Broadway productions, only one of them, *A Memory of Two Mondays*, opened there. Even the off-Broadway of today is less hospitable to the one-act than it was in the days of the Provincetown Playhouse or the

Group Theatre. The one-act thrives best in an enthusiastic atmosphere of experiment and innovation—Antoine's *Théâtre Libre*, the Abbey, the Poets' Theatre in Cambridge. Perhaps this atmosphere, breathed alike by playwright, director, actors, and audience, is as much responsible as the demands of the form for the vigor and strength of a good one-act. But enthusiasm is not enough to create such an atmosphere; discipline is also required, and the shorter the play, the greater its need. It is unfortunate that the discipline achieved by the playwright in his solitude is sometimes difficult to match in the larger group required to produce his play. Such a combination of enthusiasm and discipline most often develops under those conditions of freedom and discontent where beliefs are strongly held and vigorously asserted.

# Miss Julie

A Tragedy
by August Strindberg

Translated by
Elizabeth Sprigge

MISS JULIE, *aged 25*

JEAN, *the valet, aged 30*

KRISTIN, *the cook, aged 35*

*Scene: The large kitchen of a Swedish manor house in a country district in the eighties.*

*Midsummer eve.*

*The kitchen has three doors, two small ones into* JEAN's *and* KRISTIN's *bedrooms, and a large, glass-fronted double one, opening on to a courtyard. This is the only way to the rest of the house.*

*Through these glass doors can be seen part of a fountain with a cupid, lilac bushes in flower, and the tops of some Lombardy poplars. On one wall are shelves edged with scalloped paper on which are kitchen utensils of copper, iron, and tin.*

*To the left is the corner of a large tiled range and part of its chimney-hood, to the right the end of the servants' dinner table with chairs beside it.*

*The stove is decorated with birch boughs, the floor strewn with twigs of juniper. On the end of the table is a large Japanese spice jar full of lilac.*

*There are also an ice-box, a scullery table, and a sink. Above the double door hangs a big old-fashioned bell; near it is a speaking-tube.*

*A fiddle can be heard from the dance in the barn near-by.* KRISTIN *is standing at the stove, frying something in a pan. She wears a light-colored cotton dress and a big apron.*

*JEAN enters, wearing livery and carrying a pair of large riding-boots with spurs, which he puts in a conspicuous place.*

JEAN: Miss Julie's crazy again to-night, absolutely crazy.

KRISTIN: Oh, so you're back, are you?

JEAN: When I'd taken the Count to the station, I came back and dropped in at the Barn for a dance. And who did I see there but our young lady leading off with the game-keeper. But the moment she sets eyes on me, up she rushes and invites me to waltz with her. And how she waltzed—I've never seen anything like it! She's crazy.

KRISTIN: Always has been, but never so bad as this last fortnight since the engagement was broken off.

JEAN: Yes, that was a pretty business, to be sure. He's a decent enough chap, too, even if he isn't rich. Oh, but they're choosy! (*Sits down at the end of the table.*) In any case, it's a bit odd that our young—er—lady would rather stay at home with the yokels than go with her father to visit her relations.

KRISTIN: Perhaps she feels a bit awkward, after that bust-up with her fiancé.

JEAN: Maybe. That chap had some guts, though. Do you know the sort of thing that was going on, Kristin? I saw it with my own eyes, though I didn't let on I had.

KRISTIN: You saw them . . . ?

JEAN: Didn't I just! Came across the pair of them one evening in the stable-yard. Miss Julie was doing what she called "training" him. Know what that was? Making him jump over her riding whip—the way you teach a dog. He did it twice and got a cut each time for his pains, but when it came to the third go, he snatched the whip out of her hand and broke it into smithereens. And then he cleared off.

KRISTIN: What goings on! I never did!

JEAN: Well, that's how it was with that little affair . . . Now, what have you got for me, Kristin? Something tasty?

KRISTIN (*serving from the pan to his plate*): Well, it's just a little bit of kidney I cut off their joint.

JEAN (*smelling it*): Fine! That's my special *délice*. (*Feels the plate.*) But you might have warmed the plate.

KRISTIN: When you choose to be finicky you're worse than the Count himself. (*Pulls his hair affectionately.*)

JEAN (*crossly*): Stop pulling my hair. You know how sensitive I am.

KRISTIN: There, there! It's only love, you know.

> JEAN *eats.* KRISTIN *brings a bottle of beer.*

JEAN: Beer on Midsummer Eve? No thanks! I've got something better than that. (*From a drawer in the table brings out a bottle of red wine with a yellow seal.*) Yellow seal, see! Now get me a glass. You use a glass with a stem of course when you're drinking it straight.

KRISTIN (*giving him a wine-glass*): Lord help the woman who gets you for a husband, you old fusser! (*She puts the beer in the ice-box and sets a small saucepan on the stove.*)

JEAN: Nonsense! You'll be glad enough to get a fellow as smart as me. And I don't think it's done you any harm people calling me your fiancé. (*Tastes the wine.*) Good. Very good indeed. But not quite warmed enough. (*Warms the glass in his hand.*) We bought this in Dijon. Four francs the litre without the bottle, and duty on top of that. What are you cooking now? It stinks.

KRISTIN: Some bloody muck Miss Julie wants for Diana.

JEAN: You should be more refined in your speech, Kristin. But why should you spend a holiday cooking for that bitch? Is she sick or what?

KRISTIN: Yes, she's sick. She sneaked out with the pug at the lodge and got in the usual mess. And that, you know, Miss Julie won't have.

JEAN: Miss Julie's too high-and-mighty in some respects, and not enough in others, just like her mother before her. The Countess was more at home in the kitchen and cowsheds than anywhere else, but would she ever go driving with only one horse? She went round with her cuffs filthy, but she had to have the coronet on the cuff-links. Our young lady—to come back to her—hasn't any proper respect for herself or her position. I mean she isn't refined. In the Barn just now she dragged the gamekeeper away from Anna and made him dance with her—no waiting to be asked. We wouldn't do a thing like that. But that's what happens when the gentry try to behave like the common people—they become common . . . Still she's a fine girl. Smashing! What shoulders! And what—er—etcetera!

KRISTIN: Oh come off it! I know what Clara says, and she dresses her.

JEAN: . Clara? Pooh, you're all jealous! But I've been out riding with her . . . and as for her dancing!

KRISTIN: Listen, Jean. You will dance with me, won't you, as soon as I'm through?

JEAN: Of course I will.

KRISTIN: Promise?

JEAN: Promise? When I say I'll do a thing I do it. Well, thanks for the supper. It was a real treat. (*Corks the bottle.*)

JULIE *appears in the doorway, speaking to someone outside.*

JULIE: I'll be back in a moment. Don't wait.

JEAN *slips the bottle into the drawer and rises respectfully.* JULIE *enters and joins* KRISTIN *at the stove.*

Well, have you made it?

KRISTIN *signs that* JEAN *is near them.*

JEAN (*gallantly*): Have you ladies got some secret?

JULIE (*flipping his face with her handkerchief*): You're very inquisitive.

JEAN: What a delicious smell! Violets.

JULIE (*coquettishly*): Impertinence! Are you an expert of scent too? I must say you know how to dance. Now don't look. Go away.

*The music of a schottische begins.*

JEAN (*with impudent politeness*): Is it some witches' brew you're cooking on Midsummer Eve? Something to tell your stars by, so you can see your future?

JULIE (*sharply*): If you could see that you'd have good eyes. (*To* KRISTIN.) Put it in a bottle and cork it tight. Come and dance this schottische with me, Jean.

JEAN (*hesitating*): I don't want to be rude, but I've promised to dance this one with Kristin.

JULIE: Well, she can have another, can't you, Kristin? You'll lend me Jean, won't you?

KRISTIN (*bottling*): It's nothing to do with me. When you're so condescending, Miss, it's not his place to say no. Go on, Jean, and thank Miss Julie for the honor.

JEAN: Frankly speaking, Miss, and no offence meant, I wonder if it's wise for you to dance twice running with the same partner, specially as those people are so ready to jump to conclusions.

JULIE (*flaring up*): What did you say? What sort of conclusions? What do you mean?

JEAN (*meekly*): As you choose not to understand, Miss Julie, I'll have to speak more plainly. It looks bad to show a preference for one of your retainers when they're all hoping for the same unusual favor.

JULIE: Show a preference! The very idea! I'm surprised at you. I'm doing the people an honor by attending their ball when I'm mistress of the house, but if I'm really going to dance,

I mean to have a partner who can lead and doesn't make me look ridiculous.

JEAN: If those are your orders, Miss, I'm at your service.

JULIE (*gently*): Don't take it as an order. To-night we're all just people enjoying a party. There's no question of class. So now give me your arm. Don't worry, Kristin. I shan't steal your sweetheart.

JEAN *gives* JULIE *his arm and leads her out.*

*Left alone,* KRISTIN *plays her scene in an unhurried, natural way, humming to the tune of the schottische, played on a distant violin. She clears* JEAN's *place, washes up and puts things away, then takes off her apron, brings out a small mirror from a drawer, props it against the jar of lilac, lights a candle, warms a small pair of tongs and curls her fringe. She goes to the door and listens, then turning back to the table finds* MISS JULIE's *forgotten handkerchief. She smells it, then meditatively smooths it out and folds it.*

*Enter* JEAN.

JEAN: She really *is* crazy. What a way to dance! With people standing grinning at her too from behind the doors. What's got into her, Kristin?

KRISTIN: Oh, it's just her time coming on. She's always queer then. Are you going to dance with me now?

JEAN: Then you're not wild with me for cutting that one.

KRISTIN: You know I'm not—for a little thing like that. Besides, I know my place.

JEAN (*putting his arm round her waist*): You're a sensible girl, Kristin, and you'll make a very good wife . . .

*Enter* JULIE, *unpleasantly surprised.*

JULIE (*with forced gaiety*): You're a fine beau—running away from your partner.

JEAN: Not away, Miss Julie, but as you see back to the one I deserted.

JULIE (*changing her tone*): You really can dance, you know. But why are you wearing your livery on a holiday. Take it off at once.

JEAN: Then I must ask you to go away for a moment, Miss. My black coat's here. (*Indicates it hanging on the door to his room.*)

JULIE: Are you so shy of me—just over changing a coat? Go into your room then—or stay here and I'll turn my back.

JEAN: Excuse me then, Miss. (*He goes to his room and is partly visible as he changes his coat.*)

JULIE: Tell me, Kristin, is Jean your fiancé? You seem very intimate.

KRISTIN: My fiancé? Yes, if you like. We call it that.

JULIE: Call it?

KRISTIN: Well, you've had a fiancé yourself, Miss, and . . .

JULIE: But we really were engaged.

KRISTIN: All the same it didn't come to anything.

JEAN *returns in his black coat.*

JULIE: Très gentil, Monsieur Jean. Très gentil.

JEAN: Vous voulez plaisanter, Madame.

JULIE: Et vous voulez parler français. Where did you learn it?

JEAN: In Switzerland, when I was sommelier at one of the biggest hotels in Lucerne.

JULIE: You look quite the gentleman in that get-up. Charming. (*Sits at the table.*)

JEAN: Oh, you're just flattering me!

JULIE (*annoyed*): Flattering you?

JEAN: I'm too modest to believe you would pay real compliments to a man like me, so I must take it you are exaggerating— that this is what's known as flattery.

JULIE: Where on earth did you learn to make speeches like that? Perhaps you've been to the theatre a lot.

JEAN: That's right. And travelled a lot too.

JULIE: But you come from this neighborhood, don't you?

JEAN: Yes, my father was a laborer on the next estate—the District Attorney's place. I often used to see you, Miss Julie, when you were little, though you never noticed me.

JULIE: Did you really?

JEAN: Yes. One time specially I remember . . . but I can't tell you about that.

JULIE: Oh do! Why not? This is just the time.

JEAN: No, I really can't now. Another time perhaps.

JULIE: Another time means never. What harm in now?

JEAN: No harm, but I'd rather not. (*Points to* KRISTIN, *now fast asleep.*) Look at her.

JULIE: She'll make a charming wife, won't she? I wonder if she snores.

JEAN: No, she doesn't, but she talks in her sleep.

JULIE (*cynically*): How do you know she talks in her sleep?

JEAN (*brazenly*): I've heard her. (*Pause. They look at one another.*)

JULIE: Why don't you sit down?

JEAN: I can't take such a liberty in your presence.

JULIE: Supposing I order you to.

JEAN: I'll obey.

JULIE: Then sit down. No, wait a minute. Will you get me a drink first?

JEAN: I don't know what's in the ice-box. Only beer, I expect.

JULIE: There's no only about it. My taste is so simple I prefer it to wine.

*JEAN takes a bottle from the ice-box, fetches a glass and plate and serves the beer.*

JEAN: At your service.

JULIE: Thank you. Won't you have some yourself?

JEAN: I'm not really a beer-drinker, but if it's an order . . .

JULIE: Order? I should have thought it was ordinary manners to keep your partner company.

JEAN: That's a good way of putting it. (*He opens another bottle and fetches a glass.*)

JULIE: Now drink my health. (*He hesitates.*) I believe the man really is shy.

*JEAN kneels and raises his glass with mock ceremony.*

JEAN: To the health of my lady!

JULIE: Bravo! Now kiss my shoe and everything will be perfect. (*He hesitates, then boldly takes hold of her foot and lightly kisses it.*) Splendid. You ought to have been an actor.

JEAN (*rising*): We can't go on like this, Miss Julie. Someone might come in and see us.

JULIE: Why would that matter?

JEAN: For the simple reason that they'd talk. And if you knew the way their tongues were wagging out there just now, you . . .

JULIE: What were they saying? Tell me. Sit down.

JEAN (*sitting*): No offense meant, Miss, but . . . well, their language wasn't nice, and they were hinting . . . oh, you know quite well what. You're not a child, and if a lady's seen drinking alone at night with a man—and a servant at that—then . . .

JULIE: Then what? Besides, we're not alone. Kristin's here.

JEAN: Yes, asleep.

JULIE: I'll wake her up. (*Rises.*) Kristin, are you asleep? (KRISTIN *mumbles in her sleep.*) Kristin! Goodness, how she sleeps!

KRISTIN (*in her sleep*): The Count's boots are cleaned—put the coffee on—yes, yes, at once . . . (*Mumbles incoherently.*)

JULIE (*tweaking her nose*): Wake up, can't you!

JEAN (*sharply*): Let her sleep.

JULIE: What?

JEAN: When you've been standing at the stove all day you're likely to be tired at night. And sleep should be respected.

JULIE (*changing her tone*): What a nice idea. It does you credit. Thank you for it. (*Holds out her hand to him.*) Now come out and pick some lilac for me.

*During the following* KRISTIN *goes sleepily in to her bedroom.*

JEAN: Out with you, Miss Julie?

JULIE: Yes.

JEAN: It wouldn't do. It really wouldn't.

JULIE: I don't know what you mean. You can't possibly imagine that . . .

JEAN: I don't, but others do.

JULIE: What? That I'm in love with the valet?

JEAN: I'm not a conceited man, but such a thing's been known to happen, and to these rustics nothing's sacred.

JULIE: You, I take it, are an aristocrat.

JEAN: Yes, I am.

JULIE: And I am coming down in the world.

JEAN: Don't come down, Miss Julie. Take my advice. No one will believe you came down of your own accord. They'll all say you fell.

JULIE: I have a higher opinion of our people than you. Come and put it to the test. Come on. (*Gazes into his eyes.*)

JEAN: You're very strange, you know.

JULIE: Perhaps I am, but so are you. For that matter everything is strange. Life, human beings, everything, just scum drifting about on the water until it sinks—down and down. That reminds me of a dream I sometimes have, in which I'm on top of a pillar and can't see any way of getting down. When I look down I'm dizzy; I have to get down but I haven't the courage to jump. I can't stay there and I long to fall, but I don't fall. There's no respite. There can't be any peace at all for me until I'm down, right down on the ground. And if I did get to the ground I'd want to be under the ground . . . Have you ever felt like that?

JEAN: No. In my dream I'm lying under a great tree in a dark wood. I want to get up, up to the top of it, and look out over the bright landscape where the sun is shining and rob that high nest of its golden eggs. And I climb and climb, but the trunk is so thick and smooth and it's so far to the first branch. But I know if I can once reach that first branch I'll go to the top just as if I'm on a ladder. I haven't reached it yet, but I shall get there, even if only in my dreams.

JULIE: Here I am chattering about dreams with you. Come on. Only into the park. (*She takes his arm and they go towards the door.*)

JEAN: We must sleep on nine midsummer flowers tonight; then our dreams will come true, Miss Julie.

*They turn at the door. He has a hand to his eye.*

JULIE: Have you got something in your eye? Let me see.

JEAN: Oh, it's nothing. Just a speck of dust. It'll be gone in a minute.

JULIE: My sleeve must have rubbed against you. Sit down and let me see to it. (*Takes him by the arm and makes him sit down, bends his head back and tries to get the speck out with the corner of her handkerchief.*) Keep still now, quite still. (*Slaps his hand.*) Do as I tell you. Why, I believe you're trembling, big, strong man though you are! (*Feels his biceps.*) What muscles!

JEAN (*warning*): Miss Julie!

JULIE: Yes, Monsieur Jean?

JEAN: Attention. Je ne suis qu'un homme.

JULIE: Will you stay still! There now. It's out. Kiss my hand and say thank you.

JEAN (*rising*): Miss Julie, listen. Kristin's gone to bed now. Will you listen?

JULIE: Kiss my hand first.

JEAN: Very well, but you'll have only yourself to blame.

JULIE: For what?

JEAN: For what! Are you still a child at twenty-five? Don't you know it's dangerous to play with fire?

JULIE: Not for me. I'm insured.

JEAN (*bluntly*): No, you're not. And even if you are, there's still stuff here to kindle a flame.

JULIE: Meaning yourself?

JEAN: Yes. Not because I'm me, but because I'm a man and young and . . .

JULIE: And good-looking? What incredible conceit! A Don Juan perhaps? Or a Joseph? Good Lord, I do believe you are a Joseph!

JEAN: Do you?

JULIE: I'm rather afraid so.

JEAN *goes boldly up and tries to put his arms round her and kiss her. She boxes his ears.*

How dare you!

JEAN: Was that in earnest or a joke?

JULIE: In earnest.

JEAN: Then what went before was in earnest too. You take your games too seriously and that's dangerous. Anyhow I'm tired of playing now and beg leave to return to my work. The Count will want his boots first thing and it's past midnight now.

JULIE: Put those boots down.

JEAN: No. This is my work, which it's my duty to do. But I never undertook to be your playfellow and I never will be. I consider myself too good for that.

JULIE: You're proud.

JEAN: In some ways—not all.

JULIE: Have you even been in love?

JEAN: We don't put it that way, but I've been gone on quite a few girls. And once I went sick because I couldn't have the one I wanted. Sick, I mean, like those princes in the Arabian Nights who couldn't eat or drink for love.

JULIE: Who was she? (*No answer.*) Who was she?

JEAN: You can't force me to tell you that.

JULIE: If I ask as an equal, ask as a—friend? Who was she?

JEAN: You.

JULIE (*sitting*): How absurd!

JEAN: Yes, ludicrous if you like. That's the story I wouldn't tell you before, see, but now I will . . . Do you know what the world looks like from below? No, you don't. No more than the hawks and falcons do whose backs one hardly ever sees because they're always soaring up aloft. I lived in a laborer's hovel with seven other children and a pig, out in the gray fields where there isn't a single tree. But from the window I could see the wall round the Count's park with apple-trees above it. That was the Garden of Eden, guarded by many terrible angels with flaming swords. All the same I and the other boys managed to get to the tree of life. Does all this make you despise me?

JULIE: Goodness, all boys steal apples!

JEAN: You say that now, but all the same you do despise me. However, one time I went into the Garden of Eden with my mother to weed the onion beds. Close to the kitchen garden there was a Turkish pavilion hung all over with jasmine and honeysuckle. I hadn't any idea what it was used for, but I'd never seen such a beautiful building. People used to go in and then come out again, and one day the door was left open. I crept up and saw the walls covered with pictures of kings and emperors, and the windows had red curtains with fringes —you know now what the place was, don't you? I . . . (*Breaks off a piece of lilac and holds it for* JULIE *to smell. As he talks, she takes it from him.*) I had never been inside the manor, never seen anything but the church, and this was more beautiful. No matter where my thoughts went, they always came back—to that place. The longing went on growing in me to enjoy it fully, just once. Enfin, I sneaked in, gazed and admired. Then I heard someone coming. There was only one way out for the gentry, but for me there was another and I had no choice but to take it. (JULIE *drops the lilac on the table.*) Then I took to my heels, plunged through the raspberry canes, dashed across the strawberry beds and found myself on the rose terrace. There I saw a pink dress and a pair of white stockings—it was you. I crawled into a weed pile and lay there right under it among prickly thistles and damp rank earth. I watched you walking among the roses and said to myself: "If it's true that a thief can get to heaven and be with the angels, it's pretty strange that a laborer's child here on God's earth mayn't come in the park and play with the Count's daughter."

JULIE (*sentimentally*): Do you think all poor children feel the way you did?

JEAN (*taken aback, then rallying*): *All* poor children? . . . Yes, of course they do. Of course.

JULIE: It must be terrible to be poor.

JEAN (*with exaggerated distress*): Oh yes, Miss Julie, yes. A dog may lie on the Countess's sofa, a horse may have his nose stroked by a young lady, but a servant . . . (*Change of tone.*) well, yes, now and then you meet one with guts enough to rise in the world, but how often? Anyhow, do you know what I did? Jumped in the millstream with my clothes on, was pulled out and got a hiding. But the next Sunday, when Father and all the rest went to Granny's, I managed to get left behind. Then I washed with soap and hot water, put my best clothes on and went to church so as to see you. I did see you and went home determined to die. But I wanted to die beautifully and peacefully, without any pain. Then I remembered it was dangerous to sleep under an elder bush. We had a big one in full bloom, so I stripped it and climbed into the oats-bin with the flowers. Have you ever noticed how smooth oats are? Soft to touch as human skin . . . Well, I closed the lid and shut my eyes, fell asleep, and when they woke me I was very ill. But I didn't die, as you see. What I meant by all that I don't know. There was no hope of winning you—you were simply a symbol of the hopelessness of ever getting out of the class I was born in.

JULIE: You put things very well, you know. Did you go to school?

JEAN: For a while. But I've read a lot of novels and been to the theatre. Besides, I've heard educated folk talking—that's what's taught me most.

JULIE: Do you stand round listening to what we're saying?

JEAN: Yes, of course. And I've heard quite a bit too! On the carriage box or rowing the boat. Once I heard you, Miss Julie, and one of your young lady friends . . .

JULIE: Oh! Whatever did you hear?

JEAN: Well, it wouldn't be nice to repeat it. And I must say I was pretty startled. I couldn't think where you had learnt such words. Perhaps, at bottom, there isn't as much difference between people as one's led to believe.

JULIE: How dare you! We don't behave as you do when we're engaged.

JEAN (*looking hard at her*): Are you sure? It's no use making out so innocent to me.

JULIE: The man I gave my love to was a rotter.

JEAN: That's what you always say—afterwards.

JULIE: Always?

JEAN: I think it must be always. I've heard the expression several times in similar circumstances.

JULIE: What circumstances?

JEAN: Like those in question. The last time . . .

JULIE (*rising*): Stop. I don't want to hear any more.

JEAN: Nor did *she*—curiously enough. May I go to bed now please?

JULIE (*gently*): Go to bed on Midsummer Eve?

JEAN: Yes. Dancing with that crowd doesn't really amuse me.

JULIE: Get the key of the boathouse and row me out on the lake. I want to see the sun rise.

JEAN: Would that be wise?

JULIE: You sound as though you're frightened for your reputation.

JEAN: Why not? I don't want to be made a fool of, nor to be sent packing without a character when I'm trying to better myself. Besides, I have Kristin to consider.

JULIE: So now it's Kristin.

JEAN: Yes, but it's you I'm thinking about too. Take my advice and go to bed.

JULIE: Am I to take orders from you?

JEAN: Just this once, for your own sake. Please. It's very late and sleepiness goes to one's head and makes one rash. Go to bed. What's more, if my ears don't deceive me, I hear people coming this way. They'll be looking for me, and if they find us here, you're done for.

*The* CHORUS *approaches, singing. During the following dialogue the song is heard in snatches, and in full when the peasants enter.*

> Out of the wood two women came,
> Tridiri-ralla, tridiri-ra.
> The feet of one were bare and cold,
> Tridiri-ralla-la.
>
> The other talked of bags of gold,
> Tridiri-ralla, tridiri-ra.
> But neither had a sou to her name,
> Tridiri-ralla-la.
>
> The bridal wreath I give to you,
> Tridiri-ralla, tridiri-ra.
> But to another I'll be true,
> Tridiri-ralla-la.

JULIE: I know our people and I love them, just as they do me. Let them come. You'll see.

JEAN: No, Miss Julie, they don't love you. They take your food, then spit at it. You must believe me. Listen to them, just listen to what they're singing . . . No, don't listen.

JULIE (*listening*): What are they singing?

JEAN: They're mocking—you and me.

JULIE: Oh no! How horrible! What cowards!

JEAN: A pack like that's always cowardly. But against such odds there's nothing we can do but run away.

JULIE: Run away? Where to? We can't get out and we can't go into Kristin's room.

JEAN: Into mine then. Necessity knows no rules. And you can trust me. I really am your true and devoted friend.

JULIE: But supposing . . . supposing they were to look for you in there?

JEAN: I'll bolt the door, and if they try to break in I'll shoot. Come on. (*Pleading.*) Please come.

JULIE (*tensely*): Do you promise . . . ?

JEAN: I swear!

JULIE *goes quickly into his room and he excitedly follows her.*

*Led by the fiddler, the peasants enter in festive attire with flowers in their hats. They put a barrel of beer and a keg of spirits, garlanded with leaves, on the table, fetch glasses, and begin to carouse. The scene becomes a ballet. They form a ring and dance and sing and mime: "Out of the wood two women came." Finally they go out, still singing.*

JULIE *comes in alone. She looks at the havoc in the kitchen, wrings her hands, then takes out her powder puff and powders her face.*

JEAN *enters in high spirits.*

JEAN: Now you see! And you heard, didn't you? Do you still think it's possible for us to stay here?

JULIE: No, I don't. But what can we do?

JEAN: Run away. Far away. Take a journey.

JULIE: Journey? But where to?

JEAN: Switzerland. The Italian lakes. Ever been there?

JULIE: No. Is it nice?

JEAN: Ah! Eternal summer, oranges, evergreens . . . ah!

JULIE: But what would we do there?

JEAN: I'll start a hotel. First-class accommodation and first-class customers.

JULIE: Hotel?

JEAN: There's life for you. New faces all the time, new languages —no time for nerves or worries, no need to look for something to do—work rolling up of its own accord. Bells ringing night and day, trains whistling, buses coming and going, and all the time gold pieces rolling on to the counter. There's life for you!

JULIE: For *you*. And I?

JEAN: Mistress of the house, ornament of the firm. With your looks, and your style . . . oh, it's bound to be a success! Terrific! You'll sit like a queen in the office and set your slaves in motion by pressing an electric button. The guests will file past your throne and nervously lay their treasure on your table. You've no idea the way people tremble when they get their bills. I'll salt the bills and you'll sugar them with your sweetest smiles. Ah, let's get away from here! (*Produces a time-table.*) At once, by the next train. We shall be at Malmö at six-thirty, Hamburg eight-forty next morning, Frankfurt-Basle the following day, and Como by the St. Gothard pass in—let's see—three days. Three days!

JULIE: That's all very well. But Jean, you must give me courage. Tell me you love me. Come and take me in your arms.

JEAN (*reluctantly*): I'd like to, but I daren't. Not again in this house. I love you—that goes without saying. You can't doubt that, Miss Julie, can you?

JULIE (*shyly, very feminine*): Miss? Call me Julie. There aren't any barriers between us now. Call me Julie.

JEAN (*uneasily*): I can't. As long as we're in this house, there *are* barriers between us. There's the past and there's the Count. I've never been so servile to anyone as I am to him. I've only got to see his gloves on a chair to feel small. I've only to hear his bell and I shy like a horse. Even now, when I look at his boots, standing there so proud and stiff, I feel my back beginning to bend. (*Kicks the boots.*) It's those old, narrow-minded notions drummed into us as children . . . but they can soon be forgotten. You've only got to get to another country, a republic, and people will bend themselves double before my porter's livery. Yes, double they'll bend themselves, but I shan't. I wasn't born to bend. I've got guts. I've got character, and once I reach that first branch, you'll watch me climb. Today I'm valet, next year I'll be proprietor, in ten years I'll have made a fortune, and then I'll go to Rumania, get myself decorated and I may, I only say *may*, mind you, end up as a Count.

JULIE (*sadly*): That would be very nice.

JEAN: You see in Rumania one can buy a title, and then you'll be a Countess after all. My Countess.

JULIE: What do I care about all that? I'm putting those things behind me. Tell me you love me, because if you don't . . . if you don't, what am I?

JEAN: I'll tell you a thousand times over—later. But not here. No sentimentality now or everything will be lost. We must consider this thing calmly like reasonable people. (*Takes a cigar, cuts and lights it.*) You sit down there and I'll sit here and we'll talk as if nothing has happened.

JULIE: My God, have you no feelings at all?

JEAN: Nobody has more. But I know how to control them.

JULIE: A short time ago you were kissing my shoe. And now . . .

JEAN (*harshly*): Yes, that was then. Now we have something else to think about.

JULIE: Don't speak to me so brutally.

JEAN: I'm not. Just sensibly. One folly's been committed, don't let's have more. The Count will be back at any moment and we've got to settle our future before that. Now, what do you think of my plans? Do you approve?

JULIE: It seems a very good idea—but just one thing. Such a big undertaking would need a lot of capital. Have you got any?

JEAN (*chewing his cigar*): I certainly have. I've got my professional skill, my wide experience and my knowledge of foreign languages. That's capital worth having, it seems to me.

JULIE: But it won't buy even one railway ticket.

JEAN: Quite true. That's why I need a backer to advance some ready cash.

JULIE: How could you get that at a moment's notice?

JEAN: You must get it, if you want to be my partner.

JULIE: I can't. I haven't any money of my own. (*Pause.*)

JEAN: Then the whole thing's off.

JULIE: And . . . ?

JEAN: We go on as we are.

JULIE: Do you think I'm going to stay under this roof as your mistress? With everyone pointing at me. Do you think I can face my father after this? No. Take me away from here, away from this shame, this humiliation. Oh my God, what have I done? My God, my God! (*Weeps.*)

JEAN: So that's the tune now, is it? What have you done? Same as many before you.

JULIE (*hysterically*): And now you despise me. I'm falling, I'm falling.

JEAN: Fall as far as me and I'll lift you up again.

JULIE: Why was I so terribly attracted to you? The weak to the strong, the falling to the rising? Or was it love? Is that love? Do you know what love is?

JEAN: Do I? You bet I do. Do you think I never had a girl before?

JULIE: The things you say, the things you think!

JEAN: That's what life's taught me, and that's what I am. It's no good getting hysterical or giving yourself airs. We're both in the same boat now. Here, my dear girl, let me give you a glass of something special. (*Opens the drawer, takes out the bottle of wine and fills two used glasses.*)

JULIE: Where did you get that wine?

JEAN: From the cellar.

JULIE: My father's Burgundy.

JEAN: Why not, for his son-in-law?

JULIE: And I drink beer.

JEAN: That only shows your taste's not so good as mine.

JULIE: Thief!

JEAN: Are you going to tell on me?

JULIE: Oh God! The accomplice of a petty thief! Was I blind drunk? Have I dreamt this whole night? Midsummer Eve, the night for innocent merrymaking.

JEAN: Innocent, eh?

JULIE: Is anyone on earth as wretched as I am now?

JEAN: Why should *you* be? After such a conquest. What about Kristin in there? Don't you think she has any feelings?

JULIE: I did think so, but I don't any longer. No. A menial is a menial . . .

JEAN: And a whore is a whore.

JULIE (*falling to her knees, her hands clasped*): O God in heaven, put an end to my miserable life! Lift me out of this filth in which I'm sinking. Save me! Save me!

JEAN: I must admit I'm sorry for you. When I was in the onion bed and saw you up there among the roses, I . . . yes, I'll tell you now . . . I had the same dirty thoughts as all boys.

JULIE: You, who wanted to die because of me?

JEAN: In the oats-bin? That was just talk.

JULIE: Lies, you mean.

JEAN (*getting sleepy*): More or less. I think I read a story in some paper about a chimney-sweep who shut himself up in a chest full of lilac because he'd been summonsed for not supporting some brat . . .

JULIE: So this is what you're like.

JEAN: I had to think up something. It's always the fancy stuff that catches the women.

JULIE: Beast!

JEAN: Merde!

JULIE: Now you have seen the falcon's back.

JEAN: Not exactly its *back*.

JULIE: I was to be the first branch.

JEAN: But the branch was rotten.

JULIE: I was to be a hotel sign.

JEAN: And I the hotel.

JULIE: Sit at your counter, attract your clients, and cook their accounts.

JEAN: I'd have done that myself.

JULIE: That any human being can be so steeped in filth!

JEAN: Clean it up then.

JULIE: Menial! Lackey! Stand up when I speak to you.

JEAN: Menial's whore, lackey's harlot, shut your mouth and get out of here! Are you the one to lecture me for being coarse? Nobody of my kind would ever be as coarse as you were tonight. Do you think any servant girl would throw herself at a man that way? Have you ever seen a girl of my class asking for it like that? I haven't. Only animals and prostitutes.

JULIE (*broken*): Go on. Hit me, trample on me—it's all I deserve. I'm rotten. But help me! If there's any way out at all, help me.

JEAN (*more gently*): I'm not denying myself a share in the honor of seducing you, but do you think anybody in my place would have dared look in your direction if you yourself hadn't asked for it? I'm still amazed . . .

JULIE: And proud.

JEAN: Why not? Though I must admit the victory was too easy to make me lose my head.

JULIE: Go on hitting me.

JEAN (*rising*): No. On the contrary I apologize for what I've said. I don't hit a person who's down—least of all a woman. I can't deny there's a certain satisfaction in finding that what dazzled one below was just moonshine, that that falcon's back is gray after all, that there's powder on the lovely cheek, that polished nails can have black tips, that the handkerchief is dirty although it smells of scent. On the other hand it hurts to find that what I was struggling to reach wasn't high and isn't real. It hurts to see you fallen so low you're far lower than your own cook. Hurts like when you see the last flowers of summer lashed to pieces by rain and turned to mud.

JULIE: You're talking as if you're already my superior.

JEAN: I am. I might make you a Countess, but you could never make me a Count, you know.

JULIE: But I am the child of a Count, and you could never be that.

JEAN: True, but I might be the father of Counts if . . .

JULIE: You're a thief. I'm not.

JEAN: There are worse things than being a thief—much lower. Besides, when I'm in a place I regard myself as a member of the family to some extent, as one of the children. You don't call it stealing when children pinch a berry from over-laden bushes. (*His passion is roused again.*) Miss Julie, you're a glorious woman, far too good for a man like me. You were carried away by some kind of madness, and now you're try-ing to cover up your mistake by persuading yourself you're in love with me. You're not, although you may find me physically attractive, which means your love's no better than mine. But I wouldn't be satisfied with being nothing but an animal for you, and I could never make you love me.

JULIE: Are you sure?

JEAN: You think there's a chance? Of my loving you, yes, of course. You're beautiful, refined (*Takes her hand.*), *educated*, and you can be nice when you want to be. The fire you kindle in a man isn't likely to go out. (*Puts his arm round her.*) You're like mulled wine, full of spices, and your kisses . . . (*He tries to pull her to him, but she breaks away.*)

JULIE: Let go of me! You won't win me that way.

JEAN: Not that way, how then? Not by kisses and fine speeches, not by planning the future and saving you from shame? How then?

JULIE: How? How? I don't know. There isn't any way. I loathe you—loathe you as I loathe rats, but I can't escape from you.

JEAN: Escape with me.

JULIE (*pulling herself together*): Escape? Yes, we must escape. But I'm so tired. Give me a glass of wine. (*He pours it out. She looks at her watch.*) First we must talk. We still have a little time. (*Empties the glass and holds it out for more.*)

JEAN: Don't drink like that. You'll get tipsy.

JULIE: What's that matter?

JEAN: What's it matter? It's vulgar to get drunk. Well, what have you got to say?

JULIE: We've got to run away, but we must talk first—or rather, I must, for so far you've done all the talking. You've told me about your life, now I want to tell you about mine, so that we really know each other before we begin this journey together.

JEAN: Wait. Excuse my saying so, but don't you think you may be sorry afterwards if you give away your secrets to me?

JULIE: Aren't you my friend?

JEAN: On the whole. But don't rely on me.

JULIE: You can't mean that. But anyway everyone knows my secrets. Listen. My mother wasn't well-born; she came of quite humble people, and was brought up with all those new ideas of sex-equality and women's rights and so on. She thought marriage was quite wrong. So when my father proposed to her, she said she would never become his *wife* . . . but in the end she did. I came into the world, as far as I can make out, against my mother's will, and I was left to run wild, but I had to do all the things a boy does—to prove women are as good as men. I had to wear boys' clothes; I was taught to handle horses—and I wasn't allowed in the dairy. She made me groom and harness and go out hunting; I even had to try to plough. All the men on the estate were given the women's jobs, and the women the men's, until the whole place went to rack and ruin and we were the laughingstock of the neighborhood. At last my father seems to have come to his senses and rebelled. He changed everything and ran the place his own way. My mother got ill. I don't know what was the matter with her, but she used to have strange attacks and hide herself in the attic or the garden. Sometimes she stayed out all night. Then came the great fire which you have heard people talking about. The house and the stables and the barns—the whole place burnt to the ground. In very suspicious circumstances. Because the accident happened the very day the insurance had to be renewed, and my father had sent the new premium, but through some carelessness of the messenger it arrived too late. (*Refills her glass and drinks.*)

JEAN: Don't drink any more.

JULIE: Oh, what does it matter? We were destitute and had to sleep in the carriages. My father didn't know how to get money to rebuild, and then my mother suggested he should borrow from an old friend of hers, a local brick manufacturer. My father got the loan and, to his surprise, without having to pay interest. So the place was rebuilt. (*Drinks.*) Do you know who set fire to it?

JEAN: Your lady mother.

JULIE: Do you know who the brick manufacturer was?

JEAN: Your mother's lover?

JULIE: Do you know whose the money was?

JEAN: Wait . . . no, I don't know that.

JULIE: It was my mother's.

JEAN: In other words the Count's, unless there was a settlement.

JULIE: There wasn't any settlement. My mother had a little money of her own which she didn't want my father to control, so she invested it with her—friend.

JEAN: Who grabbed it.

JULIE: Exactly. He appropriated it. My father came to know all this. He couldn't bring an action, couldn't pay his wife's lover, nor prove it was his wife's money. That was my mother's revenge because he made himself master in his own house. He nearly shot himself then—at least there's a rumor he tried and didn't bring it off. So he went on living, and my mother had to pay dearly for what she'd done. Imagine what those five years were like for me. My natural sympathies were with my father, yet I took my mother's side, because I didn't know the facts. I'd learnt from her to hate and distrust men—you know how she loathed the whole male sex. And I swore to her I'd never become the slave of any man.

JEAN: And so you got engaged to that attorney.

JULIE: So that he should be my slave.

JEAN: But he wouldn't be.

JULIE: Oh yes, he wanted to be, but he didn't have the chance. I got bored with him.

JEAN: Is that what I saw—in the stableyard?

JULIE: What did you see?

JEAN: What I saw was him breaking off the engagement.

JULIE: That's a lie. It was I who broke it off. Did he say it was him? The cad.

JEAN: He's not a cad. Do you hate men, Miss Julie?

JULIE: Yes . . . most of the time. But when that weakness comes, oh . . . the shame!

JEAN: Then do you hate me?

JULIE: Beyond words. I'd gladly have you killed like an animal.

JEAN: Quick as you'd shoot a mad dog, eh?

JULIE: Yes.

JEAN: But there's nothing here to shoot with—and there isn't a dog. So what do we do now?

JULIE: Go abroad.

JEAN: To make each other miserable for the rest of our lives?

JULIE: No, to enjoy ourselves for a day or two, for a week, for as long as enjoyment lasts, and then—to die . . .

JEAN: Die? How silly! I think it would be far better to start a hotel.

JULIE (*without listening*): . . . die on the shores of Lake Como, where the sun always shines and at Christmas time there are green trees and glowing oranges.

JEAN: Lake Como's a rainy hole and I didn't see any oranges outside the shops. But it's a good place for tourists. Plenty of villas to be rented by—er—honeymoon couples. Profitable business that. Know why? Because they all sign a lease for six months and all leave after three weeks.

JULIE (*naïvely*): After three weeks? Why?

JEAN: They quarrel, of course. But the rent has to be paid just the same. And then it's let again. So it goes on and on, for there's plenty of love although it doesn't last long.

JULIE: You don't want to die with me?

JEAN: I don't want to die at all. For one thing I like living and for another I consider suicide's a sin against the Creator who gave us life.

JULIE: You believe in God—*you?*

JEAN: Yes, of course. And I go to church every Sunday. Look here, I'm tired of all this. I'm going to bed.

JULIE: Indeed! And do you think I'm going to leave things like this? Don't you know what you owe the woman you've ruined?

JEAN (*taking out his purse and throwing a silver coin on the table*): There you are. I don't want to be in anybody's debt.

JULIE (*pretending not to notice the insult*): Don't you know what the law is?

JEAN: There's no law unfortunately that punishes a woman for seducing a man.

JULIE: But can you see anything for it but to go abroad, get married, and then divorce?

JEAN: What if I refuse this mésalliance?

JULIE: Mésalliance?

JEAN: Yes, for me. I'm better bred than you, see! Nobody in my family committed arson.

JULIE: How do you know?

JEAN: Well, you can't prove otherwise, because we haven't any family records outside the Registrar's office. But I've seen your family tree in that book on the drawing-room table. Do you know who the founder of your family was? A miller who let his wife sleep with the King one night during the Danish war. I haven't any ancestors like that. I haven't any ancestors at all, but I might become one.

JULIE: This is what I get for confiding in someone so low, for sacrificing my family honor . . .

JEAN: Dishonor! Well, I told you so. One shouldn't drink, because then one talks. And one shouldn't talk.

JULIE: Oh, how ashamed I am, how bitterly ashamed! If at least you loved me!

JEAN: Look here—for the last time—what do you want? Am I to burst into tears? Am I to jump over your riding whip? Shall I kiss you and carry you off to Lake Como for three weeks, after which . . . What am I to do? What do you want? This is getting unbearable, but that's what comes of playing around with women. Miss Julie, I can see how miserable you are; I know you're going through hell, but I don't understand you. We don't have scenes like this; we don't go in for hating each other. We make love for fun in our spare time, but we haven't all day and all night for it like you. I think you must be ill. I'm sure you're ill.

JULIE: Then you must be kind to me. You sound almost human now.

JEAN: Well, be human yourself. You spit at me, then won't let me wipe it off—on you.

JULIE: Help me, help me! Tell me what to do, where to go.

JEAN: Jesus, as if I knew!

JULIE: I've been mad, raving mad, but there must be a way out.

JEAN: Stay here and keep quiet. Nobody knows anything.

JULIE: I can't. People do know. Kristin knows.

JEAN: They don't know and they wouldn't believe such a thing.

JULIE (*hesitating*): But—it might happen again.

JEAN: That's true.

JULIE: And there might be—consequences.

JEAN (*in panic*): Consequences! Fool that I am I never thought of that. Yes, there's nothing for it but to go. At once. I can't come with you. That would be a complete giveaway. You must go alone—abroad—anywhere.

JULIE: Alone? Where to? I can't.

JEAN: You must. And before the Count gets back. If you stay, we know what will happen. Once you've sinned you feel you might as well go on, as the harm's done. Then you get more and more reckless and in the end you're found out. No. You must go abroad. Then write to the Count and tell him everything, except that it was me. He'll never guess that—and I don't think he'll want to.

JULIE: I'll go if you come with me.

JEAN: Are you crazy, woman? "Miss Julie elopes with valet." Next day it would be in the headlines, and the Count would never live it down.

JULIE: I can't go. I can't stay. I'm so tired, so completely worn out. Give me orders. Set me going. I can't think any more, can't act . . .

JEAN: You see what weaklings you are. Why do you give yourselves airs and turn up your noses as if you're the lords of
creation? Very well, I'll give you your orders. Go upstairs
and dress. Get money for the journey and come down here
again.

JULIE (*softly*): Come up with me.

JEAN: To your room? Now you've gone crazy again. (*Hesitates
a moment.*) No! Go along at once. (*Takes her hand and
pulls her to the door.*)

JULIE (*as she goes*): Speak kindly to me, Jean.

JEAN: Orders always sound unkind. Now you know. Now you
know.

*Left alone,* JEAN *sighs with relief, sits down at the table, takes
out a notebook and pencil and adds up figures, now and then
aloud. Dawn begins to break.* KRISTIN *enters dressed for
church, carrying his white dickey and tie.*

KRISTIN: Lord Jesus, look at the state the place is in! What have
you been up to? (*Turns out the lamp.*)

JEAN: Oh, Miss Julie invited the crowd in. Did you sleep through
it? Didn't you hear anything?

KRISTIN: I slept like a log.

JEAN: And dressed for church already.

KRISTIN: Yes, you promised to come to Communion with me
today.

JEAN: Why, so I did. And you've got my bib and tucker, I see.
Come on then. (*Sits.* KRISTIN *begins to put his things on.
Pause. Sleepily.*) What's the lesson today?

KRISTIN: It's about the beheading of John the Baptist, I think.

JEAN: That's sure to be horribly long. Hi, you're choking me!
Oh Lord, I'm so sleepy, so sleepy!

KRISTIN: Yes, what have you been doing up all night? You look absolutely green.

JEAN: Just sitting here talking with Miss Julie.

KRISTIN: She doesn't know what's proper, that one. (*Pause.*)

JEAN: I say, Kristin.

KRISTIN: What?

JEAN: It's queer really, isn't it, when you come to think of it? Her.

KRISTIN: What's queer?

JEAN: The whole thing. (*Pause.*)

KRISTIN (*looking at the half-filled glasses on the table*): Have you been drinking together too?

JEAN: Yes.

KRISTIN: More shame you. Look me straight in the face.

JEAN: Yes.

KRISTIN: Is it possible? Is it possible?

JEAN (*after a moment*): Yes, it is.

KRISTIN: Oh! This I would never have believed. How low!

JEAN: You're not jealous of her, surely?

KRISTIN: No, I'm not. If it had been Clara or Sophie I'd have scratched your eyes out. But not of her. I don't know why; that's how it is though. But it's disgusting.

JEAN: You're angry with her then.

KRISTIN: No. With you. It was wicked of you, very very wicked. Poor girl. And, mark my words, I won't stay here any longer now—in a place where one can't respect one's employers.

JEAN: Why should one respect them?

KRISTIN: You should know since you're so smart. But you don't want to stay in the service of people who aren't respectable, do you? I wouldn't demean myself.

JEAN: But it's rather a comfort to find out they're no better than us.

KRISTIN: I don't think so. If they're no better there's nothing for us to live up to. Oh and think of the Count! Think of him. He's been through so much already. No, I won't stay in the place any longer. A fellow like you too! If it had been that attorney now or somebody of her own class . . .

JEAN: Why, what's wrong with . . .

KRISTIN: Oh, you're all right in your own way, but when all's said and done there is a difference between one class and another. No, this is something I'll never be able to stomach. That our young lady who was so proud and so down on men you'd never believe she'd let one come near her should go and give herself to one like you. She who wanted to have poor Diana shot for running after the lodge-keeper's pug. No, I must say. . . ! Well, I won't stay here any longer. On the twenty-fourth of October I quit.

JEAN: And then?

KRISTIN: Well, since you mention it, it's about time you began to look around, if we're ever going to get married.

JEAN: But what am I to look for? I shan't get a place like this when I'm married.

KRISTIN: I know you won't. But you might get a job as porter or caretaker in some public institution. Government rations are small but sure, and there's a pension for the widow and children.

JEAN: That's all very fine, but it's not in my line to start thinking at once about dying for my wife and children. I must say I had rather bigger ideas.

KRISTIN: You and your ideas! You've got obligations too, and you'd better start thinking about them.

JEAN: Don't *you* start pestering me about obligations. I've had enough of that. (*Listens to a sound upstairs.*) Anyway we've plenty of time to work things out. Go and get ready now and we'll be off to church.

KRISTIN: Who's that walking about upstairs?

JEAN: Don't know—unless it's Clara.

KRISTIN (*going*): You don't think the Count could have come back without our hearing him?

JEAN (*scared*): The Count? No, he can't have. He'd have rung for me.

KRISTIN: God help us! I've never known such goings on. (*Exit.*)

*The sun has now risen and is shining on the treetops. The light gradually changes until it slants in through the windows.* JEAN *goes to the door and beckons.* JULIE *enters in travelling clothes, carrying a small bird-cage covered with a cloth which she puts on a chair.*

JULIE: I'm ready.

JEAN: Hush! Kristin's up.

JULIE (*in a very nervous state*): Does she suspect anything?

JEAN: Not a thing. But, my God, what a sight you are!

JULIE: Sight? What do you mean?

JEAN: You're white as a corpse and—pardon me—your face is dirty.

JULIE: Let me wash then. (*Goes to the sink and washes her face and hands.*) There. Give me a towel. Oh! The sun is rising!

JEAN: And that breaks the spell.

JULIE: Yes. The spell of Midsummer Eve . . . But listen, Jean. Come with me. I've got the money.

JEAN (*sceptically*): Enough?

JULIE: Enough to start with. Come with me. I can't travel alone today. It's Midsummer Day, remember. I'd be packed into a suffocating train among crowds of people who'd all stare at me. And it would stop at every station while I yearned for wings. No, I can't do that, I simply can't. There will be memories too; memories of Midsummer Days when I was little. The leafy church—birch and lilac—the gaily spread dinner table, relatives, friends—evening in the park—dancing and music and flowers and fun. Oh, however far you run away—there'll always be memories in the baggage car—and remorse and guilt.

JEAN: I will come with you, but quickly now then, before it's too late. At once.

JULIE: Put on your things. (*Picks up the cage.*)

JEAN: No luggage, mind. That would give us away.

JULIE: No, only what we can take with us in the carriage.

JEAN *(fetching his hat)*: What on earth have you got there? What is it?

JULIE: Only my greenfinch. I don't want to leave it behind.

JEAN: Well, I'll be damned! We're to take a bird-cage along, are we? You're crazy. Put that cage down.

JULIE: It's the only thing I'm taking from my home. The only living creature who cares for me since Diana went off like that. Don't be cruel. Let me take it.

JEAN: Put that cage down, I tell you—and don't talk so loud. Kristin will hear.

JULIE: No, I won't leave it in strange hands. I'd rather you killed it.

JEAN: Give the little beast here then and I'll wring its neck.

JULIE: But don't hurt it, don't . . . no, I can't.

JEAN: Give it here. I *can*.

JULIE *(taking the bird out of the cage and kissing it)*: Dear little Serena, must you die and leave your mistress?

JEAN: Please don't make a scene. It's *your* life and future we're worrying about. Come on, quick now!

*He snatches the bird from her, put it on a board and picks up a chopper.* JULIE *turns away.*

You should have learnt how to kill chickens instead of target-shooting. Then you wouldn't faint at a drop of blood.

JULIE (*screaming*): Kill me too! Kill me! You who can butcher an innocent creature without a quiver. Oh, how I hate you, how I loathe you! There is blood between us now. I curse the hour I first saw you. I curse the hour I was conceived in my mother's womb.

JEAN: What's the use of cursing. Let's go.

JULIE (*going to the chopping-block as if drawn against her will*): No, I won't go yet. I can't . . . I must look. Listen! There's a carriage. (*Listens without taking her eyes off the board and chopper.*) You don't think I can bear the sight of blood. You think I'm so weak. Oh, how I should like to see your blood and your brains on a chopping-block! I'd like to see the whole of your sex swimming like that in a sea of blood. I think I could drink out of your skull, bathe my feet in your broken breast and eat your heart roasted whole. You think I'm weak. You think I love you, that my womb yearned for your seed and I want to carry your offspring under my heart and nourish it with my blood. You think I want to bear your child and take your name. By the way, what is your name? I've never heard your surname. I don't suppose you've got one. I should be "Mrs. Hovel" or "Madam Dung-hill." You dog wearing my collar, you lackey with my crest on your buttons! I share you with my cook; I'm my own servant's rival! Oh! Oh! Oh! . . . You think I'm a coward and will run away. No, now I'm going to stay—and let the storm break. My father will come back . . . find his desk broken open . . . his money gone. Then he'll ring that bell —twice for the valet—and then he'll send for the police . . . and I shall tell everything. Everything. Oh how wonderful to make an end of it all—a real end! He has a stroke and dies and that's the end of all of us. Just peace and quietness . . . eternal rest. The coat of arms broken on the coffin and the Count's line extinct . . . But the valet's line goes on in an orphanage, wins laurels in the gutter and ends in jail.

JEAN: There speaks the noble blood! Bravo, Miss Julie. But now, don't let the cat out of the bag.

KRISTIN *enters dressed for church, carrying a prayer-book. JULIE rushes to her and flings herself into her arms for protection.*

JULIE: Help me, Kristin! Protect me from this man!

KRISTIN (*unmoved and cold*): What goings-on for a feast day morning! (*Sees the board.*) And what a filthy mess. What's it all about? Why are you screaming and carrying on so?

JULIE: Kristin, you're a woman and my friend. Beware of that scoundrel!

JEAN (*embarrassed*): While you ladies are talking things over, I'll go and shave. (*Slips into his room.*)

JULIE: You must understand. You must listen to me.

KRISTIN: I certainly don't understand such loose ways. Where are you off to in those travelling clothes? And he had his hat on, didn't he, eh?

JULIE: Listen, Kristin. Listen, I'll tell you everything.

KRISTIN: I don't want to know anything.

JULIE: You must listen.

KRISTIN: What to? Your nonsense with Jean? I don't care a rap about that; it's nothing to do with me. But if you're thinking of getting him to run off with you, we'll soon put a stop to that.

JULIE (*very nervously*): Please try to be calm, Kristin, and listen. I can't stay here, nor can Jean—so we must go abroad.

KRISTIN: Hm, hm!

JULIE (*brightening*): But you see, I've had an idea. Supposing we all three go—abroad—to Switzerland and start a hotel together . . . I've got some money, you see . . . and Jean and I could run the whole thing—and I thought you would take charge of the kitchen. Wouldn't that be splendid? Say yes, do. If you come with us everything will be fine. Oh do say yes! (*Puts her arms round* KRISTIN.)

KRISTIN (*coolly thinking*): Hm, hm.

JULIE (*presto tempo*): You've never travelled, Kristin. You should go abroad and see the world. You've no idea how nice it is travelling by train—new faces all the time and new countries. On our way through Hamburg we'll go to the zoo—you'll love that—and we'll go to the theatre and the opera too . . . and when we get to Munich there'll be the museums, dear, and pictures by Rubens and Raphael—the great painters, you know . . . You've heard of Munich, haven't you? Where King Ludwig lived—you know, the king who went mad . . . We'll see his castles—some of his castles are still just like in fairy tales . . . and from there it's not far to Switzerland—and the Alps. Think of the Alps, Kristin dear, covered with snow in the middle of summer . . . and there are oranges there and trees that are green the whole year round . . .

JEAN *is seen in the door of his room, sharpening his razor on a strop which he holds with his teeth and his left hand. He listens to the talk with satisfaction and now and then nods approval.* JULIE *continues, tempo prestissimo.*

And then we'll get a hotel . . . and I'll sit at the desk, while Jean receives the guests and goes out marketing and writes letters . . . There's life for you! Trains whistling, buses driving up, bells ringing upstairs and downstairs . . . and I shall make out the bills—and I shall cook them too . . . you've no idea how nervous travellers are when it comes to paying their bills. And you—you'll sit like a queen in the kitchen . . . of course there won't be any standing at the stove for you. You'll always have to be nicely dressed and ready to be seen, and with your looks—no, I'm not flattering you—one fine day you'll catch yourself a husband . . . some rich Englishman, I shouldn't wonder—they're the ones who are easy—(*Slowing down.*)—to catch . . . and then we'll get rich and build ourselves a villa on Lake Como . . . of course it rains there a little now and then—but—(*Dully.*)—the sun must shine there too sometimes—even though it seems gloomy—and if not—then we can come home again—come back—(*Pause.*)—here—or somewhere else . . .

KRISTIN: Look here, Miss Julie, do you believe all that yourself?

JULIE (*exhausted*): Do I believe it?

KRISTIN: Yes.

JULIE (*wearily*): I don't know. I don't believe anything any more. (*Sinks down on the bench; her head in her arms on the table.*) Nothing. Nothing at all.

KRISTIN (*turning to* JEAN): So you meant to beat it, did you?

JEAN (*disconcerted, putting the razor on the table*): Beat it? What are you talking about? You've heard Miss Julie's plan, and though she's tired now with being up all night, it's a perfectly sound plan.

KRISTIN: Oh, is it? If you thought I'd work for that . . .

JEAN (*interrupting*): Kindly use decent language in front of your mistress. Do you hear?

KRISTIN: Mistress?

JEAN: Yes.

KRISTIN: Well, well, just listen to that!

JEAN: Yes, it would be a good thing if you did listen and talked less. Miss Julie is your mistress and what's made you lose your respect for her now ought to make you feel the same about yourself.

KRISTIN: I've always had enough self-respect—

JEAN: To despise other people.

KRISTIN: —not to go below my own station. Has the Count's cook ever gone with the groom or the swineherd? Tell me that.

JEAN: No, you were lucky enough to have a high-class chap for your beau.

KRISTIN: High-class all right—selling the oats out of the Count's stable.

JEAN: You're a fine one to talk—taking a commission on the groceries and bribes from the butcher.

KRISTIN: What the devil . . . ?

JEAN: And now you can't feel any respect for your employers. You, you!

KRISTIN: Are you coming to church with me? I should think you need a good sermon after your fine deeds.

JEAN: No, I'm not going to church today. You can go alone and confess your own sins.

KRISTIN: Yes, I'll do that and bring back enough forgiveness to cover yours too. The Savior suffered and died on the cross for all our sins, and if we go to Him with faith and a penitent heart, He takes all our sins upon Himself.

JEAN: Even grocery thefts?

JULIE: Do you believe that, Kristin?

KRISTIN: That is my living faith, as sure as I stand here. The faith I learnt as a child and have kept ever since, Miss Julie. "But where sin abounded, grace did much more abound."

JULIE: Oh, if I had your faith! Oh, if . . .

KRISTIN: But you see you can't have it without God's special grace, and it's not given to all to have that.

JULIE: Who is it given to then?

KRISTIN: That's the great secret of the workings of grace, Miss

Julie. God is no respecter of persons, and with Him the last shall be first . . .

JULIE: Then I suppose He does respect the last.

KRISTIN (*continuing*): . . . and it is easier for a camel to go through the eye of a needle than for a rich man to enter into the kingdom of God. That's how it is, Miss Julie. Now I'm going—alone, and on my way I shall tell the groom not to let any of the horses out, in case anyone should want to leave before the Count gets back. Goodbye. (*Exit.*)

JEAN: What a devil! And all on account of a greenfinch.

JULIE (*wearily*): Never mind the greenfinch. Do you see any way out of this, any end to it?

JEAN (*pondering*): No.

JULIE: If you were in my place, what would you do?

JEAN: In your place? Wait a bit. If I was a woman—a lady of rank who had—fallen. I don't know. Yes, I do know now.

JULIE (*picking up the razor and making a gesture*): This?

JEAN: Yes. But *I* wouldn't do it, you know. There's a difference between us.

JULIE: Because you're a man and I'm a woman? What is the difference?

JEAN: The usual difference—between man and woman.

JULIE (*holding the razor*): I'd like to. But I can't. My father couldn't either, that time he wanted to.

JEAN: No, he didn't want to. He had to be revenged first.

JULIE: And now my mother is revenged again, through me.

JEAN: Didn't you ever love your father, Miss Julie?

JULIE: Deeply, but I must have hated him too—unconsciously. And he let me be brought up to despise my own sex, to be half woman, half man. Whose fault is what's happened? My father's, my mother's, or my own? My own? I haven't any-

thing that's my own. I haven't one single thought that I
didn't get from my father, one emotion that didn't come
from my mother, and as for this last idea—about all people
being equal—I got that from him, my fiancé—that's why I
call him a cad. How can it be my fault? Push the responsibility on to Jesus, like Kristin does? No, I'm too proud and
—thanks to my father's teaching—too intelligent. As for all
that about a rich person not being able to get into heaven,
it's just a lie, but Kristin, who has money in the savings-
bank, will certainly not get in. Whose fault is it? What
does it matter whose fault it is? In any case I must take the
blame and bear the consequences.

JEAN: Yes, but . . . (*There are two sharp rings on the bell.*
JULIE *jumps to her feet.* JEAN *changes into his livery.*) The
Count is back. Supposing Kristin . . . (*Goes to the speak-
ing-tube, presses it and listens.*)

JULIE: Has he been to his desk yet?

JEAN: This is Jean, sir.(*Listens.*) Yes, sir. (*Listens.*) Yes, sir, very
good, sir. (*Listens.*) At once, sir? (*Listens.*) Very good, sir.
In half an hour.

JULIE (*in panic*): What did he say? My God, what did he say?

JEAN: He ordered his boots and his coffee in half an hour.

JULIE: Then there's half an hour . . . Oh, I'm so tired! I can't
do anything. Can't be sorry, can't run away, can't stay,
can't live—can't die. Help me. Order me, and I'll obey like
a dog. Do me this last service—save my honor, save his name.
You know what I ought to do, but haven't the strength to
do. Use your strength and order me to do it.

JEAN: I don't know why—I can't now—I don't understand . . .
It's just as if this coat made me—I can't give you orders—
and now that the Count has spoken to me—I can't quite explain, but . . . well, that devil of a lackey is bending my
back again. I believe if the Count came down now and ordered me to cut my throat, I'd do it on the spot.

JULIE: Then pretend you're him and I'm you. You did some fine acting before, when you knelt to me and played the aristocrat. Or . . . Have you ever seen a hypnotist at the theatre? (*He nods.*) He says to the person "Take the broom," and he takes it. He says "Sweep," and he sweeps . . .

JEAN: But the person has to be asleep.

JULIE (*as if in a trance*): I am asleep already . . . the whole room has turned to smoke—and you look like a stove—a stove like a man in black with a tall hat—your eyes are glowing like coals when the fire is low—and your face is a white patch like ashes. (*The sunlight has now reached the floor and lights up* JEAN.) How nice and warm it is! (*She holds out her hands as though warming them at a fire.*) And so light—and so peaceful.

JEAN (*putting the razor in her hand*): Here is the broom. Go now while it's light—out to the barn—and . . . (*Whispers in her ear.*)

JULIE (*waking*): Thank you. I am going now—to rest. But just tell me that even the first can receive the gift of grace.

JEAN: The first? No, I can't tell you that. But wait . . . Miss Julie, I've got it! You aren't one of the first any longer. You're one of the last.

JULIE: That's true. I'm one of the very last. I *am* the last. Oh! . . . But now I can't go. Tell me again to go.

JEAN: No, I can't now either. I can't.

JULIE: And the first shall be last.

JEAN: Don't think, don't think. You're taking my strength away too and making me a coward. What's that? I thought I saw the bell move . . . To be so frightened of a bell! Yes, but it's not just a bell. There's somebody behind it—a hand moving it—and something else moving the hand—and if you stop your ears—if you stop your ears—yes, then it rings louder than ever. Rings and rings until you answer—and then it's too late. Then the police come and . . . and . . . (*The bell rings twice loudly.* JEAN *flinches, then straightens himself up.*) It's horrible. But there's no other way to end it . . . Go!

JULIE *walks firmly out through the door.*

**CURTAIN**

# *Purgatory*

## by W. B. Yeats

*Scene: A ruined house and a bare tree in the background.*

BOY: Half-door, hall door,
Hither and thither, day and night,
Hill or hollow, shouldering this pack,
Hearing you talk.

OLD MAN:            Study that house.
I think about its jokes and stories;
I try to remember what the butler
Said to a drunken gamekeeper
In mid-October, but I cannot.
If I cannot, none living can.
Where are the jokes and stories of a house,
Its threshold gone to patch a pig-sty?

BOY: So you have come this path before?

OLD MAN: The moonlight falls upon the path,
The shadow of a cloud upon the house,
And that's symbolical; study that tree,
What is it like?

BOY:            A silly old man.

OLD MAN: It's like—no matter what it's like.
I saw it a year ago stripped bare as now,
So I chose a better trade.
I saw it fifty years ago
Before the thunderbolt had riven it,
Green leaves, ripe leaves, leaves thick as butter,
Fat, greasy life. Stand there and look,
Because there is somebody in that house.

*The* BOY *puts down pack and stands in the doorway.*

BOY: There's nobody here.

OLD MAN:            There's somebody there.

BOY: The floor is gone, the window's gone,

51

> And where there should be roof there's sky,
> And here's a bit of an eggshell thrown
> Out of a jackdaw's nest.

OLD MAN:                            But there are some
> That do not care what's gone, what's left:
> The souls in Purgatory that come back
> To habitations and familiar spots.

BOY: Your wits are out again.

OLD MAN:                            Re-live
> Their transgressions, and that not once
> But many times; they know at last
> The consequence of those transgressions
> Whether upon others or upon themselves;
> Upon others, others may bring help,
> For when the consequence is at an end
> The dream must end; if upon themselves,
> There is no help but in themselves
> And in the mercy of God.

BOY:                            I have had enough!
> Talk to the jackdaws, if talk you must.

OLD MAN: Stop! Sit there upon that stone.
> That is the house where I was born.

BOY: The big old house that was burnt down?

OLD MAN: My mother that was your granddam owned it,
> This scenery and this countryside,
> Kennel and stable, horse and hound—
> She had a horse at the Curragh, and there met
> My father, a groom in a training stable,
> Looked at him and married him.
> Her mother never spoke to her again,
> And she did right.

BOY:                            What's right and wrong?
> My granddad got the girl and the money.

OLD MAN: Looked at him and married him,

    And he squandered everything she had.
    She never knew the worst, because
    She died in giving birth to me,
    But now she knows it all, being dead.
    Great people lived and died in this house;
    Magistrates, colonels, members of Parliament,
    Captains and Governors, and long ago
    Men that had fought at Aughrim and the Boyne.
    Some that had gone on government work
    To London or to India came home to die,
    Or came from London every spring
    To look at the May-blossom in the park.
    They had loved the trees that he cut down
    To pay what he had lost at cards
    Or spent on horses, drink, and women;
    Had loved the house, had loved all
    The intricate passages of the house,
    But he killed the house; to kill a house
    Where great men grew up, married, died,
    I here declare a capital offence.

BOY: My God, but you had luck! Grand clothes,
    And maybe a grand horse to ride.

OLD MAN: That he might keep me upon his level
    He never sent me to school, but some
    Half-loved me for my half of her:
    A gamekeeper's wife taught me to read,
    A Catholic curate taught me Latin.
    There were old books and books made fine
    By eighteenth-century French binding, books
    Modern and ancient, books by the ton.

BOY: What education have you given me?

OLD MAN: I gave the education that befits
    A bastard that a pedlar got
    Upon a tinker's daughter in a ditch.
    When I had come to sixteen years old
    My father burned down the house when drunk

BOY: But what is my age, sixteen years old,
At the Puck Fair.

OLD MAN:                    And everything was burnt;
Books, library, all were burnt.

BOY: Is what I have heard upon the road the truth,
That you killed him in the burning house?

OLD MAN: There's nobody here but our two selves?

BOY: Nobody, Father.

OLD MAN:                    I stuck him with a knife,
That knife that cuts my dinner now,
And after that I left him in the fire.
They dragged him out, somebody saw
The knife wound but could not be certain
Because the body was all black and charred.
Then some that were his drunken friends
Swore they would put me upon trial,
Spoke of quarrels, a threat I had made.
The gamekeeper gave me some old clothes,
I ran away, worked here and there
Till I became a pedlar on the roads,
No good trade, but good enough
Because I am my father's son,
Because of what I did or may do.
Listen to the hoofbeats! Listen, listen!

BOY: I cannot hear a sound.

OLD MAN:                         Beat! Beat!
This night is the anniversary
Of my mother's wedding night,
Or of the night wherein I was begotten.
My father is riding from the public house,
A whiskey bottle under his arm.

*A window is lit showing a young girl.*

Look at the window; she stands there
Listening, the servants are all in bed,

She is alone, he has stayed late
Bragging and drinking in the public house.

BOY: There's nothing but an empty gap in the wall.
You have made it up. No, you are mad!
You are getting madder every day.

OLD MAN: It's louder now because he rides
Upon a gravelled avenue
All grass today. The hoof-beat stops,
He has gone to the other side of the house,
Gone to the stable, put the horse up.
She has gone down to open the door.
This night she is no better than her man
And does not mind that he is half drunk,
She is mad about him. They mount the stairs,
She brings him into her own chamber.
And that is the marriage-chamber now.
The window is dimly lit again.
Do not let him touch you! It is not true
That drunken men cannot beget,
And if he touch he must beget
And you must bear his murderer.
Deaf! Both deaf! If I should throw
A stick or a stone they would not hear;
And that's a proof my wits are out.
But there's a problem: she must live
Through everything in exact detail,
Driven to it by remorse, and yet
Can she renew the sexual act
And find no pleasure in it, and if not,
If pleasure and remorse must both be there,
Which is the greater?
                              I lack schooling.
Go fetch Tertullian; he and I
Will ravel all that problem out
Whilst those two lie upon the mattress
Begetting me.

Come back! Come back!
And so you thought to slip away,
My bag of money between your fingers,
And that I could not talk and see!
You have been rummaging in the pack.

*The light in the window has faded out.*

BOY: You never gave me my right share.

OLD MAN: And had I given it, young as you are,
You would have spent it upon drink.

BOY: What if I did? I had a right
To get it and spend it as I chose.

OLD MAN: Give me that bag and no more words.

BOY: I will not.

OLD MAN:                I will break your fingers.

*They struggle for the bag. In the struggle it drops, scattering
the money. The* OLD MAN *staggers but does not fall. They
stand looking at each other. The window is lit up.* A MAN
*is seen pouring whiskey into a glass.*

BOY: What if I killed you? You killed my granddad,
Because you were young and he was old.
Now I am young and you are old.

OLD MAN (*staring at window*): Better-looking, those sixteen
years—

BOY: What are you muttering?

OLD MAN:                          Younger—and yet
She should have known he was not her kind.

BOY: What are you saying? Out with it!

OLD MAN *points to window.*

My God! The window is lit up
And somebody stands there, although
The floorboards are all burnt away.

OLD MAN: The window is lit up because my father
Has come to find a glass for his whiskey.
He leans there like some tired beast.

BOY: A dead, living, murdered man!

OLD MAN: "Then the bride-sleep fell upon Adam":
Where did I read those words?
                    And yet
There's nothing leaning in the window
But the impression upon my mother's mind;
Being dead she is alone in her remorse.

BOY: A body that was a bundle of old bones
Before I was born. Horrible! Horrible!

*He covers his eyes.*

OLD MAN: That beast there would know nothing, being nothing,
If I should kill a man under the window
He would not even turn his head.

*He stabs the* BOY.

My father and my son on the same jackknife!
That finishes—there—there—there—

*He stabs again and again.*

*The window grows dark.*

"Hush-a-bye baby, thy father's a knight,
Thy mother a lady, lovely and bright."
No, that is something that I read in a book,
And if I sing it must be to my mother,
And I lack rhyme.

*The stage has grown dark except where the tree stands in
white light.*

                    Study that tree.
It stands there like a purified soul,
All cold, sweet, glistening light.
Dear mother, the window is dark again,
But you are in the light because

I finished all that consequence.
I killed that lad because had he grown up
He would have struck a woman's fancy,
Begot, and passed pollution on.
I am a wretched foul old man
And therefore harmless. When I have stuck
This old jack-knife into a sod
And pulled it out all bright again,
And picked up all the money that he dropped,
I'll to a distant place, and there
Tell my old jokes among new men.

*He cleans the knife and begins to pick up money.*

Hoof-beats! Dear God,
How quickly it returns—beat—beat—!

Her mind cannot hold up that dream.
Twice a murderer and all for nothing,
And she must animate that dead night
Not once but many times!

                    O God,
Release my mother's soul from its dream!
Mankind can do no more. Appease
The misery of the living and the remorse of the dead.

**CURTAIN**

# The Man With
# the Flower in
# His Mouth

by Luigi Pirandello

Translated by

Eric Bentley

THE MAN WITH THE FLOWER IN HIS MOUTH

A PEACEFUL CUSTOMER

*Towards the end, at the points indicated, a* WOMAN *is seen at the corner, clad in black, and wearing an old hat with drooping feathers.*

*Scene: At the back, we see the trees of an avenue and electric lights showing through the leaves. On both sides, the last houses of a street which leads into this avenue. Among the houses on the left, a cheap all-night cafe, with chairs and little tables on the sidewalk. In front of the houses on the right, a streetlamp, lit. On the left, where the street meets the avenue, there is another lamp affixed to the corner house; it too is lit. At intervals, the vibrant notes of a mandolin are heard in the distance.*

*When the curtain rises,* THE MAN WITH THE FLOWER IN HIS MOUTH *is sitting at a table and looking in silence at the* PEACEFUL CUSTOMER *who is at the next table, sucking a mint frappé through a straw.*

MAN: Well, what I was just going to say . . . Here you are, a law-abiding sort of man . . . You missed your train?

CUSTOMER: By one minute. I get to the station and see the damn thing just pulling out.

MAN: You could have run after it.

CUSTOMER: Sure—but for those damn packages. I looked like an old packhorse covered with luggage. Isn't that silly? But you know how women are. Errands, errands, errands! You're never through. God! You know how long it took me to get my fingers on the strings of all those packages—when I climbed out of the cab? Three solid minutes. Two packages to each finger.

MAN: What a sight! Know what *I'd* have done? Left 'em in the cab.

CUSTOMER: How about my wife? And my daughters? And all the other women?

MAN: They'd squawk. I'd enjoy that.

CUSTOMER: You don't seem to know how women carry on when they get out in the country.

MAN: I know exactly how they carry on. (*Pause.*) They tell you they won't need a thing, they can live on nothing.

CUSTOMER: Worse, they pretend they live there to *save* money. They go out to one of those villages*—the uglier and filthier the better—and then insist on wearing all their fanciest get-ups! Women! But I suppose it's their vocation. "If you're going into town, could you get me one of these—and one of those—and would it trouble you *too* much to get me . . ." Would it trouble you *too* much! "And since you'll be right next door to . . ." "Now really, darling, how do you expect me to get all that done in three hours?" "Why not? Can't you take a cab?" And the hell of it is—figuring on those three hours—I didn't bring the keys to our house here in town.

MAN: Quite a thing. So?

CUSTOMER: I left my pile of packages at the station—in the parcel room. Then I went to a restaurant for supper. Then I went to the theatre—to get rid of my bad temper. The heat nearly killed me. Coming out, I say: "And now, what? It's after midnight. There isn't a train till four. All that fuss for a couple of hours of sleep? Not worth the price of the ticket." So here I am. Open all night, isn't it?

MAN: All night. (*Pause.*) So you left your packages in the parcel room?

---

*The scene is rather obviously laid in Rome. The villages where "commuters" live are some ten miles out. [E.B.]

CUSTOMER: Why do you ask? Don't you think they're safe? They were tied up good and . . .

MAN: Oh, sure, sure! (*Pause.*) I feel *sure* they're safe. I know how well these salesmen wrap their stuff. They make quite a specialty of it. (*Pause.*) I can see their hands now. What hands! They take a good big piece of paper, double thickness, sort of a reddish color, wavy lines on it—a pleasure just to look at it!—so smooth, you could press it against your cheek and feel how cool and delicate it is . . . They roll it out on the counter and then place your cloth in the middle of it with *such* agility—fine cloth too, neatly folded. They raise one edge of the paper with the back of the hand, lower the other one, and bring the two edges together in an elegant fold—*that's* just thrown in for good measure . . . Then they fold the corners down in a triangle with its apex turned in like this. Then they reach out with one hand for the box of string, instinctively pull off just exactly enough, and tie up the parcel so quickly you haven't even time to admire their . . . virtuosity—the little loop is ready for your finger!

CUSTOMER: Anyone can see you've given a lot of attention to this matter.

MAN: Have I! My dear man, I spend whole days at it. What's more, I can spend a solid hour at a single store window. I lose myself in it. I seem to *be* that piece of silk, I'd *like* to be that piece of silk, that bit of braid, that ribbon—red or blue—that the salesgirls are measuring with their tape and—you've seen what they do with it before they wrap it up?—they twist it round the thumb and little finger of their left hand in a figure eight! (*Pause.*) I look at the shoppers as they come out of the store with their bundle on their finger—or in their hand—or under their arm. I watch them pass. My eyes follow them till they're out of sight. I imagine, oh, I imagine so many, many things, you've no idea, how could you have? (*Pause. Then, darkly, as to himself.*) All the same, it helps.

CUSTOMER: What helps?

MAN: Latching on—to life. With the imagination. Like a creeper around the bars of a gate. (*Pause.*) Giving it no rest—my imagination, I mean—clinging, clinging with my imagination to the lives of others—all the time. Not people I know, of course. I couldn't do that. That'd be annoying, it'd nauseate me if *they* knew. No. Just strangers. With them my imagination can work freely. Not capriciously, though. Oh no, I take account of the smallest things I can find out about them. You've no idea how my imagination functions. I work my way *in*. In! I get to see this man's house—or that man's, I live in it, I feel I belong there. And I begin to notice—you know how a house, any old house, has its own air, how there's something special about the air in it? Your house? Mine? Of course, in your own house, you don't notice it any more, it's *your* air, the air of *your* life, isn't it? Uh huh. I see you agree—

CUSTOMER: I only meant . . . well, I was thinking what a good time you must have imagining all this!

MAN (*annoyed, after thinking a moment*): Good time? I had a—!

CUSTOMER: Good time, yes. I can just see you—

MAN: Tell me something. Did you ever consult an eminent physician?

CUSTOMER: Me? Why should I? I'm not sick!

MAN: Just a moment. I ask because I'd like to know if you ever saw a fine doctor's waiting room—full of patients waiting their turn?

CUSTOMER: Well, yes. I once had to take my little girl. She's nervous.

MAN: Okay. You needn't tell me. It's the waiting rooms . . . (*Pause.*) Have you ever given them much attention? The old-fashioned couch with dark covers, the upholstered table chairs that don't match as a rule . . . the armchairs? Stuff bought at sales and auctions, coming together there by ac-

cident, for the convenience of the patients. It doesn't belong
to the house. The doctor has quite another sort of room for
himself, for his wife, his wife's friends . . . lavish . . .
lovely . . . If you took one of the chairs from the drawing
room and put it in the waiting room, why, it'd stick out like
a sore thumb. Not that the waiting room isn't just right—
nothing special of course but quite proper, quite respectable . . . I'd like to know if you—when you went with
your little girl—if you took a good look at the chair you
sat in?

CUSTOMER: Well, um, no, I guess I didn't.

MAN: Of course not. You weren't sick . . . (*Pause.*) But often
even the sick don't notice. They're all taken up with their
sickness. (*Pause.*) How many times they sit, some of them,
staring at their finger which is making meaningless markings
on the polished arm of the chair. They're thinking—so they
don't see. (*Pause.*) And what an impression you get when
you get out of the doctor's office and cross the waiting
room and see the chair you'd been sitting in awaiting sen-
tence on the as yet unknown sickness just a short time before! Now, there's another patient on it and *he's* hugging his
secret sickness too. Or it's empty—oh, how *impassive* it looks!
—waiting for Mr. X to come and sit on it. (*Pause.*) What
were we saying? Oh, yes. The pleasure of imagining things.
And I suddenly thought of a chair in one of those waiting
rooms. Why?

CUSTOMER: Yes, it certainly . . .

MAN: You don't see the connection? Neither do I. (*Pause.*) You
recall an image, you recall another image, they're unrelated,
and yet—they're *not* unrelated—for you. Oh, no, they have
their reasons, they stem from *your* experience. Of course
you have to pretend they don't. When you talk, you have
to forget them. Most often they're so illogical, these . . .
analogies. (*Pause.*) The connection could be this, maybe.
Listen. Do you think those chairs get any pleasure from
imagining which patient will sit on them next? What sick-

ness lurks inside him? Where he'll go, what he'll do after this visit? Of course they don't. And it's the same with me! I get no pleasure from it. There are those poor chairs and here am I. *They* open their arms to the doctor's patients, *I* open mine to . . . this person or that. You for instance. And yet I get no pleasure—no pleasure at all—from the train you missed, the family waiting for that train in the country, your other little troubles . . .

CUSTOMER: I've plenty, you know that?

MAN: You should thank God they're little. (*Pause.*) Some people have big troubles, my dear sir. (*Pause.*) As I was saying, I feel the need to latch on—by the skin of my . . . imagination—to the lives of others. Yet I get no pleasure from this. It doesn't even interest me. Quite the reverse, quite . . . One wants to see what their troubles are just to prove to oneself that life is idiotic and stupid! So that one won't mind being through with it!! (*With dark rage.*) Proving that to yourself takes quite a bit of doing, huh? You need evidence, you need a hundred and one instances, and—you—must—be—*implacable!* Because, well, because, my dear sir, there's something—we don't know what it's made of, but it exists—and we all feel it, we feel it like a pain in the throat—it's the hunger for life! A hunger that is never appeased—that never *can* be appeased—because life—life as we live it from moment to moment—is so hungry itself, hungry *for* itself, we never get to taste it even! The taste of life, the flavor and savor of life, is all in the past, we carry it inside us. Or rather it's always at a distance from us. We're tied to it only by a slender thread, the rope of memory. Yes, memory ties us to . . . what? that idiocy, these irritations, those silly illusions, mad pursuits like . . . yes . . . What today is idiocy, what today is an irritation, even what today is a misfortune, a grave misfortune, look! Four years pass, five years, ten, and who knows what savor or flavor it will have, what tears will be shed over it, how—it—will—*taste!* Life, life! You only have to think of giving it up—especially if it's a matter of days—(*At this point the head of* THE WOMAN IN

BLACK *is seen at the corner.*) Look! See that? At the corner! See that woman, that shadow of a woman? She's hiding now.

CUSTOMER: What? Who was it?

MAN: You didn't see? She's hiding now.

CUSTOMER: A woman?

MAN: My wife.

CUSTOMER: Ah! Your wife? (*Pause.*)

MAN: She keeps an eye on me. Oh, sometimes I could just go over and kick her! It wouldn't do any good, though. She's as stubborn as a lost dog: the more you kick it, the closer it sticks to you. (*Pause.*) What that woman is suffering on my account you could not imagine. She doesn't eat. Doesn't sleep any more. Just follows me around. Night and day. At a distance. She *might* brush her clothes once in a while—and that old shoe of a hat. She isn't a woman any more. Just—a rag doll. Her hair's going gray, yes, the white dust has settled on her temples forever, and she's only thirty-four. (*Pause.*) She annoys me. You wouldn't believe how much she annoys me. Sometimes I grab hold of her and shake her. "You're an idiot!" I shout. She takes it. She stands there looking at me. Oh, that look! It makes my fingers itch. I feel like strangling her! Nothing happens, of course. She just waits till I'm a short way off. Then she starts following me again. (THE WOMAN IN BLACK *again sticks her head out.*) Look! There's her head again!

CUSTOMER: Poor woman!

MAN: Poor woman? You know what she wants? She wants me to stay and take it easy at home—all cozy and quiet—and let her be nice to me, look after me, show me wifely tenderness . . . Home! The rooms in perfect order, the furniture elegant and neat, silence reigns . . . It used to, anyway. Silence—measured by the tick-tocking of the dining-room clock! (*Pause.*) That's what she wants! I just want you to see the absurdity of it! Isn't it absurd? It's worse: it's cruel, it's macabre! Don't you see? Think of Messina. Or Avezzano. Suppose they knew an earthquake was coming. Do you think those cities could just sit? You think they could just sit calmly in the moonlight waiting for it? Carefully preserving the lovely lines of their streets and the spaciousness of their piazzas? Not daring to deviate one inch from the plans of the City Planning Commission? You're crazy. Those cities would drop everything and take to their heels! Every house, every stone, would take to its heels! (*Wheeling on the* CUSTOMER.) You agree?

CUSTOMER (*frightened*): Well . . .

MAN: Well, just suppose the people knew? The citizens of Avezzano and Messina. Would they calmly get undressed and go to bed? Fold their clothes and put their shoes outside the door? Creep down under the bedclothes and enjoy the nice clean feeling of freshly laundered sheets? Knowing that—in a few hours—they would be dead?—You think they might?

CUSTOMER: Maybe your wife—

MAN: Let me finish. (*Starting over.*) If death, my dear sir, if death were some strange, filthy insect that just . . . settled on you, as it were, took you unawares, shall we say . . . You're walking along. All of a sudden a passerby stops you, and, with finger and thumb cautiously extended, says: "Excuse me, sir, excuse me, honored sir, but death has settled on you!" And with finger and thumb cautiously extended, he takes it and throws it in the gutter. Wouldn't that be wonderful? But death is not an insect. It has settled on many walkers in the city—however far away their thoughts may be, however carefree they may feel. They don't see it. They're thinking what they'll be doing tomorrow. But I (*He gets up.*) . . . Look, my dear sir, come here (*He gets the* CUSTOMER *up and takes him under the lighted lamp.*) under the lamp. Come over here. I'll show you something. Look! Under this side of my mustache. See that little knob?

Royal purple? Know what they call it? It has such a poetic name. It suggests something soft and sweet. Like a caramel. Epithelioma. (*The "o" is stressed.*) Try it, isn't it soft and sweet? Epithelioma. Understand? Death passed my way. He stuck this . . . flower in my mouth and said: "Keep it, old chap. I'll stop by again in eight months—or maybe ten." (*Pause.*) Now tell me. *You* tell *me.* Can I just sit quietly at home as that unhappy girl wishes me to—with this flower in my mouth? (*Pause.*) I yell at her. "So you want me to kiss you, do you?" "Yes, yes, kiss me!" You know what she did? A couple of weeks ago she took a pin and cut herself—here—on the lip—then she took hold of my head and tried to kiss me, tried to kiss me on the mouth. She said she wanted to die with me. (*Pause.*) She's insane. (*Angrily.*) I'm not home! Ever! What I want is to stand at store windows admiring the virtuosity of salesmen! Because, you see, if ever, for one second, I am not occupied, if ever I'm *empty*—know what I mean?—why, I might take a life and think nothing of it, I might destroy the life in someone . . . someone I don't even know, I'd take a gun and kill some-one—like you maybe—someone who's missed his train. (*He laughs.*) Of course, I'm only joking. (*Pause.*) I'll go now. (*Pause.*) It'd be myself I'd kill. (*Pause.*) At this time of year, there's a certain kind of apricot, it's good . . . How do *you* eat them? Skin and all? You cut them in exact halves, you take hold with finger and thumb, lengthwise, like this . . . then! (*He swallows.*) How succulent! Pure delight! Like a woman's lips! (*He laughs. Pause.*) I wish to send my best wishes to your good lady and her daughters in your country home. (*Pause.*) I imagine them . . . I imagine them dressed in white and light blue in the middle of a lovely green meadow under the shade of . . . (*Pause.*)Will you do me a favor when you arrive, tomorrow morning? As I figure it, your village is a certain distance from the station. It is dawn. You will be on foot. The first tuft of grass you see by the roadside—count the number of blades, will you? Just count the blades of grass. The number will be the number of days

I have to live. (*Pause.*) One last request: pick a big tuft! (*He laughs.*) Then: Good night!

*He walks away humming through closed lips the tune which the mandolin is playing in the distance. He is approaching the corner on the right. But at a certain point—remembering his Wife—he turns and sneaks off in the opposite direction. The* CUSTOMER *follows with his eyes—more or less dumbfounded.*

**CURTAIN**

# *Pullman Car Hiawatha*

## by Thornton Wilder

*Scene: At the back of the stage is a balcony or bridge or runway leading out of sight in both directions. Two flights of stairs descend from it to the stage. There is no further scenery.*

*At the rise of the curtain the* STAGE MANAGER *is making lines with a piece of chalk on the floor of the stage by the footlights.*

73

THE STAGE MANAGER: This is the plan of a Pullman car. Its name is Hiawatha and on December twenty-first it is on its way from New York to Chicago. Here at your left are three compartments. Here is the aisle and five lowers. The berths are all full, uppers and lowers, but for the purposes of this play we are limiting our interest to the people in the lower berths on the further side only.

The berths are already made up. It is half-past nine. Most of the passengers are in bed behind the green curtains. They are dropping their shoes on the floor, or wrestling with their trousers, or wondering whether they dare hide their valuables in the pillow slips during the night.

All right! Come on, everybody!

*The actors enter carrying chairs. Each improvises his berth by placing two chairs facing one another in his chalk-marked space. They then sit in one chair, profile to the audience, and rest their feet on the other. This must do for lying in bed.*

*The passengers in the compartments do the same.*

*Reading from left to right we have:*

COMPARTMENT THREE: *an insane woman with a male attendant and a trained nurse.*

COMPARTMENT TWO: .PHILIP *and*

COMPARTMENT ONE: HARRIET, *his young wife.*

LOWER ONE: *a maiden lady.*

LOWER THREE: *a middle-aged doctor.*

LOWER FIVE: *a stout, amiable woman of fifty.*

LOWER SEVEN: *an engineer going to California.*

LOWER NINE: *another engineer.*

LOWER ONE: Porter, be sure and wake me up at quarter of six.

PORTER: Yes, ma'am.

LOWER ONE: I know I shan't sleep a wink, but I want to be told when it's quarter of six.

PORTER: Yes, ma'am.

LOWER SEVEN (*putting his head through the curtains*): Hsst! Porter! Hsst! How the hell do you turn on this other light?

PORTER (*fussing with it*): I'm afraid it's outa order, suh. You'll have to use the other end.

THE STAGE MANAGER (*falsetto, substituting for some woman in an upper berth*): May I ask if someone in this car will be kind enough to lend me some aspirin?

PORTER (*rushing about*): Yes, ma'am.

LOWER NINE (*one of the engineers, descending the aisle and falling into Lower Five*): Sorry, lady, sorry. Made a mistake.

LOWER FIVE (*grumbling*): Never in all my born days!

LOWER ONE (*in a shrill whisper*): Porter! Porter!

PORTER: Yes, ma'am.

LOWER ONE: My hot-water bag's leaking. I guess you'll have to take it away. I'll have to do without it tonight. How awful!

LOWER FIVE (*sharply to the passenger above her*): Young man, you mind your own business, or I'll report you to the conductor.

STAGE MANAGER (*substituting for UPPER FIVE*): Sorry, ma'am, I didn't mean to upset you. My suspenders fell down and I was trying to catch them.

LOWER FIVE: Well, here they are. Now go to sleep. Everybody seems to be rushing into my berth tonight.

*She puts her head out.*

Porter! Porter! Be a good soul and bring me a glass of water, will you? I'm parched.

LOWER NINE: Bill!

*No answer.*

Bill!

LOWER SEVEN: Ye'? Wha' d'y'a want?

LOWER NINE: Slip me one of those magazines, willya?

LOWER SEVEN: Which one d'y'a want?

LOWER NINE: Either one. *Detective Stories.* Either one.

LOWER SEVEN: Aw, Fred. I'm just in the middle of one of'm in *Detective Stories.*

LOWER NINE: That's all right. I'll take the Western. Thanks.

THE STAGE MANAGER (*to the actors*): All right! Sh! Sh! Sh—

*To the audience.*

Now I want you to hear them thinking.

*There is a pause and then they all begin a murmuring-swishing noise, very soft. In turn each one of them can be heard above the others.*

LOWER FIVE (*the lady of fifty*): Let's see: I've got the doll for the baby. And the slip-on for Marietta. And the fountain pen for Herbert. And the subscription to *Time* for George . . .

LOWER SEVEN (*Bill*): God! Lillian, if you don't turn out to be what I think you are, I don't know what I'll do. I guess it's bad politics to let a woman know that you're going all the way to California to see her. I'll think up a song and dance about a business trip or something. Was I ever as hot and bothered about anyone like this before? Well, there was Martha. But that was different. I'd better try and read or I'll go cuckoo. "How did you know it was ten o'clock when the visitor left the house?" asked the detective. "Because at ten o'clock," answered the girl, "I always turn out the lights in the conservatory and in the back hall. As I was coming down the stairs I heard the master talking to someone at the front door. I heard him say, 'Well, good night . . .' "—Gee, I don't feel like reading; I'll just think about Lillian. That yellow hair. Them eyes! . .

LOWER THREE: *The* DOCTOR *reads aloud to himself from a medical journal the most hair-raising material, every now and then punctuating his reading with an interrogative "So?"*

LOWER ONE (*the maiden lady*): I know I'll be awake all night. I might just as well make up my mind to it now. I can't imagine what got hold of that hot-water bag to leak on the train of all places. Well now, I'll lie on my right side and breathe deeply and think of beautiful things, and perhaps I can doze off a bit.

*And lastly:*

LOWER NINE (*Fred*): That was the craziest thing I ever did. It's set me back three whole years. I could have saved up thirty thousand dollars by now if I'd only stayed over here. What business had I got to fool with contracts with the goddam Soviets. Hell, I thought it would be interesting. Interesting, what the hell! It's set me back three whole years. I don't even know if the company'll take me back. I'm green, that's all. I just don't grow up.

*The* STAGE MANAGER *strides toward them with lifted hand, crying "Hush," and their whispering ceases.*

THE STAGE MANAGER: That'll do! Just one minute. Porter!

THE PORTER (*appearing at the left*): Yessuh.

THE STAGE MANAGER: It's your turn to think.

THE PORTER *is very embarrassed.*

Don't you want to? You have a right to.

THE PORTER (*torn between the desire to release his thoughts and his shyness*): Ah . . . ah . . . I'm only thinkin' about my home in Chicago and . . . and my life insurance.

THE STAGE MANAGER: That's right.

THE PORTER: . . . well, thank you . . . thank you.

*He slips away, blushing violently, in an agony of self-consciousness and pleasure.*

THE STAGE MANAGER (*to the audience*): He's a good fellow, Harrison is. Just shy.

*To the actors again.*

Now the compartments, please.

*The berths fall into shadow.*

PHILIP *is standing at the door connecting his compartment with his wife's.*

PHILIP: Are you all right, angel?

HARRIET: Yes. I don't know what was the matter with me during dinner.

PHILIP: Shall I close the door?

HARRIET: Do see whether you can't put a chair against it that will hold it half open without banging.

PHILIP: There. Good night, angel. If you can't sleep, call me, and we'll sit up and play Russian bank.

HARRIET: You're thinking of that awful time when we sat up every night for a week . . . But at least I know I shall sleep tonight. The noise of the wheels has become sort of nice and homely. What state are we in?

PHILIP: We're tearing through Ohio. We'll be in Indiana soon.

HARRIET: I know those little towns full of horse blocks.

PHILIP: Well, we'll reach Chicago very early. I'll call you. Sleep tight.

HARRIET: Sleep tight, darling.

*He returns to his own compartment. In Compartment Three, the male attendant tips his chair back against the wall and smokes a cigar. The trained nurse knits a stocking. The insane woman leans her forehead against the windowpane; that is, stares into the audience.*

THE INSANE WOMAN (*Her words have a dragging, complaining sound but lack any conviction*): Don't take me there. Don't take me there.

THE FEMALE ATTENDANT: Wouldn't you like to lie down, dearie?

THE INSANE WOMAN: I want to get off the train. I want to go back to New York.

THE FEMALE ATTENDANT: Wouldn't you like me to brush your hair again? It's such a nice feeling.

THE INSANE WOMAN (*going to the door*): I want to get off the train. I want to open the door.

THE FEMALE ATTENDANT (*taking one of her hands*): Such a noise! You'll wake up all the nice people. Come and I'll tell you a story about the place we're going to.

THE INSANE WOMAN: I don't want to go to that place.

THE FEMALE ATTENDANT: Oh, it's lovely! There are lawns and gardens everywhere. I never saw such a lovely place. Just lovely.

THE INSANE WOMAN (*lies down on the bed*): Are there roses?

THE FEMALE ATTENDANT: Roses! Red, yellow, white . . . just everywhere.

THE MALE ATTENDANT (*after a pause*): That musta been Cleveland.

THE FEMALE ATTENDANT: I had a case in Cleveland once. Diabetes.

THE MALE ATTENDANT (*after another pause*): I wisht I had a radio here. Radios are good for *them*. I had a patient once that had to have the radio going every minute.

THE FEMALE ATTENDANT: Radios are lovely. My married niece has one. It's always going. It's wonderful.

THE INSANE WOMAN (*half rising*): I'm not beautiful. I'm not beautiful as she was.

THE FEMALE ATTENDANT: Oh, I think you're beautiful! Beautiful. Mr. Morgan, don't you think Mrs. Churchill is beautiful?

THE MALE ATTENDANT: Oh, fine lookin'! Regular movie star, Mrs. Churchill.

*She looks inquiringly at them and subsides.*

HARRIET *groans slightly. Smothers a cough. She gropes about with her hand and finds the bell.*

*The* PORTER *knocks at her door.*

HARRIET (*whispering*): Come in. First, please close the door into my husband's room. Softly. Softly.

PORTER (*a plaintive porter*): Yes, ma'am.

HARRIET: Porter, I'm not well. I'm sick. I must see a doctor.

PORTER: Why, ma'am, they ain't no doctor . . .

HARRIET: Yes, when I was coming out from dinner I saw a man in one of the seats on *that* side reading medical papers. Go and wake him up.

PORTER (*flabbergasted*): Ma'am, I cain't wake anybody up.

HARRIET: Yes, you can. Porter. Porter. Now don't argue with me. I'm very sick. It's my heart. Wake him up. Tell him it's my heart.

PORTER: Yes, ma'am.

*He goes into the aisle and starts pulling the shoulder of the man in Lower Three.*

LOWER THREE: Hello. Hello. What is it? Are we there?

*The* PORTER *mumbles to him.*

I'll be right there. Porter, is it a young woman or an old one?

PORTER: I dono, suh. I guess she's kinda old, suh, but not so very old.

LOWER THREE: Tell her I'll be there in a minute and to lie quietly.

*The* PORTER *enters* HARRIET'S *compartment. She has turned her head away.*

PORTER: He'll be here in a minute, ma'am. He says you lie quiet.

LOWER THREE *stumbles along the aisle muttering.*

LOWER THREE: Damn these shoes!

SOMEONE'S VOICE: Can't we have a little quiet in this car, please?

LOWER NINE: Oh, shut up!

*The* DOCTOR *passes the* PORTER *and enters* HARRIET'S *compartment. He leans over her, concealing her by his stooping figure.*

LOWER THREE: She's dead, porter. Is there anyone on the train traveling with her?

PORTER: Yessuh. Dat's her husband in dere.

LOWER THREE: Idiot! Why didn't you call him? I'll go in and speak to him.

*The* STAGE MANAGER *comes forward.*

THE STAGE MANAGER: All right. So much for the inside of the car. That'll be enough of that for the present. Now for its position geographically, meteorologically, astronomically, theologically considered.

Pullman Car Hiawatha, ten minutes of ten. December twenty-first, 1930. All ready.

*Some figures begin to appear on the balcony.*

No, no. It's not time for the planets yet. Nor the hours.

*They retire.*

*The* STAGE MANAGER *claps his hands. A grinning boy in overalls enters from the left behind the berths.*

GROVER'S CORNERS, OHIO (*in a foolish voice as though he were reciting a piece at a Sunday School entertainment*): I represent Grover's Corners, Ohio—821 souls. "There's so much good in the worst of us and so much bad in the best of us, that it ill behooves any of us to criticize the rest of us." Robert Louis Stevenson. Thankya.

*He grins and goes out right.*

*Enter from the same direction somebody in shirt sleeves. This is a field.*

THE FIELD: I represent a field you are passing between Grover's Corners, Ohio, and Parkersburg, Ohio. In this field there are fifty-one gophers, 206 field mice, six snakes and millions of bugs, insects, ants, and spiders, all in their winter sleep. "What is so rare as a day in June? Then, if ever, come perfect days." *The Vision of Sir Launfal,* William Cullen—I mean James Russell Lowell. Thank you. (*Exit.*)

*Enter a tramp.*

THE TRAMP: I just want to tell you that I'm a tramp that's been traveling under this car Hiawatha, so I have a right to be in this play. I'm going from Rochester, New York, to Joliet, Illinois. It takes a lotta people to make a world.

> On the road to Mandalay
> Where the flying fishes play
> And the sun comes up like thunder
> Over China cross the bay.

Frank W. Service. It's bitter cold. Thank you.

*Exit.*

*Enter a gentle old farmer's wife with three stringy young people.*

PARKERSBURG, OHIO: I represent Parkersburg, Ohio—2604 souls. I have seen all the dreadful havoc that alcohol has done, and I hope no one here will ever touch a drop of the curse of this beautiful country.

*She beats a measure and they all sing unsteadily:*

"Throw out the life line! Throw out the life line! Someone is sinking today-ay . . ."

THE STAGE MANAGER *moves them away tactfully.*

*Enter a workman.*

THE WORKMAN: Ich bin der Arbeiter der hier sein Leben verlor. Bei der Sprengung für diese Brücke über die Sie in dem Moment fahren—

*The engine whistles for a trestle crossing.*

—erschlug mich ein Felsbock. Ich spiele jetzt als Geist in diesem Stuck mit. "Vor sieben und achtzig Jahren haben unsere Väter auf diesem Continent eine neue Nation hervorgebracht . . ."

THE STAGE MANAGER (*helpfully, to the audience*): I'm sorry; that's in German. He says that he's the ghost of a workman who was killed while they were building the trestle over which the car Hiawatha is now passing—

*The engine whistles again.*

—and he wants to appear in this play. A chunk of rock hit him while they were dynamiting. His motto you know: "Four score and seven years ago our fathers brought forth upon this continent a new nation dedicated," and so on. Thank you, Mr. Krüger.

*Exit the ghost.*

*Enter another worker.*

THIS WORKER: I'm a watchman in a tower near Parkersburg, Ohio. I just want to tell you that I'm not asleep and that the signals are all right for this train. I hope you all have a fine trip. "If you can keep your heads when all about you are losing theirs and blaming it on you . . ." Rudyard Kipling. Thank you. (*Exit.*)

*The STAGE MANAGER comes forward.*

THE STAGE MANAGER: All right. That'll be enough of that. Now the weather.

*Enter a mechanic.*

A MECHANIC: It is eleven degrees above zero. The wind is north-northwest, velocity, 57. There is a field of low barometric pressure moving eastward from Saskatchewan to the eastern coast. Tomorrow it will be cold with some snow in the Middle Western States and northern New York. (*Exit.*)

THE STAGE MANAGER: All right. Now for the hours.

*Helpfully to the audience.*

The minutes are gossips; the hours are philosophers; the years are theologians. The hours are philosophers with the exception of Twelve O'clock who is also a theologian. Ready, Ten O'clock!

*The hours are beautiful girls dressed like Elihu Vedder's Pleiades. Each carries a great gold roman numeral. They pass slowly across the balcony at the back, moving from right to left.*

What are you doing, Ten O'clock? Aristotle?

TEN O'CLOCK: No, Plato, Mr. Washburn.

THE STAGE MANAGER: Good. "Are you not rather convinced that he who thus . . ."

TEN O'CLOCK: "Are you not rather convinced that he who sees beauty as only it can be seen will be specially favored? And since he is in contact not with images but with realities . . ."

*She continues the passage in a murmur as* ELEVEN O'CLOCK *appears.*

ELEVEN O'CLOCK: "What else can I, Epictetus, do, a lame old man, but sing hymns to God? If then I were a nightingale, I would do the nightingale's part. If I were a swan, I would do a swan's. But now I am a rational creature . . ."

*Her voice too subsides to a murmur.* TWELVE O'CLOCK *appears.*

THE STAGE MANAGER: Good. Twelve O'clock, what have you?

TWELVE O'CLOCK: Saint Augustine and his mother.

THE STAGE MANAGER: So. "And we began to say: If to any the tumult of the flesh were hushed . . ."

TWELVE O'CLOCK: "And we began to say: If to any the tumult of the flesh were hushed; hushed the images of earth; of waters and of air; . . ."

THE STAGE MANAGER: Faster. "Hushed also the poles of heaven."

TWELVE O'CLOCK: "Yea, were the very soul to be hushed to herself."

STAGE MANAGER: A little louder, Miss Foster.

TWELVE O'CLOCK (*a little louder*): "Hushed all dreams and imaginary revelations . . ."

THE STAGE MANAGER (*waving them back*): All right. All right. Now the planets. December twenty-first, 1930, please.

*The hours unwind and return to their dressing rooms at the right. The planets appear on the balcony. Some of them take their place halfway on the steps. These have no words, but each has a sound. One has a pulsating, zinging sound. Another has a thrum. One whistles ascending and descending scales. Saturn does a slow, obstinate:*

M—M—M—M—

Louder, Saturn—Venus, higher. Good. Now, Jupiter. Now the Earth.

*He turns to the beds on the train.*

Come, everybody. This is the Earth's sound.

*The towns, workmen, etc., appear at the edge of the stage. The passengers begin their "thinking" murmur.*

Come, Grover's Corners. Parkersburg. You're in this.
Watchman. Tramp. This is the Earth's sound.

*He conducts it as the director of an orchestra would. Each
of the towns and workmen does his motto.*

THE INSANE WOMAN *breaks into passionate weeping. She rises
and stretches out her arms to the* STAGE MANAGER.

THE INSANE WOMAN: Use me. Give me something to do.

*He goes to her quickly, whispers something in her ear, and
leads her back to her guardians. She is unconsoled.*

THE STAGE MANAGER: Now sh-sh-sh! Enter the archangels. (*To the
audience.*) We have now reached the theological position of
Pullman car Hiawatha.

*The towns and workmen have disappeared. The planets, off
stage, continue a faint music. Two young men in blue serge
suits enter along the balcony and descend the stairs at the
right. As they pass each bed the passenger talks in his sleep.*
GABRIEL *points out* BILL *to* MICHAEL *who smiles with raised
eyebrows. They pause before* LOWER FIVE, *and* MICHAEL
*makes the sound of assent that can only be rendered "Hn-
Hn." The remarks that the characters make in their sleep
are not all intelligible, being lost in the sound of sigh or groan
or whisper by which they are conveyed. But we seem to
hear:*

LOWER NINE (*loud*): Some people are slower than others, that's
all.

LOWER SEVEN: It's no fun, y'know. I'll try.

LOWER FIVE (*the lady of the Christmas presents, rapidly*): You
know best, of course. I'm ready whenever you are. One
year's like another.

LOWER ONE: I can teach sewing. I can sew.

*They approach* HARRIET'S *compartment.*

THE INSANE WOMAN *sits up and speaks to them.*

THE INSANE WOMAN: Me?

THE ARCHANGELS *shake their heads.*

THE INSANE WOMAN: What possible use can there be in my simply waiting? Well, I'm grateful for anything. I'm grateful for being so much better than I was. The old story, the terrible story, doesn't haunt me as it used to. A great load seems to have been taken off my mind. But no one understands me any more. At last I understand myself perfectly, but no one else understands a thing I say. So I must wait?

THE ARCHANGELS *nod, smiling.*

THE INSANE WOMAN (*resignedly, and with a smile that implies their complicity*): Well, you know best. I'll do whatever is best; but everyone is so childish, so absurd. They have no logic. These people are all so mad . . . These people are like children; they have never suffered.

*She returns to her bed and sleeps. The* ARCHANGELS *stand beside* HARRIET. *The doctor has drawn* PHILIP *into the next compartment and is talking to him in earnest whispers.*

HARRIET'S *face has been toward the wall; she turns it slightly and speaks toward the ceiling.*

HARRIET: I wouldn't be happy there. Let me stay dead down here. I belong here. I shall be perfectly happy to roam about my house and be near Philip. You know I wouldn't be happy there.

GABRIEL *leans over and whispers into her ear. After a short pause she bursts into fierce tears.*

I'm ashamed to come with you. I haven't done anything. I haven't done anything with my life. Worse than that: I was angry and sullen. I never realized anything. I don't dare go a step in such a place.

*They whisper to her again.*

But it's not possible to forgive such things. I don't want to be forgiven so easily. I want to be punished for it all. I won't stir until I've been punished a long, long time. I want to be freed of all that—by punishment. I want to be all new.

*They whisper to her. She puts her feet slowly on the ground.*

But no one else could be punished for me. I'm willing to face it all myself. I don't ask anyone to be punished for me.

*They whisper to her again. She sits long and brokenly looking at her shoes and thinking it over.*

It wasn't fair. I'd have been willing to suffer for it myself, if I could have endured such a mountain.

*She smiles.*

Oh, I'm ashamed! I'm just a stupid and you know it. I'm just another American. But then what wonderful things must be beginning now. You really want me? You really want me?

*They start leading her down the aisle of the car.*

Let's take the whole train. There are some lovely faces on this train. Can't we all come? You'll never find anyone better than Philip. Please, please, let's all go.

*They reach the steps. The* ARCHANGELS *interlock their arms as a support for her as she leans heavily on them, taking the steps slowly. Her words are half singing and half babbling.*

But look at how tremendously high and far it is. I've a weak heart. I'm not supposed to climb stairs. "I do not ask to see the distant scene; one step enough for me." It's like Switzerland. My tongue keeps saying things. I can't control it. Do let me stop a minute: I want to say good-by.

*She turns in their arms.*

Just a minute, I want to cry on your shoulder.

*She leans her forehead against* GABRIEL'S *shoulder and laughs long and softly.*

Good-by, Philip. I begged him not to marry me, but he would. He believed in me just as you do. Good-by, 1312

Ridgewood Avenue, Oaksbury, Illinois. I hope I remember all its steps and doors and wallpapers forever. Good-by, Emerson Grammar School on the corner of Forbush Avenue and Wherry Street. Good-by, Miss Walker and Miss Cramer who taught me English and Miss Matthewson who taught me biology. Good-by, First Congregational Church on the corner of Meyerson Avenue and Sixth Street and Dr. McReady and Mrs. McReady and Julia. Good-by, Papa and Mama . . .

*She turns.*

Now I'm tired· of saying good-by. I never used to talk like this. I was so homely I never used to have the courage to talk. Until Philip came. I see now. I see now. I understand everything now.

*The* STAGE MANAGER *comes forward.*

THE STAGE MANAGER (*to the actors*): All right. All right. Now we'll have the whole world together, please. The whole solar system, please.

*The complete cast begins to appear at the edges of the stage. He claps his hands.*

The whole solar system, please. Where's the tramp? Where's the moon?

*He gives two raps on the floor, like the conductor of an orchestra attracting the attention of his forces, and slowly lifts his hand. The human beings murmur their thoughts; the hours discourse; the planets chant or hum.* HARRIET's *voice finally rises above them all saying:*

HARRIET: "I was not ever thus, nor asked that Thou
Shouldst lead me on . . . and spite of fears,
Pride ruled my will: remember not past years."

*The* STAGE MANAGER *waves them away.*

THE STAGE MANAGER: Very good. Now clear the stage, please.

Now we're at Englewood Station, South Chicago. See the University's towers over there! The best of them all.

LOWER ONE (*the spinster*): Porter, you promised to wake me up at quarter of six.

PORTER: Sorry, ma'am, but it's been an awful night on this car. A lady's been terrible sick.

LOWER ONE: Oh! Is she better?

PORTER: No'm. She ain't one jot better.

LOWER FIVE: Young man, take your foot out of my face.

THE STAGE MANAGER (*again substituting for* UPPER FIVE): Sorry, lady, I slipped—

LOWER FIVE (*grumbling not unamiably*): I declare, this trip's been one long series of insults.

THE STAGE MANAGER: Just one minute, ma'am, and I'll be down and out of your way.

LOWER FIVE: Haven't you got anybody to darn your socks for you? You ought to be ashamed to go about that way.

THE STAGE MANAGER: Sorry, lady.

LOWER FIVE: You're too stuck up to get married. That's the trouble with you.

LOWER NINE: Bill! Bill!

LOWER SEVEN: Ye'? Wha' d'y'a want?

LOWER NINE: Bill, how much d'y'a give the porter on a train like this? I've been outa the country so long . . .

LOWER SEVEN: Hell, Fred, I don't know myself.

THE PORTER: CHICAGO, CHICAGO. All out. This train don't go no further.

*The passengers jostle their way out and an army of old women with mops and pails enters and prepares to clean up the car.*

**CURTAIN**

# Hello Out There

## by William Saroyan

*For George Bernard Shaw*

*Scene: There is a fellow in a small-town prison cell, tapping slowly on the floor with a spoon. After tapping half a minute, as if he were trying to telegraph words, he gets up and begins walking around the cell. At last he stops, stands at the center of the cell, and doesn't move for a long time. He feels his head, as if it were wounded. Then he looks around. Then he calls out dramatically, kidding the world.*

YOUNG MAN: Hello—out there! (*Pause.*) Hello—out there! Hello—out there! (*Long pause.*) Nobody out there. (*Still more dramatically, but more comically, too.*) Hello—out there! Hello—out there!

*A* GIRL'S VOICE *is heard, very sweet and soft.*

THE VOICE: Hello.

YOUNG MAN: Hello—out there.

THE VOICE: Hello.

YOUNG MAN: Is that you, Katey?

THE VOICE: No—this here is Emily.

YOUNG MAN: Who? (*Swiftly.*) Hello out there.

THE VOICE: Emily.

YOUNG MAN: Emily who? I don't know anybody named Emily. Are you that girl I met at Sam's in Salinas about three years ago?

93

THE VOICE: No—I'm the girl who cooks here. I'm the cook. I've never been in Salinas. I don't even know where it is.

YOUNG MAN: Hello out there. You say you cook here?

THE VOICE: Yes.

YOUNG MAN: Well, why don't you study up and learn to cook? How come I don't get no jello or anything good?

THE VOICE: I just cook what they tell me to. (*Pause.*) You lonesome?

YOUNG MAN: Lonesome as a coyote. Hear me hollering? Hello out there!

THE VOICE: Who you hollering to?

YOUNG MAN: Well—nobody, I guess. I been trying to think of somebody to write a letter to, but I can't think of anybody.

THE VOICE: What about Katey?

YOUNG MAN: I don't know anybody named Katey.

THE VOICE: Then why did you say, Is that you, Katey?

YOUNG MAN: Katey's a good name. I always did like a name like Katey. I never *knew* anybody named Katey, though.

THE VOICE: *I* did.

YOUNG MAN: Yeah? What was she like? Tall girl, or little one?

THE VOICE: Kind of medium.

YOUNG MAN: Hello out there. What sort of a looking girl are *you?*

THE VOICE: Oh, I don't know.

YOUNG MAN: Didn't anybody ever tell you? Didn't anybody ever talk to you that way?

THE VOICE: What way?

YOUNG MAN: You know. Didn't they?

THE VOICE: No, they didn't.

YOUNG MAN: Ah, the fools—they should have. I can tell from your voice you're O.K.

THE VOICE: Maybe I am and maybe I ain't.

YOUNG MAN: I never missed yet.

THE VOICE: Yeah, I know. That's why you're in jail.

YOUNG MAN: The whole thing was a mistake.

THE VOICE: They claim it was rape.

YOUNG MAN: No—it wasn't.

THE VOICE: That's what they claim it was.

YOUNG MAN: They're a lot of fools.

THE VOICE: Well, you sure are in trouble. Are you scared?

YOUNG MAN: Scared to death. (*Suddenly.*) Hello out there!

THE VOICE: What do you keep saying that for all the time?

YOUNG MAN: I'm lonesome. I'm as lonesome as a coyote. (*A long one.*) Hello—out there!

THE GIRL *appears, over to one side. She is a plain girl in plain clothes.*

THE GIRL: I'm kind of lonesome, too.

YOUNG MAN (*turning and looking at her*): Hey—No fooling? Are you?

THE GIRL: Yeah—I'm almost as lonesome as a coyote myself.

YOUNG MAN: Who *you* lonesome for?

THE GIRL: I don't know.

YOUNG MAN: It's the same with me. The minute they put you in a place like this you remember all the girls you ever knew, and all the girls you didn't get to know, and it sure gets lonesome.

THE GIRL: I bet it does.

YOUNG MAN: Ah, it's awful. (*Pause.*) You're a pretty kid, you know that?

THE GIRL: You're just talking.

YOUNG MAN: No, I'm not just talking—you *are* pretty. Any fool could see that. You're just about the prettiest kid in the whole world.

THE GIRL: I'm not—and you know it.

YOUNG MAN: No—you are. I never saw anyone prettier in all my born days, in all my travels. I knew Texas would bring me luck.

THE GIRL: Luck? You're in jail, aren't you? You've got a whole gang of people all worked up, haven't you?

YOUNG MAN: Ah, that's nothing. I'll get out of this.

THE GIRL: Maybe.

YOUNG MAN: No, I'll be all right—*now.*

THE GIRL: What do you mean—now?

YOUNG MAN: I mean after seeing you. I got something now. You know for a while there I didn't care one way or another. Tired. (*Pause.*) Tired of trying for the best all the time and never getting it. (*Suddenly.*) Hello out there!

THE GIRL: Who you calling now?

YOUNG MAN: You.

THE GIRL: Why, I'm right here.

YOUNG MAN: I know. (*Calling.*) Hello out there!

THE GIRL: Hello.

YOUNG MAN: Ah, you're sweet. (*Pause.*) I'm going to marry *you.* I'm going away with *you.* I'm going to take you to San Francisco or some place like that. I *am,* now. I'm going to win myself some real money, too. I'm going to study 'em real

careful and pick myself some winners, and we're going to
have a lot of money.

THE GIRL: Yeah?

YOUNG MAN: Yeah. Tell me your name and all that stuff.

THE GIRL: Emily.

YOUNG MAN: I know that. What's the rest of it? Where were you
born? Come on, tell me the whole thing.

THE GIRL: Emily Smith.

YOUNG MAN: Honest to God?

THE GIRL: Honest. That's my name—Emily Smith.

YOUNG MAN: Ah, you're the sweetest girl in the whole world.

THE GIRL: Why?

YOUNG MAN: I don't know why, but you are, that's all. Where
were you born?

THE GIRL: Matador, Texas.

YOUNG MAN: Where's that?

THE GIRL: Right here.

YOUNG MAN: Is this Matador, Texas?

THE GIRL: Yeah, it's Matador. They brought you here from
Wheeling.

YOUNG MAN: Is that where I was—Wheeling?

THE GIRL: Didn't you even know what town you were in?

YOUNG MAN: All towns are alike. You don't go up and ask somebody what town you're in. It doesn't make any difference.
How far away is Wheeling?

THE GIRL: Sixteen or seventeen miles. Didn't you know they
moved you?

YOUNG MAN: How could I know, when I was out—cold? Somebody hit me over the head with a lead pipe or something. What'd they hit me for?

THE GIRL: Rape—that's what they *said*.

YOUNG MAN: Ah, that's a lie. (*Amazed, almost to himself.*) She wanted me to give her money.

THE GIRL: Money?

YOUNG MAN: Yeah, if I'd have known she was a woman like that —well, by God, I'd have gone on down the street and stretched out in a park somewhere and gone to sleep.

THE GIRL: Is that what she wanted—money?

YOUNG MAN: Yeah. A fellow like me hopping freights all over the country, trying to break his bad luck, going from one poor little town to another, trying to get in on something good somewhere, and she asks for money. I thought she was lonesome. She *said* she was.

THE GIRL: Maybe she was.

YOUNG MAN: She was *something*.

THE GIRL: I guess I'd never see you, if it didn't happen, though.

YOUNG MAN: Oh, I don't know—maybe I'd just mosey along this way and see you in this town somewhere. I'd recognize you, too.

THE GIRL: Recognize me?

YOUNG MAN: Sure, I'd recognize you the minute I laid eyes on you.

THE GIRL: Well, who would I be?

YOUNG MAN: Mine, that's who.

THE GIRL: Honest?

YOUNG MAN: Honest to God.

THE GIRL: You just say that because you're in jail.

YOUNG MAN: No, I mean it. You just pack up and wait for me. We'll high-roll the hell out of here to Frisco.

THE GIRL: You're just lonesome.

YOUNG MAN: I been lonesome all my life—there's no cure for that —but you and me—we can have a lot of fun hanging around together. You'll bring me luck. I know it.

THE GIRL: What are you looking for luck for all the time?

YOUNG MAN: I'm a gambler. I don't work. I've *got* to have luck, or I'm a bum. I haven't had any decent luck in years. Two whole years now—one place to another. Bad luck all the time. That's why I got in trouble back there in Wheeling, too. That was no accident. That was my bad luck following me around. So here I am, with my head half busted. I guess it was her old man that did it.

THE GIRL: You mean her father?

YOUNG MAN: No, her husband. If I had an old lady like that, I'd throw her out.

THE GIRL: Do you think you'll have better luck, if I go with you?

YOUNG MAN: It's a cinch. I'm a good handicapper. All I need is somebody good like you with me. It's no good always walking around in the streets for anything that might be there at the time. You got to have somebody staying with you all the time—through winters when it's cold, and springtime when it's pretty, and summertime when it's nice and hot and you can go swimming—through *all* the times—rain and snow and all the different kinds of weather a man's got to go through before he dies. You got to have somebody who's right. Somebody who knows you, from away back. You got to have somebody who even knows you're wrong but likes you just the same. I know I'm wrong, but I just don't want anything the hard way, working like a dog, or the *easy* way, working like a dog—working's the hard way and the easy way both. All I got to do is beat the price, always—and then I don't feel lousy and don't hate anybody. If you go along with me, I'll be the finest guy anybody ever saw. I won't be wrong any more. You know when you get enough of that money, you *can't* be wrong any more—you're right because the money says so. I'll have a lot of money and you'll be just about the prettiest, most wonderful kid in the whole world. I'll be proud walking around Frisco with you on my arm and people turning around to look at us.

THE GIRL: Do you think they will?

YOUNG MAN: Sure they will. When I get back in some decent clothes, and you're on my arm—well, Katey, they'll turn around and look, and they'll see something, too.

THE GIRL: Katey?

YOUNG MAN: Yeah—that's your name from now on. You're the first girl I ever called Katey. I've been saving it for you. O.K.?

THE GIRL: O.K.

YOUNG MAN: How long have I been here?

THE GIRL: Since last night. You didn't wake up until late this morning, though.

YOUNG MAN: What time is it now? About nine?

THE GIRL: About ten.

YOUNG MAN: Have you got the key to this lousy cell?

THE GIRL: No. They don't let me fool with any keys.

YOUNG MAN: Well, can you get it?

THE GIRL: No.

YOUNG MAN: Can you *try?*

THE GIRL: They wouldn't let me get near any keys. I cook for this jail, when they've got somebody in it. I clean up and things like that.

YOUNG MAN: Well, I want to get out of here. Don't you know the guy that runs this joint?

THE GIRL: I know him, but he wouldn't let you out. They were talking of taking you to another jail in another town.

YOUNG MAN: Yeah? Why?

THE GIRL: Because they're afraid.

YOUNG MAN: What are they afraid of?

THE GIRL: They're afraid these people from Wheeling will come over in the middle of the night and break in.

YOUNG MAN: Yeah? What do they want to do that for?

THE GIRL: Don't *you* know what they want to do it for?

YOUNG MAN: Yeah, I know all right.

THE GIRL: Are you scared?

YOUNG MAN: Sure I'm scared. Nothing scares a man more than ignorance. You can argue with people who ain't fools, but you can't argue with fools—they just go to work and do what they're set on doing. Get me out of here.

THE GIRL: How?

YOUNG MAN: Well, go get the guy with the key, and let me talk to him.

THE GIRL: He's gone home. Everybody's gone home.

YOUNG MAN: You mean I'm in this little jail all alone?

THE GIRL: Well—yeah—except me.

YOUNG MAN: Well, what's the big idea—doesn't anybody stay here all the time?

THE GIRL: No, they go home every night. I clean up and then I go, too. I hung around tonight.

YOUNG MAN: What made you do that?

THE GIRL: I wanted to talk to you.

YOUNG MAN: Honest? What did you want to talk about?

THE GIRL: Oh, I don't know. I took care of you last night. You were talking in your sleep. You liked me, too. I didn't think you'd like me when you woke up, though.

YOUNG MAN: Yeah? Why not?

THE GIRL: I don't know.

YOUNG MAN: Yeah? Well, you're wonderful, see?

THE GIRL: Nobody ever talked to me that way. All the fellows in town—(*Pause.*)

YOUNG MAN: What about 'em? (*Pause.*) Well, what about 'em? Come on—tell me.

THE GIRL: They laugh at me.

YOUNG MAN: Laugh at *you?* They're fools. What do they know about anything? You go get your things and come back here. I'll take you with me to Frisco. How old are you?

THE GIRL: Oh, I'm of age.

YOUNG MAN: How old are you?—Don't lie to me! Sixteen?

THE GIRL: I'm seventeen.

YOUNG MAN: Well, bring your father and mother. We'll get married before we go.

THE GIRL: They wouldn't let me go.

YOUNG MAN: Why not?

THE GIRL: I don't know, but they wouldn't. I know they wouldn't.

YOUNG MAN: You go tell your father not to be a fool, see? What is he, a farmer?

THE GIRL: No—nothing. He gets a little relief from the government because he's supposed to be hurt or something—his side hurts, he says. I don't know what it is.

YOUNG MAN: Ah, he's a liar. Well, I'm taking you with me, see?

THE GIRL: He takes the money I earn, too.

YOUNG MAN: He's got no right to do that.

THE GIRL: I know it, but he does it.

YOUNG MAN (*almost to himself*): This world stinks. You shouldn't have been born in this town, anyway, and you shouldn't have had a man like that for a father, either.

THE GIRL: Sometimes I feel sorry for him.

YOUNG MAN: Never mind feeling sorry for him. (*Pointing a finger.*) I'm going to talk to your father some day. I've got a few things to tell that guy.

THE GIRL: I know you have.

YOUNG MAN (*suddenly*): Hello—out there! See if you can get that fellow with the keys to come down and let me out.

THE GIRL: Oh, I couldn't.

YOUNG MAN: Why not?

THE GIRL: I'm nobody here—they give me fifty cents every day I work.

YOUNG MAN: How much?

THE GIRL: Fifty cents.

YOUNG MAN (*to the world*): You see? They ought to pay money to *look* at you. To breathe the *air* you breathe. I don't know. Sometimes I figure it never is going to make sense. Hello—out there! I'm scared. You try to get me out of here. I'm scared them fools are going to come here from Wheeling and go crazy, thinking they're heroes. Get me out of here, Katey.

THE GIRL: I don't know what to do. Maybe I could break the door down.

YOUNG MAN: No, you couldn't do that. Is there a hammer out there or anything?

THE GIRL: Only a broom. Maybe they've locked the broom up, too.

YOUNG MAN: Go see if you can find anything.

THE GIRL: All right. (*She goes.*)

YOUNG MAN: Hello—out there! Hello—out there! (*Pause.*) Hello
—out there! Hello—out there! (*Pause.*) Putting me in jail.
(*With contempt.*) Rape! Rape? *They* rape everything good
that was ever born. His side hurts. They laugh at her. Fifty
cents a day. Little punk people. Hurting the only good thing
that ever came their way. (*Suddenly.*) Hello—out there!

THE GIRL (*returning*): There isn't a thing out there. They've
locked everything up for the night.

YOUNG MAN: Any cigarettes?

THE GIRL: Everything's locked up—all the drawers of the desk, all
the closet doors—everything.

YOUNG MAN: I ought to have a cigarette.

THE GIRL: I could get you a package maybe, somewhere. I guess
the drug store's open. It's about a mile.

YOUNG MAN: A mile? I don't want to be alone that long.

THE GIRL: I could run all the way, and all the way back.

YOUNG MAN: You're the sweetest girl that ever lived.

THE GIRL: What kind do you want?

YOUNG MAN: Oh, any kind—Chesterfields or Camels or Lucky
Strikes—any kind at all.

THE GIRL: I'll go get a package. (*She turns to go.*)

YOUNG MAN: What about the money?

THE GIRL: I've got some money. I've got a quarter I been saving.
I'll run all the way. (*She is about to go.*)

YOUNG MAN: Come here.

THE GIRL (*going to him*): What?

YOUNG MAN: Give me your hand. (*He takes her hand and looks
at it, smiling. He lifts it and kisses it.*) I'm scared to death.

THE GIRL: I am, too.

YOUNG MAN: I'm not lying—I don't care what happens to me, but
I'm scared nobody will ever come out here to this God-
forsaken broken-down town and find you. I'm scared you'll
get used to it and not mind. I'm scared you'll never get to
Frisco and have 'em all turning around to look at you. Listen—go get me a gun, because if they come, I'll kill 'em!
They don't understand. Get me a gun!

THE GIRL: I could get my father's gun. I know where he hides it.

YOUNG MAN: Go get it. Never mind the cigarettes. Run all the way.
(*Pause, smiling but seriously.*) Hello, Katey.

THE GIRL: Hello. What's *your* name?

YOUNG MAN: Photo-Finish is what they *call* me. My races are
always photo-finish races. You don't know what that means,
but it means they're very close. So close the only way they
can tell which horse wins is to look at a photograph after
the race is over. Well, every race I bet turns out to be a
photo-finish race, and my horse never wins. It's my bad
luck, all the time. That's why they call me Photo-Finish. Say
it before you go.

THE GIRL: Photo-Finish.

YOUNG MAN: Come here. (THE GIRL *moves close and he kisses
her.*) Now, hurry. Run all the way.

THE GIRL: I'll run. (THE GIRL *turns and runs. The* YOUNG MAN
*stands at the center of the cell a long time.* THE GIRL *comes
running back in. Almost crying.*) I'm afraid. I'm afraid I
won't see you again. If I come back and you're not here, I—

YOUNG MAN: Hello—out there!

THE GIRL: It's so lonely in this town. Nothing here but the lonesome wind all the time, lifting the dirt and blowing out to
the prairie. I'll stay *here*. I won't *let* them take you away.

YOUNG MAN: Listen, Katey. Do what I tell you. Go get that gun and come back. Maybe they won't come tonight. Maybe they won't come at all. I'll hide the gun and when they let me out you can take it back and put it where you found it. And then we'll go away. But if they come, I'll kill 'em! Now, hurry—

THE GIRL: All right. (*Pause.*) I want to tell you something.

YOUNG MAN: O.K.

THE GIRL (*very softly*): If you're not here when I come back, well, I'll have the gun and I'll know what to do with it.

YOUNG MAN: You know how to handle a gun?

THE GIRL: I know how.

YOUNG MAN: Don't be a fool. (*Takes off his shoe, brings out some currency.*) Don't be a fool, see? Here's some money. Eighty dollars. Take it and go to Frisco. Look around and find somebody. Find somebody alive and halfway human, see? Promise me—if I'm not here when you come back, just throw the gun away and get the hell to Frisco. Look around and find somebody.

THE GIRL: I don't *want* to find anybody.

YOUNG MAN (*swiftly, desperately*): Listen, if I'm not here when you come back, how do you know I haven't gotten away? Now, do what I tell you. I'll meet you in Frisco. I've got a couple of dollars in my other shoe. I'll see you in San Francisco.

THE GIRL (*with wonder*): San Francisco?

YOUNG MAN: That's right—San Francisco. That's where you and me belong.

THE GIRL: I've always wanted to go to *some* place like San Francisco—but how could I go alone?

YOUNG MAN: Well, you're not alone any more, see?

THE GIRL: Tell me a little what it's like.

YOUNG MAN (*very swiftly, almost impatiently at first, but grad-*

*ually slower and with remembrance, smiling, and* THE GIRL *moving closer to him as he speaks*): Well, it's on the Pacific to begin with—ocean water all around. Cool fog and sea-gulls. Ships from all over the world. It's got seven hills. The little streets go up and down, around and all over. Every night the fog-horns bawl. But they won't be bawling for you and me.

THE GIRL: What else?

YOUNG MAN: That's about all, I guess.

THE GIRL: Are people different in San Francisco?

YOUNG MAN: People are the same everywhere. They're different only when they love somebody. That's the only thing that makes 'em different. More people in Frisco love somebody, that's all.

THE GIRL: Nobody anywhere loves anybody as much as I love you.

YOUNG MAN (*shouting, as if to the world*): You see? Hearing you say that, a man could die and still be ahead of the game. Now, hurry. And don't forget, if I'm not here when you come back, get the hell to San Francisco where you'll have a chance. Do you hear me?

THE GIRL *stands a moment looking at him, then backs away, turns and runs. The* YOUNG MAN *stares after her, troubled and smiling. Then he turns away from the image of her and walks about like a lion in a cage. After a while he sits down suddenly and buries his head in his hands. From a distance the sound of several automobiles approaching is heard. He listens a moment, then ignores the implications of the sound, whatever they may be. Several automobile doors are slammed. He ignores this also. A wooden door is opened with a key and closed, and footsteps are heard in a hall. Walking easily, almost casually and yet arrogantly, a* MAN *comes in.*

YOUNG MAN (*jumps up suddenly and shouts at* THE MAN, *almost scaring him*): What the hell kind of a jailkeeper are you, anyway? Why don't you attend to your business? You get paid for it, don't you? Now, get me out of here.

THE MAN: But I'm not the jailkeeper.

YOUNG MAN: Yeah? Well, who are you, then?

THE MAN: I'm the husband.

YOUNG MAN: What husband you talking about?

THE MAN: You know what husband.

YOUNG MAN: Hey! (*Pause, looking at* THE MAN.) Are you the guy that hit me over the head last night?

THE MAN: I am.

YOUNG MAN (*with righteous indignation*): What do you mean going around hitting people over the head?

THE MAN: Oh, I don't know. What do you *mean* going around— the way you do?

YOUNG MAN (*rubbing his head*): You hurt my head. You got no right to hit anybody over the head.

THE MAN (*suddenly angry, shouting*): Answer my question! What do you mean?

YOUNG MAN: Listen, you—don't be hollering at me just because I'm locked up.

THE MAN (*with contempt, slowly*): You're a dog!

YOUNG MAN: Yeah, well, let me tell you something. You *think* you're the husband. You're the husband of nothing. (*Slowly.*) What's more, your wife—if you want to call her that—is a tramp. Why don't you throw her out in the street where she belongs?

THE MAN (*draws a pistol*): Shut up!

YOUNG MAN: Yeah? Go ahead, shoot—(*Softly.*) and spoil the fun.

What'll your pals think? They'll be disappointed, won't they. What's the fun hanging a man who's already dead? (THE MAN *puts the gun away*.) That's right, because now you can have some fun yourself, telling me what you're going to do. That's what you came here for, isn't it? Well, you don't need to tell me. I *know* what you're going to do. I've read the papers and I know. They have fun. A mob of 'em fall on one man and beat him, don't they? They tear off his clothes and kick him, don't they? And women and little children stand around watching, don't they? Well, before you go on *this* picnic, I'm going to tell you a few things. Not that that's going to send you home with your pals— the other heroes. No. You've been outraged. A stranger has come to town and violated your women. Your pure, innocent, virtuous women. You fellows have got to set this thing right. You're men, not mice. You're home-makers, and you beat your children. (*Suddenly*.) Listen, you—I didn't know she was your wife. I didn't know she was anybody's wife.

THE MAN: You're a liar!

YOUNG MAN: Sometimes—when it'll do somebody some good— but not this time. Do you want to hear about it? (THE MAN *doesn't answer*.) All right, I'll tell you. I met her at a lunch counter. She came in and sat next to me. There was plenty of room, but she sat next to me. Somebody had put a nickel in the phonograph and a fellow was singing *New San Antonio Rose*. Well, she got to talking about the song. I thought she was talking to the waiter, but *he* didn't answer her, so after a while *I* answered her. That's how I met her. I didn't think anything of it. We left the place together and started walking. The first thing I knew she said, This is where I live.

THE MAN: You're a dirty liar!

YOUNG MAN: Do you want to hear it? Or not? (THE MAN *does not answer*.) O.K. She asked me to come in. Maybe she had something in mind, maybe she didn't. Didn't make any difference to me, one way or the other. If she was lonely, all right. If not, all right.

THE MAN: You're telling a lot of dirty lies!

YOUNG MAN: I'm telling the truth. Maybe your wife's out there with your pals. Well, call her in. I got nothing against her, or you—or any of you. Call her in, and ask her a few questions. Are you in love with her? (THE MAN *doesn't answer.*) Well, that's too bad.

THE MAN: What do you mean, too bad?

YOUNG MAN: I mean this may not be the first time something like this has happened.

THE MAN (*swiftly*): Shut up!

YOUNG MAN: Oh, you know it. You've always known it. You're afraid of your pals, that's all. She asked me for money. That's all she wanted. I wouldn't be here now if I had given her the money.

THE MAN (*slowly*): How much did she ask for?

YOUNG MAN: I didn't ask her how much. I told her I'd made a mistake. She said she would make trouble if I didn't give her money. Well, I don't like bargaining, and I don't like being threatened, either. I told her to get the hell away from me. The next thing I knew she'd run out of the house and was hollering. (*Pause.*) Now, why don't you go out there and tell 'em they took me to another jail—go home and pack up and leave her. You're a pretty good guy, you're just afraid of your pals.

THE MAN *draws his gun again. He is very frightened. He moves a step toward the* YOUNG MAN, *then fires three times. The* YOUNG MAN *falls to his knees.* THE MAN *turns and runs, horrified.*

YOUNG MAN: Hello—out there! (*He is bent forward.*)

THE GIRL *comes running in, and halts suddenly, looking at him.*

THE GIRL: There were some people in the street, men and women

and kids—so I came in through the back, through a window.
I couldn't find the gun. I looked all over but I couldn't find
it. What's the matter?

YOUNG MAN: Nothing—nothing. Everything's all right. Listen.
Listen, kid. Get the hell out of here. Go out the same way
you came in and run—run like hell—run all night. Get to
another town and get on a train. Do you hear me?

THE GIRL: What's happened?

YOUNG MAN: Get away—just get away from here. Take any
train that's going—you can get to Frisco later.

THE GIRL (*almost sobbing*): I don't want to go any place without
you.

YOUNG MAN: I can't go. Something's happened. (*He looks at her.*)
But I'll be with you always—God damn it. Always!

*He falls forward.* THE GIRL *stands near him, then begins to
sob softly, walking away. She stands over to one side, stops
sobbing, and stares out. The excitement of the mob outside
increases.* THE MAN, *with two of his pals, comes running in.*
THE GIRL *watches, unseen.*

THE MAN: Here's the son of a bitch!

ANOTHER MAN: O.K. Open the cell, Harry.

*The* THIRD MAN *goes to the cell door, unlocks it, and swings
it open.*

*A* WOMAN *comes running in.*

THE WOMAN: Where is he? I want to see him. Is he dead? (*Looking down at him, as the* MEN *pick him up.*) There he is.
(*Pause.*) Yeah, that's him.

*Her husband looks at her with contempt, then at the dead
man.*

THE MAN (*trying to laugh*): All right—let's get it over with.

THIRD MAN: Right you are, George. Give me a hand, Harry.

*They lift the body.*

THE GIRL (*suddenly, fiercely*): Put him down!

THE MAN: What's this?

SECOND MAN: What are you doing here? Why aren't you out in the street?

THE GIRL: Put him down and go away.

*She runs toward the* MEN.

THE WOMAN *grabs her.*

THE WOMAN: Here—where do you think *you're* going?

THE GIRL: Let me go. You've no right to take him away.

THE WOMAN: Well, listen to her, will you? (*She slaps* THE GIRL *and pushes her to the floor.*) Listen to the little slut, will you?

*They all go, carrying the* YOUNG MAN's *body.* THE GIRL *gets up slowly, no longer sobbing. She looks around at everything, then looks straight out, and whispers.*

THE GIRL: Hello—out—there! Hello—out there!

**CURTAIN**

# 27 Wagons Full of Cotton

## A Mississippi Delta Comedy

### by Tennessee Williams

*Now Eros shakes my soul, a wind on the mountain, falling on the oaks.*

SAPPHO

CHARACTERS

JAKE MEIGHAN, *a cotton-gin owner.*

FLORA MEIGHAN, *his wife.*

SILVA VICARRO, *superintendent of the Syndicate Plantation.*

*All of the action takes place on the front porch of the Meig-hans' residence near Blue Mountain, Mississippi.*

*Scene: The front porch of the* MEIGHANS' *cottage near Blue Mountain, Mississippi. The porch is narrow and rises into a single narrow gable. There are spindling white pillars on either side supporting the porch roof and a door of Gothic design and two Gothic windows on either side of it. The peaked door has an oval of richly stained glass, azure, crimson, emerald, and gold. At the windows are fluffy white curtains gathered coquettishly in the middle by baby-blue satin bows. The effect is not unlike a doll's house.*

SCENE I

*It is early evening and there is a faint rosy dusk in the sky. Shortly after the curtain rises,* JAKE MEIGHAN, *a fat man of sixty, scrambles out the front door and races around the corner of the house carrying a gallon can of coal-oil. A dog barks at him. A car is heard starting and receding rapidly in the distance. A moment later* FLORA *calls from inside the house.*

FLORA: Jake! I've lost m' white kid purse! (*Closer to the door.*) Jake? Look'n see 'f uh laid it on th' swing. (*There is a pause.*) Guess I could've left it in th' Chevy? (*She comes up to screen door.*) Jake. Look'n see if uh left it in th' Chevy. Jake? (*She steps outside in the fading rosy dusk. She switches on the porch light and stares about, slapping at gnats attracted by the light. Locusts provide the only answering voice.* FLORA *gives a long nasal call.*) Ja-ay—a-a-ake!

115

*A cow moos in the distance with the same inflection. There is muffled explosion somewhere about half a mile away. A strange flickering glow appears, the reflection of a burst of flame. Distant voices are heard exclaiming.*

VOICES (*shrill, cackling like hens*):

You heah that noise?

Yeah! Sound like a bomb went off!

Oh, look!

Why, it's a fire!

Where's it at? You tell?

Th' Syndicate Plantation!

Oh, my God! Let's go!

*A fire whistle sounds in the distance.*

Henry! Start th' car! You all wanta go with us?

Yeah, we'll be right out!

Hurry, honey!

*A car can be heard starting up.*

Be right there!

Well, hurry.

VOICE (*just across the dirt road*): Missus Meighan?

FLORA: Ye-ah?

VOICE: Ahn't you goin' th' fire?

FLORA: I wish I could but Jake's gone off in th' Chevy.

VOICE: Come awn an' go with us, honey!

FLORA: Oh, I cain't an' leave th' house wide open! Jake's gone off with th' keys. What do you all think it is on fire?

VOICE: Th' Syndicate Plantation!

FLORA: Th' Syndicate Plan-*ta*-tion?

*The car starts off and recedes.*

Oh, my Go-od! (*She climbs laboriously back up on the porch and sits on the swing which faces the front. She speaks tragically to herself.*) Nobody! Nobody! Never! Never! Nobody!

*Locusts can be heard. A car is heard approaching and stopping at a distance back of house. After a moment Jake ambles casually up around the side of the house.*

FLORA (*in a petulant babyish tone*): Well!

JAKE: Whatsamatter, Baby?

FLORA: I never known a human being could be that mean an' thoughtless!

JAKE: Aw, now, that's a mighty broad statement fo' you to make, Mrs. Mcighan. What's the complaint this time?

FLORA: Just flew out of the house without even sayin' a word!

JAKE: What's so bad about that?

FLORA: I told you I had a headache comin' on an' had to have a dope, there wassen a single bottle lef' in th' house, an' you said, Yeah, get into yuh things 'n' we'll drive in town right away! So I get into m' things an' I cain't find m' white kid purse. Then I remember I left it on th' front seat of th' Chevy. I come out here t' git it. Where are you? Gone off! Without a word! Then there's a big explosion! Feel my heart!

JAKE: Feel my baby's heart? (*He puts a hand on her huge bosom.*)

FLORA: Yeah, just you feel it, poundin' like a hammer! How'd I know what happened? You not here, just disappeared somewhere!

JAKE (*sharply*): Shut up! (*He pushes her head roughly.*)

FLORA: Jake! What did you do that fo'?

JAKE: I don't like how you holler! Holler ev'ry thing you say!

FLORA: What's the matter with you?

JAKE: Nothing's the matter with me.

FLORA: Well, why did you go off?

JAKE: I didn' go off!

FLORA: You certainly *did* go off! Try an' tell me that you never went off when I just now seen an' heard you drivin' back in th' car? What uh you take me faw? No sense a-tall?

JAKE: If you got sense you keep your big mouth shut!

FLORA: Don't talk to me like that!

JAKE: Come on inside.

FLORA: I won't. Selfish an' inconsiderate, that's what you are! I told you at supper, There's not a bottle of Coca-Cola left on th' place. You said, Okay, right after supper we'll drive on over to th' White Star drugstore an' lay in a good supply. When I come out of th' house—

JAKE (*He stands in front of her and grips her neck with both hands*): Look here! Listen to what I tell you!

FLORA: *Jake!*

JAKE: Shhh! Just listen, Baby.

FLORA: Lemme go! G'damn you, le' go my throat!

JAKE: Jus' try an' concentrate on what I tell yuh!

FLORA: Tell me what?

JAKE: I ain't been off th' po'ch.

FLORA: Huh!

JAKE: I ain't been off th' front po'ch! Not since supper! Understand that, now?

FLORA: Jake, honey, you've gone out of you' mind!

JAKE: Maybe so. Never you mind. Just get that straight an'

keep it in your haid. I ain't been off the porch of this house since supper.

FLORA: But you sure as God *was* off it! (*He twists her wrist.*) Ouuuu! Stop it, stop it, stop it!

JAKE: Where have I been since supper?

FLORA: Here, here! On th' porch! Fo' God's sake, quit that twistin'!

JAKE: Where have I been?

FLORA: Porch! Porch! Here!

JAKE: Doin' what?

FLORA: *Jake!*

JAKE: Doin' what?

FLORA: Lemme go! Christ, Jake! Let loose! Quit twisting, you'll break my wrist!

JAKE (*laughing between his teeth*): Doin' what? What doin'? Since supper?

FLORA (*crying out*): How in hell do I know!

JAKE: 'Cause you was right here with me, all the time, for every second! You an' me, sweetheart, was sittin' here together on th' swing, just swingin' back an' forth every minute since supper! You got that in your haid good now?

FLORA (*whimpering*): Le'-go!

JAKE: Got it? In your haid good now?

FLORA: Yeh, yeh, yeh—leggo!

JAKE: What was I doin', then?

FLORA: Swinging! For Christ's sake—swingin'!

*He releases her. She whimpers and rubs her wrist but the impression is that the experience was not without pleasure for both parties. She groans and whimpers. He grips her loose curls in his hand and bends her head back. He plants a long wet kiss on her mouth.*

FLORA (*whimpering*): Mmmm-hmmmm! Mmmm! Mmmm!

JAKE (*huskily*): Tha's my swee' baby girl.

FLORA: Mmmmm! Hurt! Hurt!

JAKE: Hurt?

FLORA: Mmmm! Hurt!

JAKE: Kiss?

FLORA: Mmmm!

JAKE: Good?

FLORA: Mmmm . . .

JAKE: Good! Make little room.

FLORA: Too hot!

JAKE: Go on, make little room.

FLORA: Mmmmm . . .

JAKE: Cross patch?

FLORA: Mmmmmm.

JAKE: Whose baby? Big? Sweet?

FLORA: Mmmmm! Hurt!

JAKE: Kiss! (*He lifts her wrist to his lips and makes gobbling sounds.*)

FLORA (*giggling*): Stop! Silly! Mmmm!

JAKE: What would I do if you was a big piece of cake?

FLORA: Silly.

JAKE: Gobble! Gobble!

FLORA: Oh, you—

JAKE: What would I do if you was angel food cake? Big white piece with lots of nice thick icin'?

FLORA (*giggling*): Quit!

JAKE: Gobble, gobble, gobble!

FLORA (*squealing*): Jake!

JAKE: Huh?

FLORA: You *tick*-le!

JAKE: Answer little question!

FLORA: Wh-at?

JAKE: Where I been since supper?

FLORA: Off in the Chevy!

*He instantly seizes the wrist again. She shrieks.*

JAKE: Where've I been since supper?

FLORA: Po'ch! Swing!

JAKE: Doin' what?

FLORA: *Swingin'!* Oh, Christ, Jake, let loose!

JAKE: Hurt?

FLORA: Mmmmm . . .

JAKE: Good?

FLORA (*whimpering*): Mmmmm . . .

JAKE: Now you know where I been an' what I been doin' since supper?

FLORA: Yeah . . .

JAKE: Case anybody should ask?

FLORA: Who's going to ast?

JAKE: Never mind who's goin' t' ast, just you know the answers! Uh-huh?

FLORA: Uh-huh. (*Lisping babyishly.*) This is where you been. Settin' on th' swing since we had supper. Swingin'—back an' fo'th—back an' fo'th . . . You didn' go off in th' Chevy. (*Slowly.*) An' you was awf'ly surprised w'en th' syndicate fire broke out! (JAKE *slaps her.*) Jake!

JAKE: Everything you said is awright. But don't you get ideas.

FLORA: Ideas?

JAKE: A woman like you's not made to have ideas. Made to be hugged an' squeezed!

FLORA (*babyishly*): Mmmm . . .

JAKE: But not for ideas. So don't you have ideas. (*He rises.*) Go out an' get in th' Chevy.

FLORA: We goin to th' fire?

JAKE: No. We ain' goin' no fire. We goin' in town an' get us a case a dopes because we're hot an' thirsty.

FLORA (*vaguely, as she rises*): I lost m' white—kid—purse . . .

JAKE: It's on the seat of th' Chevy whe' you left it.

FLORA: Whe' *you* goin'?

JAKE: I'm goin in t' th' toilet. I'll be right out.

*He goes inside, letting the screen door slam.* FLORA *shuffles to the edge of the steps and stands there with a slight idiotic smile. She begins to descend, letting herself down each time with the same foot, like a child just learning to walk. She stops at the bottom of the steps and stares at the sky, vacantly and raptly, her fingers closing gently around the bruised wrist.* JAKE *can be heard singing inside.*

> "My baby don' care fo' rings
> or other expensive things—
> My baby just care—fo'—me!"

**CURTAIN**

## Scene II

*It is just after noon. The sky is the color of the satin bows
on the window curtains—a translucent, innocent blue. Heat
devils are shimmering over the flat Delta country and the
peaked white front of the house is like a shrill exclamation.*
JAKE's *gin is busy; heard like a steady pulse across the road.
A delicate lint of cotton is drifting about in the atmosphere.*

JAKE *appears, a large and purposeful man with arms like
hams covered with a fuzz of fine blond hair. He is followed
by* SILVA VICARRO *who is the Superintendent of the Syndicate
Plantation where the fire occurred last night.* VICARRO *is a
rather small and wiry man of dark Latin looks and nature.
He wears whipcord breeches, laced boots, and a white
undershirt. He has a Roman Catholic medallion on a chain
about his neck.*

JAKE (*with the good-natured condescension of a very large man
for a small one*): Well, suh, all I got to say is you're a mighty
lucky little fellow.

VICARRO: Lucky? In what way?

JAKE: That I can take on a job like this right now! Twenty-seven
wagons full of cotton 's a pretty big piece of bus'ness, Mr.
Vicarro. (*Stopping at the steps.*) Baby! (*He bites off a piece
of tobacco plug.*) What's yuh firs' name?

VICARRO: Silva.

JAKE: How do you spell it?

VICARRO: S-I-L-V-A.

JAKE: Silva! Like a silver lining! Ev'ry cloud has got a silver lining. What does that come from? The Bible?

VICARRO (*sitting on the steps*): No. The Mother Goose Book.

JAKE: Well, suh, you sure are lucky that I can do it. If I'd been
busy like I was two weeks ago I would 've turned it down.
*BABY! COME OUT HERE A MINUTE!*

*There is a vague response from inside.*

VICARRO: Lucky. Very lucky.

*He lights a cigarette.* FLORA *pushes open the screen door and comes out. She has on her watermelon pink silk dress and is clutching against her body the big white kid purse with her initials on it in big nickel plate.*

JAKE (*proudly*): Mr. Vicarro—I want you to meet Mrs. Meighan. Baby, this is a very down-at-the-mouth young fellow I want you to cheer up fo' me. He thinks he's out of luck because his cotton gin burnt down. He's got twenty-seven wagons full of cotton to be ginned out on a hurry-up order from his most impo'tant customers in Mobile. Well, suh, I said to him, Mr. Vicarro, you're to be congratulated—not because it burnt down, but because I happen to be in a situation to take the business over. Now you tell him just how lucky he is!

FLORA (*nervously*): Well, I guess he don't see how it was lucky to have his gin burned down.

VICARRO (*acidly*): No, ma'am.

JAKE (*quickly*): Mr. Vicarro. Some fellows marry a girl when she's little an' tiny. They like a small figure. See? Then, when the girl gets comfo'tably settled down—what does she do? Puts on flesh—of cou'se!

FLORA (*bashfully*): Jake!

JAKE: Now then! How do they react? Accept it as a matter of cou'se, as something which 'as been ordained by nature? Nope! No, suh, not a bit! They sta't to feeling abused. They think that fate must have a grudge against them because the little woman is not so little as she used to be. Because she's gone an' put on a matronly figure. Well, suh, that's at the root of a lot of domestic trouble. However, Mr. Vicarro, I never made that mistake. When I fell in love with this baby-doll I've got here, she was just the same size then that you see her today.

FLORA (*crossing shyly to porch rail*): Jake . . .

JAKE (*grinning*): A woman not large but tremendous! That's how I liked her—tremendous! I told her right off, when I slipped th' ring on her finger, one Satiddy night in a boathouse on Moon Lake—I said to her, Honey, if you take off one single pound of that body—I'm going to quit yuh! I'm going to quit yuh, I said, the minute I notice you've started to take off weight!

FLORA: Aw, Jake—please!

JAKE: I don't want nothing little, not in a woman. I'm not after nothing *petite*, as the Frenchmen call it. This is what I wanted—and what I *got!* Look at her, Mr. Vicarro. Look at her blush! (*He grips the back of* FLORA's *neck and tries to turn her around.*)

FLORA: Aw, quit, Jake! Quit, will yuh?

JAKE: See what a doll she is? (FLORA *turns suddenly and spanks him with the kid purse. He cackles and runs down the steps. At the corner of the house, he stops and turns.*) Baby, you keep Mr. Vicarro comfo'table while I'm ginnin' out that twenty-seven wagons full of cotton. Th' good-neighbor policy, Mr. Vicarro. You do me a good turn an' I'll do you a good one! Be see'n yuh! So long, Baby! (*He walks away with an energetic stride.*)

VICARRO: The good-neighbor policy! (*He sits on the porch steps.*)

FLORA (*sitting on the swing*): Izzen he out-*ray*-juss! (*She laughs foolishly and puts the purse in her lap.*)

VICARRO *stares gloomily across the dancing brilliance of the fields. His lip sticks out like a pouting child's. A rooster crows in the distance.*

FLORA: I wouldn't dare to expose myself like that.

VICARRO: Expose? To what?

FLORA: The sun. I take a terrible burn. I'll never forget the burn

I took one time. It was on Moon Lake one Sunday before
I was married. I never did like t' go fishin' but this young
fellow, one of the Peterson boys, insisted that we go fishin'.
Well, he didn't catch nothin' but jus' kep' fishin' an' fishin'
an' I set there in th' boat with all that hot sun on me. I said,
Stay under the willows. But he would'n' lissen to me, an' sure
enough I took such an awful burn I had t' sleep on m' stum-
mick th' nex' three nights.

VICARRO (*absently*): What did you say? You got sun-burned?

FLORA: Yes. One time on Moon Lake.

VICARRO: That's too bad. You got over it all right?

FLORA: Oh, yes. Finally. Yes.

VICARRO: That must 've been pretty bad.

FLORA: I fell in the lake once, too. Also with one of the Peterson
boys. On another fishing trip. That was a wild bunch of
boys, those Peterson boys. I never went out with 'em but
something happened which made me wish I hadn't. One
time, sunburned. One time, nearly drowned. One time—
poison ivy! Well, lookin' back on it, now, we had a good
deal of fun in spite of it, though.

VICARRO: The good-neighbor policy, huh? (*He slaps his boot
with the riding crop. Then he rises from steps.*)

FLORA: You might as well come up on th' po'ch an' make you'-
self as comfo'table as you can.

VICARRO: Uh-huh.

FLORA: I'm not much good at—makin' conversation.

VICARRO (*finally noticing her*): Now don't you bother to make
conversation for my benefit, Mrs. Meighan. I'm the type that
prefers a quiet understanding. (FLORA *laughs uncertainly*.)
One thing I always notice about you ladies . . .

FLORA: What's that, Mr. Vicarro?

VICARRO: You always have something in your hands—to hold
onto. Now that kid purse . . .

FLORA: My purse?

VICARRO: You have no reason to keep that purse in your hands.
You're certainly not afraid that I'm going to snatch it!

FLORA: Oh, God, no! I wassen afraid of that!

VICARRO: That wouldn't be the good-neighbor policy, would it?
But you hold onto that purse because it gives you something
to get a grip on. Isn't that right?

FLORA: Yes. I always like to have something in my hands.

VICARRO: Sure you do. You feel what a lot of uncertain things
there are. Gins burn down. The volunteer fire department
don't have decent equipment. Nothing is any protection.
The afternoon sun is hot. It's no protection. The trees are
back of the house. They're no protection. The goods that
dress is made of—is no protection. So what do you do, Mrs.
Meighan? You pick up the white kid purse. It's solid. It's
sure. It's certain. It's something to hold *on* to. You get what
I mean?

FLORA: Yeah. I think I do.

VICARRO: It gives you a feeling of being attached to something.
The mother protects the baby? No, no, no—the baby protects the mother! From being lost and empty and having
nothing but lifeless things in her hands! Maybe you think
there isn't much connection!

FLORA: You'll have to excuse me from thinking. I'm too lazy.

VICARRO: What's your name, Mrs. Meighan?

FLORA: Flora.

VICARRO: Mine is Silva. Something not gold but—Silva!

FLORA: Like a silver dollar?

VICARRO: No, like a silver dime! It's an Italian name. I'm a native of New Orleans.

FLORA: Then it's not sun-burn. You're natcherally dark.

VICARRO (*raising his undershirt from his belly*): Look at this!

FLORA: Mr. Vicarro!

VICARRO: Just as dark as my arm is!

FLORA: You don't have to show me! I'm not from Missouri!

VICARRO (*grinning*): Excuse me.

FLORA (*She laughs nervously*): Whew! I'm sorry to say we don't have a coke in the house. We meant to get a case of cokes las' night, but what with all the excitement going on—

VICARRO: What excitement was that?

FLORA: Oh, the fire and all.

VICARRO (*lighting a cigarette*): I shouldn't think you all would of been excited about the fire.

FLORA: A fire is always exciting. After a fire, dogs an' chickens don't sleep. I don't think our chickens got to sleep all night.

VICARRO: No?

FLORA: They cackled an' fussed an' flopped around on the roost —took on something awful! Myself, I couldn't sleep neither. I jus' lay there an' sweated all night long.

VICARRO: On account of th' fire?

FLORA: An' the heat an' mosquitoes. And I was mad at Jake.

VICARRO: Mad at Mr. Meighan? What about?

FLORA: Oh, he went off an' left me settin' here on this ole po'ch last night without a Coca-Cola on the place.

VICARRO: Went off an' left you, did he?

FLORA: Yep. Right after supper. An' when he got back the fire 'd already broke out an' instead of drivin' in to town like he said, he decided to go an' take a look at your burnt-down cotton gin. I got smoke in my eyes an' my nose an' throat. It hurt my sinus an' I was in such a wo'n out, nervous condition, it made me cry. I cried like a baby. Finally took two teaspoons of paregoric. Enough to put an elephant to sleep. But still I stayed awake an' heard them chickens carryin' on out there!

VICARRO: It sounds like you passed a very uncomfortable night.

FLORA: Sounds like? Well, it *was*.

VICARRO: So Mr. Meighan—you say—disappeared after supper?

*There is a pause while* FLORA *looks at him blankly.*

FLORA: Huh?

VICARRO: You say Mr. Meighan was out of the house for a while after supper? (*Something in his tone makes her aware of her indiscretion.*)

FLORA: Oh—uh—just for a moment.

VICARRO: Just for a moment, huh? How long a moment? (*He stares at her very hard.*)

FLORA: What are you driving at, Mr. Vicarro?

VICARRO: Driving at? Nothing.

FLORA: You're looking at me so funny.

VICARRO: He disappeared for a moment! Is that what he did? How long a moment did he disappear for? Can you remember, Mrs. Meighan?

FLORA: What difference does that make? What's it to you, anyhow?

VICARRO: Why should you mind me asking?

FLORA: You make this sound like I was on trial for something!

VICARRO: Don't you like to pretend like you're a witness?

FLORA: Witness of what, Mr. Vicarro?

VICARRO: Why—for instance—say—a case of arson!

FLORA (*wetting her lips*): Case of—? What is—arson?

VICARRO: The willful destruction of property by fire. (*He slaps his boots sharply with the riding crop.*)

FLORA (*startled*): Oh! (*She nervously fingers the purse.*) Well, now, don't you go and be getting any—funny ideas.

VICARRO: Ideas about what, Mrs. Meighan?

FLORA: My husband's disappearin'—after supper. I can explain that.

VICARRO: Can you?

FLORA: Sure I can.

VICARRO: Good! How do you explain it? (*He stares at her. She looks down.*) What's the matter? Can't you collect your thoughts, Mrs. Meighan?

FLORA: No, but—

VICARRO: Your mind's a blank on the subject?

FLORA: Look here, now—(*She squirms on the swing.*)

VICARRO: You find it impossible to remember just what your husband disappeared for after supper? You can't imagine what kind of errand it was that he went on, can you?

FLORA: No! No, I can't!

VICARRO: But when he returned—let's see . . . The fire had just broken out at the Syndicate Plantation?

FLORA: Mr. Vicarro, I don't have the slightest idear what you could be driving at.

VICARRO: You're a very unsatisfactory witness, Mrs. Meighan.

FLORA: I never can think when people—stare straight at me.

VICARRO: Okay. I'll look away, then. (*He turns his back to her.*)

Now does that improve your memory any? Now are you able to concentrate on the question?

FLORA: Huh . . .

VICARRO: No? You're not? (*He turns around again, grinning evilly.*) Well . . . shall we drop the subject?

FLORA: I sure do wish you would.

VICARRO: It's no use crying over a burnt-down gin. This world is built on the principle of tit for tat.

FLORA: What do you mean?

VICARRO: Nothing at all specific. Mind if I . . . ?

FLORA: What?

VICARRO: You want to move over a little an' make some room? (FLORA *edges aside on the swing. He sits down with her.*) I like a swing. I've always liked to sit an' rock on a swing. Relaxes you . . . You relaxed?

FLORA: Sure.

VICARRO: No, you're not. Your nerves are all tied up.

FLORA: Well, you made me feel kind of nervous. All of them questions you ast me about the fire.

VICARRO: I didn' ask you questions about the fire. I only asked you about your husband's leaving the house after supper.

FLORA: I explained that to you.

VICARRO: Sure. That's right. You did. The good-neighbor policy. That was a lovely remark your husband made about the good-neighbor policy. I see what he means by that now.

FLORA: He was thinking about President Roosevelt's speech. We sat up an' lissened to it one night last week.

VICARRO: No, I think that he was talking about something closer to home, Mrs. Meighan. You do me a good turn and I'll do you one, that was the way that he put it. You have a piece of cotton on your face. Hold still—I'll pick it off. (*He delicately removes the lint.*) There now.

FLORA (*nervously*): Thanks.

VICARRO: There's a lot of fine cotton lint floating round in the air.

FLORA: I know there is. It irritates my nose. I think it gets up in my sinus.

VICARRO: Well, you're a delicate woman.

FLORA: Delicate? Me? Oh, no. I'm too big for that.

VICARRO: Your size is part of your delicacy, Mrs. Meighan.

FLORA: How do you mean?

VICARRO: There's a lot of you, but every bit of you is delicate. Choice. Delectable, I might say.

FLORA: Huh?

VICARRO: I mean you're altogether lacking in any—coarseness. You're soft. Fine-fibered. And smooth.

FLORA: Our talk is certainly taking a personal turn.

VICARRO: Yes. You make me think of cotton.

FLORA: Huh?

VICARRO: Cotton!

FLORA: Well! Should I say thanks or something?

VICARRO: No, just smile, Mrs. Meighan. You have an attractive smile. Dimples!

FLORA: No . . .

VICARRO: Yes, you have! Smile, Mrs. Meighan! Come on—smile! (FLORA *averts her face, smiling helplessly.*) There now. See? You've got them! (*He delicately touches one of the dimples.*)

FLORA: Please don't touch me. I don't like to be touched.

VICARRO: Then why do you giggle?

FLORA: Can't help it. You make me feel kind of hysterical, Mr. Vicarro. Mr. Vicarro—

VICARRO: Yes?

FLORA: I hope you don't think that Jake was mixed up in that fire. I swear to goodness he never left the front porch. I remember it perfeckly now. We just set here on the swing till the fire broke out and then we drove in town.

VICARRO: To celebrate?

FLORA: No, no, no.

VICARRO: Twenty-seven wagons full of cotton's a pretty big piece of business to fall in your lap like a gift from the gods, Mrs. Meighan.

FLORA: I thought you said that we would drop the subjeck.

VICARRO: You brought it up that time.

FLORA: Well, please don't try to mix me up any more. I swear to goodness the fire had already broke out when he got back.

VICARRO: That's not what you told me a moment ago.

FLORA: You got me all twisted up. We went in town. The fire broke out an' we didn't know about it.

VICARRO: I thought you said it irritated your sinus.

FLORA: Oh, my God, you sure put words in my mouth. Maybe I'd better make us some lemonade.

VICARRO: Don't go to the trouble.

FLORA: I'll go in an' fix it direckly, but right at this moment I'm too weak to get up. I don't know why, but I can't hardly hold my eyes open. They keep falling shut . . . I think it's a little too crowded, two on a swing. Will you do me a favor an' set back down over there?

VICARRO: Why do you want me to move?

FLORA: It makes too much body heat when we're crowded together.

VICARRO: One body can borrow coolness from another.

FLORA: I always heard that bodies borrowed heat.

VICARRO: Not in this case. I'm cool.

FLORA: You don't seem like it to me.

VICARRO: I'm just as cool as a cucumber. If you don't believe it, touch me.

FLORA: Where?

VICARRO: Anywhere.

FLORA (*rising with great effort*): Excuse me. I got to go in. (*He pulls her back down.*) What did you do that for?

VICARRO: I don't want to be deprived of your company yet.

FLORA: Mr. Vicarro, you're getting awf'ly familiar.

VICARRO: Haven't you got any fun-loving spirit about you?

FLORA: This isn't fun.

VICARRO: Then why do you giggle?

FLORA: I'm ticklish! Quit switching me, will yuh?

VICARRO: I'm just shooing the flies off.

FLORA: Leave 'em be, then, please. They don't hurt nothin'.

VICARRO: I think you like to be switched.

FLORA: I don't. I wish you'd quit.

VICARRO: You'd like to be switched harder.

FLORA: No, I wouldn't.

VICARRO: That blue mark on your wrist—

FLORA: What about it?

VICARRO: I've got a suspicion.

FLORA: Of what?

VICARRO: It was twisted. By your husband.

FLORA: You're crazy.

VICARRO: Yes, it was. And you liked it.

FLORA: I certainly didn't. Would you mind moving your arm?

VICARRO: Don't be so skittish.

FLORA: Awright. I'll get up then.

VICARRO: Go on.

FLORA: I feel so weak.

VICARRO: Dizzy?

FLORA: A little bit. Yeah. My head's spinning round. I wish you would stop the swing.

VICARRO: It's not swinging much.

FLORA: But even a little's too much.

VICARRO: You're a delicate woman. A pretty big woman, too.

FLORA: So is America. Big.

VICARRO: That's a funny remark.

FLORA: Yeah. I don't know why I made it. My head's so buzzy.

VICARRO: Fuzzy?

FLORA: Fuzzy an'—buzzy . . . Is something on my arm?

VICARRO: No.

FLORA: Then what 're you brushing?

VICARRO: Sweat off.

FLORA: Leave it alone.

VICARRO: Let me wipe it. (*He brushes her arm with a handkerchief.*)

FLORA (*laughing weakly*): No, please, don't. It feels funny.

VICARRO: How does it feel?

FLORA: It tickles me. All up an' down. You cut it out now. If you don't cut it out I'm going to call.

VICARRO: Call who?

FLORA: I'm going to call that nigger. The nigger that's cutting the grass across the road.

VICARRO: Go on. Call, then.

FLORA (*weakly*): Hey! Hey, boy!

VICARRO: Can't you call any louder?

FLORA: I feel so funny. What is the matter with me?

VICARRO: You're just relaxing. You're big. A big type of woman. I like you. Don't get so excited.

FLORA: I'm not, but you—

VICARRO: What am I doing?

FLORA: Suspicions. About my husband and ideas you have about me.

VICARRO: Such as what?

FLORA: He burnt your gin down. He didn't. And I'm not a big piece of cotton. (*She pulls herself up.*) I'm going inside.

VICARRO (*rising*): I think that's a good idea.

FLORA: I said I was. Not you.

VICARRO: Why not me?

FLORA: Inside it might be crowded, with you an' me.

VICARRO: Three's a crowd. We're two.

FLORA: You stay out. Wait here.

VICARRO: What'll you do?

FLORA: I'll make us a pitcher of nice cold lemonade.

VICARRO: Okay. You go on in.

FLORA: What'll you do?

VICARRO: I'll follow.

FLORA: That's what I figured you might be aiming to do. We'll both stay out.

VICARRO: In the sun?

FLORA: We'll sit back down in th' shade. (*He blocks her.*) Don't stand in my way.

VICARRO: You're standing in mine.

FLORA: I'm dizzy.

VICARRO: You ought to lie down.

FLORA: How can I?

VICARRO: Go in.

FLORA: You'd follow me.

VICARRO: What if I did?

FLORA: I'm afraid.

VICARRO: You're starting to cry.

FLORA: I'm afraid!

VICARRO: What of?

FLORA: Of you.

VICARRO: I'm little.

FLORA: I'm dizzy. My knees are so weak they're like water. I've got to sit down.

VICARRO: Go in.

FLORA: I can't.

VICARRO: Why not?

FLORA: You'd follow.

VICARRO: Would that be so awful?

FLORA: You've got a mean look in your eyes and I don't like the whip. Honest to God he never. He didn't, I swear!

VICARRO: Do what?

FLORA: The fire . . .

VICARRO: Go on.

FLORA: Please don't!

VICARRO: Don't what?

FLORA: Put it down. The whip, please put it down. Leave it out here on the porch.

VICARRO: What are you scared of?

FLORA: You.

VICARRO: Go on.

*She turns helplessly and moves to the screen. He pulls it open.*

FLORA: Don't follow. Please don't follow!

*She sways uncertainly. He presses his hand against her. She moves inside. He follows. The door is shut quietly. The gin pumps slowly and steadily across the road. From inside the house there is a wild and despairing cry. A door is slammed. The cry is repeated more faintly.*

### CURTAIN

## Scene III

*It is about nine o'clock the same evening. Although the sky behind the house is a dusky rose color, a full September moon of almost garish intensity gives the front of the house a ghostly brilliance. Dogs are howling like demons across the prostrate fields of the Delta.*

*The front porch of the* MEIGHANS *is empty.*

*After a moment the screen door is pushed slowly open and* FLORA MEIGHAN *emerges gradually. Her appearance is rav-*

*aged. Her eyes have a vacant limpidity in the moonlight, her lips are slightly apart. She moves with her hands stretched gropingly before her till she has reached a pillar of the porch. There she stops and stands moaning a little. Her hair hangs loose and disordered. The upper part of her body is unclothed except for a torn pink band about her breasts. Dark streaks are visible on the bare shoulders and arms and there is a large discoloration along one cheek. A dark trickle, now congealed, descends from one corner of her mouth. These more apparent tokens she covers with one hand when* JAKE *comes up on the porch. He is now heard approaching, singing to himself.*

JAKE: By the light—by the light—by the light—Of the sil-very mo-o-on!

*Instinctively* FLORA *draws back into the sharply etched shadow from the porch roof.* JAKE *is too tired and triumphant to notice her appearance.*

How's a baby? (FLORA *utters a moaning grunt.*) Tired? Too tired t' talk? Well, that's how I feel. Too tired t' talk. Too goddam tired t' speak a friggin' word! (*He lets himself down on the steps, groaning and without giving* FLORA *more than a glance.*) Twenty-seven wagons full of cotton. That's how much I've ginned since ten this mawnin'. A man-size job.

FLORA (*huskily*): Uh-huh ... A man-size—job ...

JAKE: *Twen-ty sev-en wa-*gons *full of cot-*ton!

FLORA (*senselessly repeating*): *Twen-ty sev-en wa-*gons *full of cot-*ton!

*A dog howls.* FLORA *utters a breathless laugh.*

JAKE: What're you laughin' at, honey? Not at me, I hope.

FLORA: No ...

JAKE: That's good. The job that I've turned out is nothing to laugh at. I drove that pack of niggers like a mule-skinner. They don't have a brain in their bodies. All they got is bodies. You got to drive, drive, drive. I don't even see how niggers eat without somebody to tell them to put the food in their moufs!

*She laughs again, like water spilling out of her mouth.*

Huh! You got a laugh like a—Christ. A terrific day's work I finished.

FLORA (*slowly*): I would'n' brag—about it. . . .

JAKE: I'm not braggin' about it, I'm just sayin' I done a big day's work, I'm all wo'n out an' I want a little appreciation, not cross speeches. Honey . . .

FLORA: I'm not—(*She laughs again.*)—makin' cross speeches.

JAKE: To take on a big piece of work an finish it up an' mention the fack that it's finished I wouldn't call braggin'.

FLORA: You're not the only one's—done a big day's—work.

JAKE: Who else that you know of? (*There is a pause.*)

FLORA: Maybe you think that I had an easy time. (*Her laughter spills out again.*)

JAKE: You're laughin' like you been on a goddam jag. (FLORA *laughs.*) What did you get pissed on? Roach poison or citronella? I think I make it pretty easy for you, workin' like a mule-skinner so you can hire you a nigger to do the wash an' take the house-work on. An elephant woman who acks as frail as a kitten, that's the kind of a woman I got on m' hands.

FLORA: Sure . . . (*She laughs.*) You make it easy!

JAKE: I've yet t' see you lift a little finger. Even gotten too lazy t' put you' things on. Round the house ha'f naked all th' time. Y' live in a cloud. All you can think of is "Give me a Coca-Cola!" Well, you better look out. They got a new bureau in the guvamint files. It's called U.W. Stands for Useless Wimmen. Tha's secret plans on foot t' have 'em shot! (*He laughs at his joke.*)

FLORA: Secret—plans—on foot?

JAKE: T' have 'em *shot*.

FLORA: That's good. I'm glad t' hear it. (*She laughs again.*)

JAKE: I come home tired an' you cain't wait t' peck at me. What 're you cross about now?

FLORA: I think it was a mistake.

JAKE: What was a mistake?

FLORA: Fo' you t' fool with th' Syndicate—Plantation . . .

JAKE: I don't know about that. We wuh kind of up-against it, honey. Th' Syndicate buyin' up all th' lan' aroun' here an' turnin' the ole croppers off it without their wages—mighty near busted ev'ry mercantile store in Two Rivers County! An' then they build their own gin to gin their own cotton. It looked for a while like I was stuck up high an' dry. But when the gin burnt down an' Mr. Vicarro decided he'd better throw a little bus'ness my way—I'd say the situation was much improved!

FLORA (*She laughs weakly*): Then maybe you don't understand th' good-neighbor—policy.

JAKE: Don't understand it? Why, I'm the boy that invented it.

FLORA: Huh-huh! What an—*invention!* All I can say is—I hope you're satisfied now that you've ginned out—twenty-seven wagons full of—cotton.

JAKE: Vicarro was pretty well pleased w'en he dropped over.

FLORA: Yeah. He was—pretty well—pleased.

JAKE: How did you all get along?

FLORA: We got along jus' fine. Jus' fine an'—dandy.

JAKE: He didn't seem like a such a bad little guy. He takes a sensible attitude.

FLORA (*laughing helplessly*): He—sure—does!

JAKE: I hope you made him comfo'table in the house?

FLORA (*giggling*): I made him a pitcher—of nice cold—lemonade!

JAKE: With a little gin in it, huh? That's how you got pissed. A nice cool drink don't sound bad to me right now. Got any left?

FLORA: Not a bit, Mr. Meighan. We drank it *a-a-ll* up! (*She flops onto the swing.*)

JAKE: So you didn't have such a tiresome time after all?

FLORA: No. Not tiresome a bit. I had a nice conversation with Mistuh—Vicarro . . .

JAKE: What did you all talk about?

FLORA: Th' good-neighbor policy.

JAKE (*chuckling*): How does he feel about th' good-neighbor policy?

FLORA: Oh—(*She giggles.*)—He thinks it's a—good idea! He says—

JAKE: Huh? (FLORA *laughs weakly.*) Says what?

FLORA: Says—(*She goes off into another spasm of laughter.*)

JAKE: What ever he said must've been a panic!

FLORA: He says—(*Controlling her spasm.*)—he don't think he'll build him a new cotton gin any more. He's gonna let you do a-a-lll his ginnin'—fo' him!

JAKE: I told you he'd take a sensible attitude.

FLORA: Yeah. Tomorrow he plans t' come back—with lots more cotton. Maybe another twenty-seven wagons.

JAKE: Yeah?

FLORA: An' while you're ginnin' it out—he'll have me entertain him with—nice lemonade! (*She has another fit of giggles.*)

JAKE: The more I hear about that lemonade the better I like it. Lemonade highballs, huh? Mr. Thomas Collins?

FLORA: I guess it's—gonna go on fo'—th' rest of th'—summer . . .

JAKE (*rising and stretching happily*): Well, it'll . . . it'll soon be fall. Cooler nights comin' on.

FLORA: I don't know that that will put a—stop to it—though . . .

JAKE (*obliviously*): The air feels cooler already. You shouldn't be settin' out here without you' shirt on, honey. A change in the air can give you a mighty bad cold.

FLORA: I couldn't stan' nothin' on me—nex' to my—skin.

JAKE: It ain't the heat that gives you all them hives, it's too much liquor. Grog-blossoms, that's what you got! I'm goin' inside to the toilet. When I come out—(*He opens the screen door and goes in.*)—We'll drive in town an' see what's at th' movies.
You go hop in the Chevy!

FLORA *laughs to herself. She slowly opens the huge kid purse and removes a wad of Kleenex. She touches herself tenderly here and there, giggling breathlessly.*

FLORA (*aloud*): I really oughtn' t' have a white kid purse. It's wadded full of—Kleenex—to make it big—like a baby! Big—in my arms—like a baby!

JAKE (*from inside*): What did you say, Baby?

FLORA (*dragging herself up by the chain of the swing*): I'm not —Baby. Mama! Ma! That's—me . . . (*Cradling the big white purse in her arms, she advances slowly and tenderly to the edge of the porch. The moon shines full on her smiling and ravaged face. She begins to rock and sway gently, rocking the purse in her arms and crooning.*)
Rock-a-bye Baby—in uh tree-tops!
If a wind blows—a cradle will rock! (*She descends a step.*)
If a bough bends—a baby will fall! (*She descends another step.*)
Down will come Baby—cradle—an'—all! (*She laughs and stares raptly and vacantly up at the moon.*)

**CURTAIN**

# Bedtime Story

## An Anatol Burlesque

by Sean O'Casey

JOHN JO MULLIGAN, *a clerk*

ANGELA NIGHTINGALE, *a gay lass*

DANIEL HALIBUT, *a clerk—friend to Mulligan*

MISS MOSSIE, *a very respectable lodging-house keeper*

A POLICEMAN

A DOCTOR

A NURSE

TIME.—*The present.*

*Scene: The sitting-room of the bachelor-flat rented by* JOHN
JO MULLIGAN *from* MISS MOSSIE, *owner of one of the old houses
of Dublin, decayed a little, but still sternly respectable, and
kept presentable by her rigid attention to it. She has divided it
into lodgings for respectable young gentlemen. A rather dull
though lofty room. To the right is an ordinary gas fire; over
it a mantelpiece on which is a clock, flanked on either side
by a colored vase; over these, on the wall, a square, gilt-
framed mirror. Further up, towards back, is a door leading
to* MULLIGAN'S *bedroom. By the back wall, near this door, is
a small bookcase with a few books sprawled out on its
shelves; and on top is a pale-green vase holding a bunch of
white pampas grass. To the left of this is a window, now
heavily curtained with dull, brown hangings. In the window's
center is a stand holding a colored flower-pot containing some
kind of a palm plant. Further on is a picture of a white-
washed cottage, well thatched with straw, a brown pathway
before the door, with purple heather growing in tufts on its
edges, and, in the distance, the dark-blue peaks of hills, all
surmounted by a bright blue sky. In the side wall on the left
is the door leading to the rest of the house. On this door several overcoats are hanging. To the left of it is an umbrella-
stand in which are a walking-stick and two umbrellas, one*

*newer than the other. Close to the fireplace is an armchair clad in dark-green leather, and further away, at an angle, is a settee to hold two, clad in the same color. In the room's center is a round table covered with a red table-cloth. On the table are a photograph or two, a vase of chrysanthemums, and a book, open, with its face turned down, so that the place might not be lost when the reader left it aside. The room is lighted from a bulb hanging from the center of the ceiling; the light is softened by being covered with a yellow parchment shade. A standard lamp stands on the floor a little way from the sitting-room door, towards the window, its light mollified by a deeply-fringed red silk shade. A key is sticking in the keyhole of the sitting-room door. A pair of* MULLIGAN'S *tan shoes are beside the fireplace. It is three or four of a cold, sleety January morning.*

*The fire is unlit, the room in darkness, when, presently, the bedroom door opens, and* MULLIGAN *comes into the sitting-room, showing the way to himself by the light of an electric torch. He is but half dressed, in blue shirt, bright-checked, baggy plus-fours, and colored-top stockings. He is a young man of twenty-four or -five; tall, but not thin. His hair is almost blond, and he wears it brushed back from his forehead, which is too high for the rather stolid face, giving him, at times, the look of a clown having a holiday. His upper lip has a close-cropped mustache. He is a constitutionally frightened chap, never able to take the gayer needs of life in his stride—though he would be glad to do it, if he could; but he can never become convalescent from a futile sense of sin. His clean-shaven face shows a very worried look. He comes into the room cautiously, waving the light over the floor, the table, the chairs, as if looking for something—as a matter of fact, he is; then returns to the door to peep into the bedroom.*

MULLIGAN (*sticking his head into the room—in a cautious whisper*): I can't see the thing anywhere. Sure you left it out here? (*There is no reply to the question.*) I say I can't find it anywhere out here. (*There is no reply. He mutters to himself as if half in prayer.*) I shouldn't have done it; I shouldn't have done it! I musta been mad. Oh, forgive me! (*He clicks his tongue, and peeps into the room again.*) Dtch dtch! Gone asleep again! (*Whispering*) Angela! Angela! (*In a louder whisper.*) Are you awake? Eh, Angela?

ANGELA (*within the room—sleepily*): Wha'?

MULLIGAN (*echoing her*): Wha', wha'! (*To himself.*) Oh, it was a mad thing to do. Miserere mei. (*Speaking into room with irritation.*) Have you forgotten what you sent me out to get? (*Appealingly.*) Please try to arouse yourself, Angela!

ANGELA (*within*): Wha'?

*Silence again for a few moments while* MULLIGAN *flashes the light on to the clock.*

MULLIGAN: It's going to four o'clock in the morning, Angela.

ANGELA (*within*): Didja get the lipstick?

MULLIGAN (*testily*): I've told you I can't see it anywhere.

ANGELA (*sleepily*): Have another look—there's a dear. I know I I left it out there somewhere.

MULLIGAN (*shivering a little*): It's nothing like a tropical climate out here, you know.

ANGELA (*sleepily*): It's easy to li' the fire, isn't it?

*Mulligan crosses to the fireplace, turns the gas tap, and sees that the meter wants another shilling. He irritatedly turns the tap off, and, crossing quickly back to the bedroom, knocks over the vase of flowers on the table, sending the water spilling over the table and on to the floor.*

MULLIGAN (*half to himself and half to* ANGELA—*with annoyance*): There's the vase down! Wather into me shoes and all over the floor! (*Putting his head into the bedroom again.*) I've knocked the vase down now! The place is flooded! And I can't light the fire—the meter needs another shilling.

ANGELA (*sleepily*): Look in me han'bag, somewhere about. Maybe there's a bob in it.

*In desperation,* MULLIGAN *goes to the cupboard, opens it, takes out a wallet from which he takes a shilling, goes back to fire-place, puts it in the slot, and lights the fire. Then he returns to the bedroom door.*

MULLIGAN (*putting his head into the bedroom again*): Angela, are you up yet? The whole place is flooded. (*He gets no answer.*) You're not going asleep again, are you? Angela!

ANGELA (*within—sleepily*): What time is it?

MULLIGAN (*in a loud and impatient whisper*): I told you long ago. It's going to four o'clock in the morning. That friend of mine I told you of, will be back any minute from his all-night dance, before you slip away, if you don't hurry.

ANGELA (*from within*): And what if he is? If he knew what had been going on in here, he'd be sorry he ever went to the dance.

MULLIGAN: Looka, Angela, I don't feel a bit funny about it. We should never have done it. Please get up, and face the situation. Remember your solemn promise to slip off when things were still.

ANGELA *appears at the door. She is a girl of twenty-five to twenty-seven, tall, trimly-formed, and not without dignity. Her hair is auburn, inclining towards redness. She is something of a pagan.*

*At present, she is dressed in her cami-knickers, covered by* MULLIGAN's *brown dressing-gown, and her bare feet are thrust into* MULLIGAN's *slippers. Far and away too good a companion of an hour, a year, or a life, for a fellow like* MUL-LIGAN.

ANGELA (*from the doorway*): D'ye like the dark because your deeds are evil, or what? Switch on the light for God's sake, man, and let's have a look at each other before you banish your poor Eve from her Mulligan paradise.

MULLIGAN (*as he switches on the light*): I was afraid someone out-side might see it, stay to look, might hear our voices, and wonder.

ANGELA: Wonder at what?

MULLIGAN: At hearing a girl's voice in my room at this time of night or morning.

ANGELA (*mockingly*): And isn't it a sweet thing for a girl's voice to be heard in a man's room at this time o' the night or morning?

MULLIGAN (*almost tearfully*): You know it's not; not as we're situated. You know you did wrong to practice on a body who didn't know enough. Situated as we are, without divine warrant, it's not proper. We're in the midst of a violent sin, and you should be ashamed and sorry, instead of feeling sinfully gay about it. It's necessary to feel sorry for a sin of this kind.

ANGELA: You were quite gay when we were coming in, boy, weren't you? You've had your few bright moments, and you've given a sparkle to your life, so don't spoil it all. It may well be more serious for me than it is for you. (*She shivers.*) Burrr! It's cold here! I'll come back when the room's warmer, and make myself ready to meet the respectable world.

*She goes back into the bedroom, while he stands at the bed-room door for a few moments, not knowing what to do.*

MULLIGAN (*eyes raised appealing to the ceiling*): Oh, that one'll be well punished for her gaiety and carelessness in sin! Oh, when will I forget this night's doings! Shattering fall! The very next day after me Novena too! (*He peeps into the bed-room.*) Don't get too cosy there, or you won't want to move. Move we must, and soon. (*He goes to the cupboard, relocks it, and puts the key in his pocket; then he goes to the arm-chair, sits down in it, and starts to put on his shoes. Putting on a shoe— in a half-prayer.*) Sweet Saint Panteemalaria, get

me outa this without exposure.( *He clicks his tongue.*) Dtch
dtch! Soaking wet! and I'll be a cautious goer from this out
—I promise. (*He goes over to bedroom door again with but
one shoe on, and peeps in.*) Angela, room's warm now; quite
warm. The time's flying, mind you. (*There is no reply.*) Aw,
God, have you gone to sleep again! Please, Miss Nightingale,
please have some regard for others!

ANGELA (*from within—sleepily*): Did you find it?

MULLIGAN: Find what, find what?

ANGELA: Me lipstick you were looking for?

MULLIGAN: No, no, I didn't; must be in there somewhere.

ANGELA: I remember I had it when you had me perched on your
lap. Remember?

MULLIGAN (*as if to someone in sitting-room*): Oh, don't be re-
minding me of things! (*Into the bedroom.*) No, I don't remember. Oh, for goodness' sake, get up!

ANGELA: All right, all right. Put out a glass of wine, and I'll be out
in a minute.

MULLIGAN *goes to the cupboard, unlocks it, and takes out a
bottle of wine and a glass. He locks the cupboard again, leaving
the key in the keyhole. He goes to the table, fills out a glass of
wine, and leaves it, with the bottle, on the table, in readiness
for* ANGELA.

*He sits down in the armchair, puts on the other shoe, then
winds a woolen muffler round his neck, puts on a pullover and
coat that have been hanging over the back of a chair, and
finally places a trilby hat on his head. As he does these things,
he occasionally mutters to himself.*

MULLIGAN (*busy with the wine for* ANGELA): Not a single
thought has she for what might happen to me if discovery
came. Utterly abandoned to her own intherests. (*As he sits
in chair putting on the second shoe—in a full-blown prayer.*)
Oh, gentle Saint Camisolinus, guardianess of all good young

people, get between me and this petticoated demonsthrator of sinful delusion, and I'll be O.K. for evermore. I will, I promise!

ANGELA *comes into the room at last, and makes quick for the fire. She has put on her stockings—silk ones—and skirt, a short, well-tailored one of darkish green, with broad belt of dark red and black buckle. She carries a brown jersey over her arm, and her shoes in her hand.*

ANGELA (*throwing her shoes on to the armchair, and stretching her hands to the fire*): Burrr! It's cold out here still! I thought you said the room was warm? (*She notices how he's dressed.*) All ready for the journey, eh? Soon we'll be skiing down the stairs, wha'? Praying to all the saints you know to see me out, eh?

*She puts the jersey on over her head before the mirror over the fireplace, and pats it down smoothly over her breast and*

ANGELA: We have to face the hard, cold facts now, haven't we, dear?

MULLIGAN: We've got to think now of what would become of me if you were discovered here.

ANGELA (*mockingly*): Really? Of course, when one thinks of it, that becomes the one important problem.

MULLIGAN (*not noticing the mockery*): It is, actually. You see, Angela, the head of my department's a grand Knight of Columbanus, an uncompromising Catholic, strict in his thought of life, and if he heard of anything like this, I'd—I'd be out in the bleaker air, quick; the little gilt I have on life would be gone; I'd run to ruin! God help me!

ANGELA (*prompting him*): And then there's Father Demsey?

MULLIGAN: Then there's Father Demsey whose right-hand man I am in the Confraternity and at all Saint Vincent de Paul meetings, with his "We can safely leave that matter with Mr. Mulligan," or "John Jo will do this for us." You see, it's a *shoulders.*

matter of importance to more than me. So, come on—we betther get off at once.

ANGELA (*rising from the chair, and drinking the glass of wine*):
Angela's bright eyes, her scarlet lip, fine foot, straight leg, and quivering thigh have lost their charm for Mr. Mulligan. He's all for go-ahead godliness now! (*She pours out another glass of wine and drinks it.*) And what is to become of me? You don't care, and I don't care either.

*She moves about the room in a slow, semi-reckless rhythm as she lilts—* MULLIGAN *following her trying to get her quiet again.*

ANGELA (*lilting and moving about*):
I don't care what becomes of me,
I don't care what becomes of me.

MULLIGAN (*shuffling after her as she moves as well as he can—in a low, anguished voice*): Angela, please! Sit down, do!

ANGELA (*lilting*):
I don't care if I'm out till two,
I don't care for the man in blue.

MULLIGAN (*following her*): Please, Miss Nightingale, be serious! The landlady'll hear you, and then we'll be done!

ANGELA (*lilting*):
I don't care what the people say,
Here, there, and everywhere;

MULLIGAN (*appealing to the ceiling*): Saint Curberisco, help me!

ANGELA (*in a final burst*):
For I'm going to be married in the morning,
So tonight, boys, I don't care!
(*Facing towards* MULLIGAN.) Sometime or other, we have to face out of all we get into: face out of getting into bed with a woman no less than face out into silence from the glamor of prayer; face out of summer into winter; face out of life into death!

MULLIGAN (*crossing himself*): Your talk's near blasphemy, Angela! Now you're going where you shouldn't venture. You'll bring a curse down on me, if you're not careful! Please be more discreet.

ANGELA: They're facts.

MULLIGAN: We're not fit for facts now.

ANGELA (*facing him fiercely*): You stand there mustering up moans for yourself, and never once realize that you've ruined me! Yes, ruined me!

MULLIGAN (*startled*): Oh, God, d'ye hear her! Ruined you? Oh, come, now, don't thry to act the innocent.

ANGELA: It's you who's acting the innocent, but it won't work. I was only an innocent kid till I met you. You led me on and destroyed all confidence in the goodness of me own nature! You never, never ceased from persuasion till you got me here. I wasn't even to take off my hat, if I was the least bit suspicious. We were just to sit quiet discussing Yeats's poems. You were to sit ice-bound in your chair.

MULLIGAN (*indignantly*): I led you on! Angela Nightingale, you're inventing things. It was you insisted on coming, because you didn't like restaurants. A sorry thing for me I ever listened to you!

ANGELA (*ignoring his remarks*): It's me's the sorry soul for listening to you. You promised a quiet hour of poetry, but we were hardly here when you began to move. Yeats's poems soon flew out of your head and hand. You got as far as "I will arise and go now, and go to Innisfree"; then before the echo of the line was hushed, you had me clapped down on your knee. (*She becomes tearful.*) That was the start of my undoing. What am I going to do!

MULLIGAN (*lifting his eyes to the ceiling*): There's lies! (*Facing her.*) Astounded I was, when without a word of warning, I found you fitting into me lap! (*Coming closer to her—fervently.*) The thruth is, if you want to know, that all the way to here, I was silently praying to a bevy of saints that you'd stay torpid in any and every emergency of look or motion!

ANGELA: You took care to leave your saints out on the doorstep; ay, and shut the door in their faces, too. You gave your solemn word, before I'd take one step to this place, that you'd be as harmless as an image in a looking-glass. I trusted you. I had heard you were a good boy. I thought you were a gentleman.

MULLIGAN: What about your uplifting can-can round the table while I was reading Yeats's poem?

ANGELA (*going her own way*): You made me believe you'd keep the width of a world between us while we were together, so's to avoid accidents. You said anyone who knew you would tell me you had a profound respect for girls; that you were slow in love-making.

MULLIGAN (*with insistence*): The can-can; what about the can-can around the table?

ANGELA (*with a great wail in her voice*): And then you stunned me with your speed!

MULLIGAN (*with greater insistence*): I'm asking you what about the can-can you danced around the table while I was thrying to read "I will arise and go now, and go to Innisfree"?

ANGELA (*acting the innocent*): What can-can? What are you talking about? I don't know what you mean by can-can.

MULLIGAN: I mean the dance that uplifted your skirt out of the way of your movements and juggled a vision of spiritual desolation into a mirage of palpitating enjoyments.

ANGELA (*appealing to the world at large*): Oh, d'ye hear the like o' that! Meanness is most of you to try to put the cloak of your own dark way round my poor shoulders! The dance I did could be done by an innocent figure in a nursery rhyme. You were bent on this awful mischief from the first. I sensed it when I walked with you—something evil hovering near. Oh, why didn't I follow me intuition! (*She begins to be hysterical.*) And I thought you such a nice man; and now,

after fencing me in with shame, you're making out I gave
you the stuff to make the fence around me. Oh, the infamy
of it! (*She moves rapidly up and down the room, clasping
and unclasping her hands.*) Oh, what shall I do, where shall
I go, what shall I say!

MULLIGAN (*getting very frightened*): Angela, calm yourself.
Speak lower, or you'll wake Miss Mossie, and we'll be
ruined. Sit down; do, please!

ANGELA (*fluttering about and staggering a little*): I'm undone,
undone completely. I won't be able to look any honest
woman in the face; I won't be able to shake the hand of any
honest man I meet; my future's devastated! (*She presses a
hand to her heart.*) I'm not feeling well; not at all well; you'd
better get Miss Mossie.

MULLIGAN (*horrified and very agitated*): Angela!

ANGELA (*staggering towards the chair*): Not well at all. I feel I'm
going to faint! No, no; yes, yes—I am going to faint!

*She sinks down on the chair, stretches out, and closes her
eyes.*

MULLIGAN (*falling on a knee before her—well frightened now*):
Angela, don't! Angela, dear, wake up! (*Lifting his eyes to
the ceiling.*) Saint Correlliolanus, come on, and deliver us
from utther desthruction!

ANGELA (*plaintively and faintly*): Wather!

MULLIGAN (*panic-stricken*): No, wine! (*He rises from his knee,
pours out a glass of wine, and brings it to her.*) Oh, Angela,
why did you let yourself get into such a state? Here, take it
quietly in sips. (*As she drinks it.*) Sip, sip, sip. That should
do you good. Hope no one heard you. Miss Mossie sleeps
with one ear cocked. (*He strokes her hand.*) You'll soon be
all right, and able to slip away in a few minutes.

ANGELA (*noticing the ring on the hand stroking hers*): Pretty
ring; garnet set in gold; precious garnet, didn't you say?

MULLIGAN (*none too sure of what he should say*): Yep. Not much value though.

ANGELA: Why's it on the little finger?

MULLIGAN: Knuckle's too big on the right one; won't go over it.

ANGELA (*fingering it*): Let me see it in me hand. (*He hesitates, then takes it off, and gives it to her with reluctance. Putting it on the engagement finger.*) Fits me to a nicety. How did you come by it?

MULLIGAN: An uncle left it in my care when he went on a job to Hong Kong. He never came back, and as no one asked about it, I made it my own.

ANGELA: Oh? Lucky one. (*She looks up into his face, smiling archly, displaying the finger with the ring on it.*) Looks like we were an engaged couple, John Jo, dear, wha'?

MULLIGAN: An engaged couple? (*With an uneasy and constrained laugh.*) Yis! Funny thought, that; quite. Feeling betther?

ANGELA: Seem to; hope it won't come over me again.

MULLIGAN (*fervently*): God forbid! What about taking off our shoes, and making a start?

*He takes off his.*

ANGELA (*taking off her shoes*): I suppose we must go sometime.

MULLIGAN (*trying to speak carelessly*): Let's have the ring back, dear.

ANGELA (*as if she'd forgotten it*): The ring? Oh, yes; I near forgot. (*She fiddles with it; then suddenly straightens herself to listen.*) Is that the sound of someone at the door below?

MULLIGAN (*agitated again*): Oh God, if it's Halibut home from the dance we'll have to wait till he settles down! I wish you'd gone when the going was good!

ANGELA (*who has taken off her shoes—rising from the chair*):
Come on, we'll chance it!

MULLIGAN (*pushing her back*): Chance it! We can't afford to
chance it. (*Going over to the door leading to rest of the
house.*) I'll reconnoiter down, and make sure the way's clear,
before we chance it.

*He goes out of the room, is absent for a few moments, while
ANGELA swallows another glass of wine; then he returns
hastily, a hand held up warningly for silence.*

MULLIGAN (*in a frightened whisper*): Near ran into him on the
stairs. Thank God it was so dark. Just had time to turn back.
We'll have to wait now till he settles in. (*He listens at the door,
shuts it suddenly, and glides over to ANGELA.*) Quick! He's
gone by his own place, and is coming up here! (*He catches
her by the arm, hurries her across the room, and shoves her
into the bedroom.*) Get in, and keep silent for God's sake!

*As he shoves her in, a knock is heard at the sitting-room
door. MULLIGAN shuts the bedroom door, slides over to the
chair, sits down, takes the book from the table, and pretends
to be reading.*

*Another knock is heard at the door, then it opens, and Mr.
DANIEL HALIBUT is seen standing there. He is a man of twenty-
five, a little below medium height, inclining to be plump. His
hair is reddish, and a thick mustache flowing from his upper
lip hides his mouth. Sometimes his hand tries to brush it
aside, but the moment the hand is removed, it falls back into its
old place at once. A fawn-colored overcoat covers an infor-
mal evening-suit—dinner-jacket and black tie. A black Hom-
burg hat is on his head. He comes in as one who is full of himself as if he had done himself well at the dance, and as one who
feels himself a man of the world above the cautious and
timorous MULLIGAN. His hat and coat are damp.*

HALIBUT (*coming into the room*): Ha, there you are, me son,
rotten night out; sleet. Coming up, I could have sworn I seen
you coming down the stairs.

MULLIGAN (*in pretended surprise*): Me coming down the stairs? At this time of the morning? What would I be doing on the stairs at this hour?

HALIBUT: Well, what are you doing up at this time of the morning?

MULLIGAN: I found it impossible to sleep, so got up to see if a bit of Yeats's poetry would make me drowsy.

HALIBUT: Is it Yeats, is it? God, man, he wouldn't let you sleep; drive you nuts! All people liking Yeats are all queer. He's all questions. What am I? Why am I? What is it? How did it come? Where will it go? All bubbles. Stuck up in the top of his ould tower, he sent the bubbles sailing out through a little loophole to attract the world outside. And all the little writers copied them, and blew bubbles of their own, till you could see them glistening among the things of the althar, or shining in the hair of the girl you were courting.

MULLIGAN (*with an obvious yawn*): Well, Yeats has made me sleepy, anyway. (*He flings the book on the table, and goes to get out of the chair.*) I'll be off to bed again.

HALIBUT (*shoving him back into the chair*): Wait till I tell you. You should ha' been at the dance. There never was a grander occasion; divel a grander ever! The place was fair gushing with girls. And only a few who'd make you shut your eyes if they were sitting on your knee. A hilariously hopeful whirlwind of skirt and petticoat, John Jo, when a waltz was on!

MULLIGAN (*getting up and edging* HALIBUT *towards the sitting-room door*): Go to bed, now, like a good fellow. I'm tired. We'll talk about it tomorrow. Goodnight.

HALIBUT (*edging* MULLIGAN *back towards the fireplace*): Wait till I tell you. You are a boyo. You'd never guess who was there? Your old flame of a week—Jessie! She told me things! When will you wake up? When he asked me out for the first time, says she, I expected a hilarious night at a dance or a music-hall, says she; I near fainted, says she, when, instead, he asked me to go with him to Benediction! Mulligan's management of maidens! Oh, John Jo, when will you wake up?

MULLIGAN (*annoyed, pushing* HALIBUT *towards the door*): If I elect to keep from danger, that's my affair. Looka, Dan, I've got to get up early to go to Mass on my way to the office, so be a good fellow, and go. I'm not concerned with girls.

HALIBUT: Betther if you were. (*He pushes* MULLIGAN *back toward the fireplace again.*) You'd sleep betther at night for one thing. (*He puts an arm around* MULLIGAN *and forces him into being a partner.*) Roamin' in th' gloamin', eh? Oh, boy! (*Lilting.*) With a lassie by yeer side. Oh, it's lovely to go roamin' in th' gloamin'!

MULLIGAN (*angrily—struggling from* HALIBUT's *hold, and rather roughly forcing him to the door*): Aw, lay off it, damn it, Dan! I'm in no mood for a Highland fling! Please go to your own room, and leave me in peace—I'm done in!

*He shoves him out and closes the sitting-room door.*

HALIBUT (*as he's being shoved out*): All right, if that's the way you feel. It'd be a good thing to put your hand on a girl's knee, and chance it.

MULLIGAN *listens at the door for a few moments. Then he gets down on his knees, and puts an ear to the floor. He rises, goes to the bedroom door, opens it, and calls* ANGELA *out.*

MULLIGAN: Now, Angela; now's our time. No delay, please.

ANGELA (*going behind the curtains on the windows*): What kind of a night or morning is it? (*From behind the curtains.*) Mother o' God! It's snowing or something! (*She comes from behind them, goes to the door, and takes one of* MULLIGAN's *coats hanging there.*) I must have a coat.

*Angela puts the coat on.*

MULLIGAN (*in a faint protest*): Eh, Angela, that's me best one.

ANGELA (*taking an umbrella from the stand*): And an umbrella, too.

MULLIGAN: That's me best umbrella.

ANGELA: Never mind, dear. I'll let you have it back when you hand me into the taxi on the all-night rank. Let's hurry now, boy.

MULLIGAN *opens the door cautiously, listens a moment; takes a torch from a pocket, and shines it forth, then leads the way from the room, shutting the door gently behind him. Both of them are in their stockinged feet. After a few moments have passed, the door suddenly flies open, and* ANGELA *hurries in, followed by* MULLIGAN *wearing a look of agony on his face. They carry their shoes under their arms. As she comes in:*

You louser, you'd have let me go off without it! Didn't care a damn once you were rid of me. And all I have for another fortnight is in that handbag!

MULLIGAN (*appealingly*): Speak lower, Angela, or you'll have the Mossie one down on top of us! I just can't remember you having a handbag when you first came in.

ANGELA (*angrily*): You can't remember! Well, I had one, and a good one, too, and I've got to get it—see! D'ye mean to hint I'm making it up?

MULLIGAN (*in agony*): No, no; but for God's sake, speak easy; please, Angela!

ANGELA (*leaving her shoes down, and pulling the cushions off the settee and throwing them on the floor*): Well, then, find it for me. Mind you, had I been down the street when I missed it, I'd have banged the door down to get in to get it!

MULLIGAN (*leaving his shoes down, and pulling the table about, pulling the chairs from the wall, and pulling the umbrella-stand away, to look behind them*): This is terrible! I'll be ruined if I'm discovered. What color was it? Where had you it last? Where d'ye think you could have put it?

ANGELA: I don't know, fool. It was a dark-green one I bought last week, and gave five pounds for. I got confused and forgot about everything when you started to pull me on to your knee.

MULLIGAN: But we can't stay to look for it. Miss Mossie'll soon be going about with her candle in her hand.

ANGELA: I'm not going without it! I think I remember you snatching it outa me hand when you started to pull me on to your lap.

MULLIGAN: Oh, give over about me pulling you on to me lap, and give us a hand to look for it! (*He runs into the bedroom, and starts to search there, flinging the bedclothes about. In bedroom.*) I can't see it anywhere here, so I can't.

ANGELA (*tearfully*): And I was to come here only for a quiet glass of wine and a biscuit. That's what you said, and kept repeating; and I believed you, oh, I believed you!

MULLIGAN (*coming out of bedroom*): No sign of it there.

ANGELA (*marching up and down the room, clasping and unclasping her hands*): Oh, isn't this a nice end to a quiet glass of wine and a biscuit!

MULLIGAN: Get a hold of yourself. What sort was it?

ANGELA: A pure morocco leather one, dark green, with initials on it filigreed in mother o' pearl.

MULLIGAN (*impatiently*): Yis, yis; (*Anxiously.*) but how much was in it altogether?

ANGELA: Fifteen pounds odd.

MULLIGAN (*aghast*): Good Lord!

ANGELA: And the lipstick you couldn't find musta been in it too; silver-cased and all; and a lovely bracelet watch waiting to be mended. Oh, what will I do! Oh, yes, and a silver brooch I wanted to get a pin for. What will I do, what will I do?

MULLIGAN: You slip off, and when I come back, I'll search high and low for it.

ANGELA (*with rising nervous tension*): And how am I to fare till you find it? You wouldn't turn a hair if I was willing to go in my shift! John Jo Mulligan, you're a dasthard! It would be the price of you to let Miss Mossie and the whole house know the sort you are!

MULLIGAN: For God's sake, Angela! What d'ye want me to do; only tell me what you want me to do?

ANGELA (*moving about distracted*): And to think I thought I was safe with you! (*Her glance falls on the cupboard, and she makes a bee-line for it.*) Could it have got in here?

MULLIGAN (*hastily*): No, no; it couldn't have got in there.

ANGELA (*drawing out a leather wallet*): What's this?

MULLIGAN (*going over to take wallet from her*): Nothing there but a few private letters, and a lot of bills.

*But before he can reach her to get it away, she has whisked a bundle of notes from it.*

ANGELA (*giggling—a little hysterical*): John Jo's hidden treasure. (*She counts them rapidly.*) Eighteen pounds ten. All fresh ones too. Nice to handle.

MULLIGAN: They're not mine. I'm minding them for a friend. You can put them back.

ANGELA (*mockingly*): At once, dear. I'll mind them for you, dear. (*She takes a checkbook out of the wallet.*) A check-book, too. (*As he comes closer.*) Keep your distance, keep your distance, or I'll claw the gob off you!

MULLIGAN: I was only going to give you a few of them to tide you over, dear.

ANGELA (*fiercely*): You were? How sweet of you! I'll have them all, you primly-born yahoo. And more. (*She raises her voice.*) And more!

MULLIGAN (*whisperingly*): All right, all right, only keep calm; keep quiet.

ANGELA (*indicating the checkbook*): Make me out a check for five pounds like a decent, honest man.

MULLIGAN (*taking a fountain pen from his pocket, and settling down to write*): All right; anything to pacify you.

ANGELA (*patronizingly patting his head*): You're not the worst, John Jo. You're really a pleasant chap when you get going. Make a check out for ten, darling, to compensate for the goods in the handbag. Ten, dear; that's all now. Well, we've had a right good time together. Pity I can't stay longer. See you again soon, when you're feeling frisky, eh? Naughty boy! (*She has taken the check from the dazed* MULLIGAN, *put it in his wallet, and now straightens herself to go, taking her shoes off the floor, and putting them under an arm. At the door.*) I know my way down, so don't you stir. I'll steal away like a maid of Araby. I'll be seeing you. Be good.

*Dazed and stunned,* MULLIGAN *sits still for a few seconds; then he gets up from the chair to look around him.*

MULLIGAN (*rising from the chair*): Fully-fledged for hell, that one, and you never noticed it! Oh, John Jo, John Jo! (*He suddenly stiffens.*) She had no handbag! She never had a handbag! Oh, Mother o' God, she's codded me! (*He looks in the cupboard, then looks over the table.*) She's taken away me wallet, too! Me umbrella!

*He runs out of the room to follow her, so agitated that he leaves door wide open behind him. There are a few moments of silence; then* MISS MOSSIE *appears at the open door with a lighted candle in a candlestick in her hand. She is a short, stout woman of thirty-five or so. She is dressed in a brown skirt reaching to her ankles, and we get a glimpse of black stockings sinking into a pair of stout black shoes. Her dark hair is gathered into a knob, and made to lie quiet on the nape of her neck. She wears a yellow jumper, and a brown Jaeger topcoat is flung over her shoulders. She wears spectacles. She looks into the room for a moment, a look of perplexed anxiety on her face, then turns aside to call to* HALIBUT.

MISS MOSSIE: Mr. Halibut, Mr. Halibut, come up, come up quick! (HALIBUT *appears at the door. He is now wearing a pair of blue pajamas, covered by a dressing-gown of dark red, and his bare feet are slippered.*) Oh, Mr. Halibut, what can the matter be? Oh, dear, what can the matter be?

HALIBUT (*agog with excitement*): What's up, Miss Mossie?

MISS MOSSIE (*coming into the sitting-room, followed by* HALIBUT): Looka the state of the room; and Mr. Mulligan's just run out into the street in his stockinged feet!

HALIBUT (*astonished*): No? How d'ye know he went out into the street?

MISS MOSSIE: I seen him go. I heard something stirring when I was putting on me jumper, so I looked out, and there was Mr. Mulligan scuttling down the stairs. Walking in his sleep, he musta been. He had an air on him as if he was enraptured within himself; a look as if he was measuring life and death together to see which was tallest.

HALIBUT: Is that right? Coming back from the dance, I thought I saw him on the stairs, too, but when I came up, he was sitting reading Yeats's poems. Said he couldn't sleep. I warned him against the poems.

MISS MOSSIE (*coming over to the bedroom door, and opening it*): Oh, looka the state of this room, too! Everything flung about.

HALIBUT (*awed*): Looks like he had a wild fit, or something!

MISS MOSSIE: Something terrific! This isn't just disarray, Mr. Halibut—it's an upheaval! You don't think it could be that something suddenly went wrong in him?

HALIBUT (*startled by a thought*): Wrong in him, Miss Mossie? What could go wrong in him?

MISS MOSSIE: A quietly-disposed man like Mr. Mulligan doesn't do this (*Indicating disorder of rooms.*) without something whizzing within him.

HALIBUT (*frightened*): You mean in his mind?

MISS MOSSIE (*firmly*): We must act. We can't let him roam the streets or do any harm here. I'll phone the police and a doctor, and I'll slip out for the constable that usually stands at the street corner. (*They move to the sitting-room door.*) I'll go now. You stay on the lobby here in the dark, and watch over him if he comes back.

HALIBUT (*dubiously*): I'm not a strong man, Miss Mossie.

MISS MOSSIE: After all, Mr. Halibut, we don't want to be murdhered in our beds.

HALIBUT (*crossing himself*): God forbid, Miss Mossie!

MISS MOSSIE: And the odd thing is, he'd be doing it with the best intentions. If he comes back, he may still be asleep, so don't shout at him and wake him too suddenly. Just humor him, unless he gets violent.

HALIBUT (*picturing in his mind all that might happen*): Ay, violent—that's the danger!

MISS MOSSIE: Then you'll just have to close with him, and hold him till the constable comes.

HALIBUT (*panic-stricken*): Close with him? Hold him till the constable comes? But, woman alive, I'm not gifted that way!

MISS MOSSIE: You'll do your best, I know; if he overcomes you, it won't be your fault.

HALIBUT: Don't you think it would be only prudent to have a poker handy?

MISS MOSSIE: Too violent-looking. (*Indicating a corner of the lobby.*) There's the bit of curtain pole I use to push the window up—you can keep that handy; but don't let him guess why you have it. (*She takes the key from the inside and puts it in the keyhole on the outside of the door.*) There now, if the worst comes, you can fly out and lock him safely within the room.

HALIBUT: It sounds easy, but it's really a desperate situation.

MISS MOSSIE: Don't let him see you're frightened. Keep him under command. That's what me sisther did with me when I used to walk in my sleep a few years ago.

HALIBUT (*stricken with confused anxiety*): What, you used to sleepwalk, too?

MISS MOSSIE: That's why I dhread the habit coming back to me, for then you never know whether you're always asleep and never awake, or always awake and never asleep. I'll be off now. You'll be quite safe if you only keep your wits about you.

*She goes off with her candle, leaving a world of darkness to poor* HALIBUT. *There is a silence for a few moments, then the watcher in the darkness, and any who are listening, hear a patter of feet on stairs outside, and the voice of* MULLIGAN *calling out loudly the name of* MISS MOSSIE *several times. Then a great bang of a closing door; dead silence for a moment, till* MULLIGAN *is heard calling again.*

MULLIGAN (*outside*): Dan, Dan, are you awake? Dan Halibut, are you awake, man? (MULLIGAN *appears on the lobby just outside the sitting-room door. He is talking to himself, a haggard, lost, and anxious look on his face, and he is a little out of breath. His coat and hat are damped by the falling sleet outside; his feet wet. He pauses on the lobby, and waves his electric torch about till its beam falls on the silent and semi-crouching* HALIBUT.) Oh, it's here you are? Thought you were in bed fast asleep. Called you, but got no answer. What a night! Twenty-eight pounds ten gone with the wind! (*He lifts a cushion from the floor to look under it.*) It's not there! (*He flings it viciously away. To* HALIBUT.) What has you here in the dark and the cold?

HALIBUT: Just shutting the window to keep it from rattling.

MULLIGAN (*going into the sitting-room*): We must do something. Miss Mossie's gone rushing hatless out into the darkness and the sleet. Hatless, mind you! Looked as if she was sleepwalk-

ing again. A one-time habit of hers, did you know? You'll
have to go after her.

HALIBUT (*coming a little way into the room, but staying close to
the door, holding the sprig of curtain pole behind his back*):
I know, I know; but what were you doing out in the sleet
and the darkness *yourself?* And in your stockinged feet, too,
look at them!

MULLIGAN: Me? Couldn't sleep; felt stifled; went out for some
fresh air. Didn't think of shoes. Something whizzing in me
mind. (*A little impatiently.*) But you dress and go after
Mossie. See what's wrong with her. Several times, before you
came, she came into my room, fast asleep, at dead of the
night, with a loving look on her face. We can't afford to let
ourselves be murdhered in our sleep, Dan. (*He flops into
chair.*) Saint Fairdooshius, succor me this night.

HALIBUT (*bewildered with anxiety, eyes lifted to ceiling in a low
appeal*): Oh, sweet Saint Slumbersnorius, come to me help
now! (*To* MULLIGAN.) All right; yes. I'll settle you in first.
You go to bed, John Jo, quiet. Go to bed, go to bed, and go
asleep, and go asleep!

MULLIGAN (*looking at* HALIBUT *curiously—a little impatiently*):
I've told you I can't sleep. Twenty-eight pounds ten, and my
fine leather wallet gone forever!

HALIBUT (*in a commandingly sing-song way*): Never mind. Put
them out of your thoughts, and go to bed, go to bed, and go
to sleep, and go to sleep—I command!

MULLIGAN (*half rising from his chair so that* HALIBUT *backs towards the door—staring at* HALIBUT *in wonderment*): What's
wrong with you, Halibut? (*He sinks back into the chair
again, and* HALIBUT *returns into the room.*) Me best coat and
best umbrella, too! Gone.

*His glance happens to fall on his hand, and he springs out of
the chair with a jump, sending* HALIBUT *backing swiftly from
the room again.*

MULLIGAN: Me ring! I never got it back!

HALIBUT (*straying cautiously back into the room again*): Money, best coat, best umbrella, wallet, and ring! When did you lose all these things, man?

MULLIGAN: A minute or so ago; no, no, an hour ago; two hours ago; more. (*He leans his arms dejectedly on the table, and buries his head on them.*) I di'n't lost them, Dan; I gave them away, flung them all away!

HALIBUT: In an excess of charity of having too many possessions, or what? You know, I've warned you, John Jo; often warned you.

MULLIGAN (*raising his head from his arms—resentfully and suspiciously*): Warned me? How warned me?

HALIBUT: I warned you that running out to devotions morning and night, and too much valuable time spent on your knees, would upset you one day or another. And, now, you'll have to admit that these things couldn't have happened to you if you had had a girl with you tonight.

MULLIGAN (*with a wail of resentment*): Oooh! Don't be a blasted fool! (*He notices that* HALIBUT *has something behind his back.*) What's that you have behind you?

HALIBUT (*trying to be carelessly funny*): Me tail. Didn't you know? I'm a wild animal (*He wags the piece of curtain pole.*) Now, the wild animal says you're to go to bed, go to bed, and go to sleep, and go to sleep. Obey the wild animal at once!

MULLIGAN (*slowly rising from the chair, staring anxiously and suspiciously at* HALIBUT): What's amiss with you, Halibut? Are you sleepwalking, too? Leave down that curtain pole. Don't be acting the goat, man. (*Coaxingly—as* HALIBUT *brings the piece of curtain pole to his front.*) Go on, Dan, oul' son, leave the thing down!

HALIBUT: As soon as you're safely settled in bed, John Jo. Then

I'll pop out after Mossie. To bed; to bed; and go to sleep, go to sleep—I command!

MULLIGAN (*fear having come on him—suddenly seizes the wine-bottle by the neck, and holds it as a club, running to window, swinging back the curtains, and trying to open it*): God Almighty, I'm alone with a lunatic! (*Shouting—as he tries to open the window.*) Help!

HALIBUT: I'll not let you destroy yourself—come away from that window, or I'll flatten you!

MULLIGAN (*wheeling round, still holding bottle by the neck to use it as a club, and facing towards* HALIBUT): Looka, Halibut, leave that club down. (*Coaxingly.*) Now, be sensible, Dan, like a good chap, and drop that club.

HALIBUT: Drop that bottle first, I say; drop that bottle first!

MULLIGAN: Drop that club, I tell you. (*Fiercely.*) Drop that club!

HALIBUT (*dancing up and down—panic-stricken*): Put that bottle down! Put it down, and go to bed, I tell you!

MULLIGAN (*dodging about*): Drop that club at once, Halibut!

HALIBUT: Put that bottle down immediately!

MULLIGAN: I command you!

HALIBUT: I command you!

*They have been dodging about without coming near to each other;* HALIBUT *swinging the piece of curtain pole to and fro in front of him for protection. In one of the blind swings, the pole slips from his hand, and sails out through the window, causing a great sound of falling glass. They both stare at the window—dumbfounded for a few moments.*

MULLIGAN (*exultingly*): Aha, I've got you now!

*But* HALIBUT *has fled from the room, banged the door after him, and locked it from the outside.* MULLIGAN *hurries to the door and presses his back to it. Then* MISS MOSSIE'S *voice is heard outside.*

MISS MOSSIE (*outside*): Oh, what's happened? I feared it would end in violence! Mr. Halibut, Mr. Halibut, are you much hurted?

MULLIGAN (*shouting through the door to* MISS MOSSIE): Miss Mossie; here, Miss Mossie!

MISS MOSSIE (*from outside*): Oh, Mr. Mulligan, what have you done to poor, innocent Mr. Halibut? We've found him lying in a dead faint out here on the lobby.

MULLIGAN (*indignantly—shouting outwards*): Poor, innocent Mr. Halibut! What has he not tried to do to me! He rushed in here, lunacy looking out of his eyes, and tried to shatther me with a club, with a club; tried to murdher me! Now he's locked me in.

MISS MOSSIE (*soothingly*): Now isn't that a shame! What a naughty man he is! Never mind now. You go to your chair and sit down by the fire, and I'll get the key to open your door. Everything will be all right, Mr. Mulligan.

MULLIGAN (*indignantly*): Everything isn't all right now! I'll live no longer in the same house with Halibut!

MISS MOSSIE (*coaxingly*): Do go and sit down by the fire, Mr. Mulligan, there's a dear. I'll bring you a hot drink, and we'll talk about things; do, now, like a good man.

MULLIGAN *goes to the fireplace, and sits down in the armchair. He lights a cigarette and puffs it indignantly. After a few moments, the door opens, and* MISS MOSSIE *lets into the room a big, topcoated and helmeted policeman, the doctor with his case, wearing an anxious look on his face, and a nurse, enveloped with a dark-blue cloak on the left side of which is a white circle surrounding a large red cross. She carries the usual nursing-suitcase in her hand.* MISS MOSSIE *is in the midst of them, and* HALIBUT, *in the rear, with a ghastly pale face, rises on his tiptoes to gaze over their shoulders. All but* HALIBUT *form a semicircle round* MULLIGAN's *back, who puffs away, unconscious of the entrance of the crowd. Bend-*

*ing sidewise from behind the policeman to speak to the sitting* MULLIGAN.

MISS MOSSIE: Now, Mr. Mulligan, we'll see what all this little disturbance was about, and what was the cause of it, and then we'll be all—er—O.K., eh? And I've brought in a few kind friends to help me.

MULLIGAN (*rising from his chair in blank surprise, and almost echoing* MISS MOSSIE): A few friends to help you? (*He turns around to face* MISS MOSSIE, *but is confronted by the big, helmeted* POLICEMAN, *the* DOCTOR, *and the* NURSE. *He slides back into the chair almost in a dead faint. Falling back into the chair.*) Good God!

**CURTAIN**

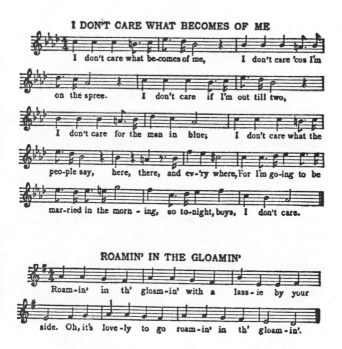

# *Cecile*
# or
# *The School for Fathers*

by Jean Anouilh

English version by
Luce and Arthur Klein

## CHARACTERS

MONSIEUR ORLAS

CECILE, *his daughter*

ARAMINTHE, *governess of* CECILE

THE CHEVALIER

MONSIEUR DAMIENS, *father of* ARAMINTHE

VALETS *and* BODYGUARDS

*Scene: A garden framed by boxed orange trees. The house is on the left, a small Chinese pavilion on the right.*

MONSIEUR ORLAS *is seated in the pavilion and* ARAMINTHE *is standing beside him. Costumes are either Louis XVth or perhaps Louis XVIth of the bourgeois class. In either case they are as false as possible.*

MONSIEUR ORLAS: Araminthe, I am very disturbed. I have always thought you were too young and much too charming to take care of my daughter.

ARAMINTHE: If you remember, Monsieur, there were four candidates for the position of governess. The three others were old and uglier than sin. Why then did you choose me, Monsieur?

MONSIEUR ORLAS: Precisely because you were young and beautiful. And yet sometimes I fear that I chose you only for my own sake. I could not bear the thought of dining with an old hag at my table. Still I believe I have been a bad father. I ought to have confided Cecile to an old dragon of a woman and to have borne it stoically. I ought to have taken my meals apart or else read the newspapers while eating.

ARAMINTHE: Among other things, Monsieur, you insisted that I teach Mademoiselle Cecile that nothing was more rude than to read while eating.

MONSIEUR ORLAS: I have been a fool! In the first place you are the same age.

ARAMINTHE: Mademoiselle Cecile is seventeen years old and I will soon be twenty-three.

MONSIEUR ORLAS: It is the same thing.

ARAMINTHE: Allow me to contradict you, Monsieur. I feel I have learned very many things in five years. And particularly to be suspicious of men.

MONSIEUR ORLAS (*suddenly*): Why do you say that to me?

ARAMINTHE: So that you will not be troubled by what seems to upset you. I am very capable of protecting Mademoiselle Cecile whose youth and inexperience could so easily be deceived by lovely words. You should at least give me credit, Monsieur, for not being deceived myself.

MONSIEUR ORLAS: I wonder why you insist on being so disagreeable with me, Araminthe?

ARAMINTHE: Have I said anything disagreeable?

MONSIEUR ORLAS: "You should at least give me credit, Monsieur, for not being deceived myself." Just what do you mean by that? That I try to deceive you? The rhetoric of young girls has always sounded Greek to me! It is true I have paid you several compliments! So what? You are no longer a child, Araminthe. You are twenty-three years old. I am a man for whom love has always been the chief interest, and although the father of Cecile I am still capable of loving. Thank God for that! Do you suppose it is easy to live in the same house with so ravishing a creature as yourself? To have you opposite me at table each day, to have you smile at me while Cecile is dreaming of heaven knows only what! . . . And then in the evening to have all three of us climb the stairs together to our respective rooms. And yours only next door to mine! I am a fool! I should have chosen a hag!

ARAMINTHE: You still have time.

MONSIEUR ORLAS: Yes, there is always time to make myself unhappy needlessly. I do not speak only of the grief Cecile would feel. You know how attached she is to you. But my entire existence would be saddened. I would gulp my meals to shorten the torture, and I would develop ulcers . . . You know what that does to one's temper. Besides I could never bear to know you were living in another home where you would be the prey to men's desires. You are a child, Araminthe. Do not forget you are only twenty-three! What do you know of life, my dear? Here you live with a well-bred gentleman who respects you. Imagine yourself governess of the baron's daughter who I know has suggested it. And on my life I wager two days would not pass before he came and knocked at your chamber door!

ARAMINTHE: Render unto Caesar the things which are Caesar's, Monsieur. You waited an entire week before you did it yourself!

MONSIEUR ORLAS: I am a well-bred man. Besides you did not open the door.

ARAMINTHE: As I would not open it for the baron were I to lose your confidence and find myself at his home.

MONSIEUR ORLAS: All the same you do not mean to compare me with this old fogy, this graybeard?

ARAMINTHE: I thought I heard you say you studied together and except for a year or so were the same age.

MONSIEUR ORLAS: Yes, but he looks it! I don't! Anyway that has no importance. Still if I had not paid you some attention one way or another you would have been the first to feel offended. I have come to know the contradictions in a woman's heart. (*He rises thoughtfully.*) I do not mind telling you, Araminthe, that I am very upset by this young chevalier. He comes here much too much.

ARAMINTHE: He loves your daughter and your daughter loves him.

MONSIEUR ORLAS: What do they know at their age? In the first

place he doesn't have a sou! His father is in straitened circumstances, besides which he already supports two older
sons. And even if he made nuns out of his three daughters he
still could not give the boy a sou! If his great-uncle died in
time he might perhaps become a Knight of Malta. But that
is all he can expect. Therefore from every point of view the
marriage is an impossibility for him. I will not permit them to
see each other!

ARAMINTHE: Then they will do so behind your back.

MONSIEUR ORLAS: Thunder and blazes, Mademoiselle, are you here
to tell me that! You are here to prevent it!

ARAMINTHE: It would be beyond my powers even if I wanted to.
Their passion will overcome all obstacles. And besides, Monsieur, I would not want to. I cannot see anyone in love
unhappy.

MONSIEUR ORLAS: So you would find the suffering of this silly fop
unbearable if I prevent him from seeing Cecile? And yet I have
been pining away at your door these six months past, and it
does not trouble you in the least! Does it?

ARAMINTHE: If I had opened my door to you, Monsieur, do you
believe you still could have entrusted Mademoiselle Cecile to
me?

MONSIEUR ORLAS: Do not confuse the issue. I simply demand that
you be very strict with Cecile who is still a child, and . . .

ARAMINTHE: We are the same age.

MONSIEUR ORLAS: The same age? Ridiculous! You are twenty-
three and she is only seventeen. In five years a young lady
has the time to learn to know the world, to judge the virtue
of a man and the sincerity of a feeling. I do not understand
you, Araminthe. After all, you must plainly see that I am
madly in love with you.

ARAMINTHE: Indeed, I believe that one cannot help but see it,
Monsieur. You are as indiscreet about it as possible. I must
exercise every ingenuity so that Mademoiselle Cecile will not

perceive it. And if you do not stop trying to touch my knee under the table, one of these days you will surely touch hers!

MONSIEUR ORLAS: A friendly caress from her father would not astonish this child. I kiss her a hundred times a day.

ARAMINTHE: If she happened to suspect that this friendly caress from her father was meant for another knee, I fear she would be offended, Monsieur. And more seriously than your frivolousness is able to imagine.

MONSIEUR ORLAS (*grumbling dreamily*): My frivolousness . . . my frivolousness . . . (*He asks in another tone.*) So according to you, Araminthe, I am a bad father? I shall never get over it.

ARAMINTHE: You have the desire to be the best father in the world, Monsieur. And I believe it is my duty to see that at least this one of your desires is fulfilled. I assure you that is why I put my knees under my chair in the most uncomfortable of positions. And I never hear your little knocks on my door at night.

MONSIEUR ORLAS (*approaching her with a lascivious look in his eye*): And if I should put Cecile in a convent—and I mean a very gay convent—or if I should send her to spend some time with her aunt who is a canoness? She would have many young cousins there with whom to play . . .

ARAMINTHE: Would you want to cause her this grief by separating her from her young chevalier? And furthermore, if Mademoiselle Cecile is gone then my place will no longer be in this home. I take care of her, Monsieur, but she takes care of me as well. We could not do without each other midst all the dangers that surround us.

MONSIEUR ORLAS (*sighs*): Life is an abyss full of contradictions, Araminthe! I am going into my study and think of all that. I am unwilling to believe that there is no solution and that duty and happiness can not be reconciled.

ARAMINTHE: I believe that is what men have always been seeking,

Monsieur, ever since they left their caves to try and live in society. They have only invented marriage to try and reconcile these two notions for a time.

MONSIEUR ORLAS: For a very short time, Araminthe. Believe a man who has gone through the venture. Afterwards it is like these chemical tests our neighbor Monsieur de Voltaire enjoys making. At first the mixture is very effervescent; then happiness which is vaporous vanishes like smoke, and the pipette contains only the large gray stone of duty. (*He asks thoughtfully.*) Is the Chevalier coming again today?

ARAMINTHE: Just as every afternoon.

MONSIEUR ORLAS: Do not leave them alone for a minute! These children caress and embrace each other as soon as your back is turned.

ARAMINTHE: One does that at their age.

MONSIEUR ORLAS (*a bit dryly*): One does it at mine and yet I do without. (*He starts to go, changes his mind, then goes to her.*) You are too cruel, Araminthe. Let me take you just once in my arms?

ARAMINTHE (*pushing him back firmly and with a smile*): No, Monsieur. Not even for the tiniest second.

MONSIEUR ORLAS (*feeling vexed, starts to leave*): Be merciless with them! See that their chairs do not even touch! And keep a close eye on the tablecloth if they should take tea! It is so easy to stretch your leg under it. Listen, Araminthe, why not teach my daughter how to sit on a chair so that no knee could possibly touch hers?

ARAMINTHE (*smiling*): I think such a gymnastic exercise is less important for her than for me, Monsieur.

MONSIEUR ORLAS (*exits with a sigh*): I am indeed an unhappy man, Araminthe.

THE CHEVALIER (*entering*): Araminthe!

ARAMINTHE: Monsieur?

THE CHEVALIER: Do you think I have come too soon?

ARAMINTHE: You always come too soon, Monsieur le Chevalier. We have just finished eating.

THE CHEVALIER: And yet I have waited more than an hour in the street before coming in. Such time lost, Araminthe! I can see that you have never loved. Ah yes, Araminthe, when you will be my age . . .

ARAMINTHE: I am afraid that will never happen again, Monsieur.

THE CHEVALIER (*protesting*): What? To love and to be loved as beautiful as you are? (*He takes her hands and kisses them.*)

ARAMINTHE (*withdrawing her hands and laughing*): No, Monsieur. To be your age. It is an experience I underwent three years ago. I am told it happens only once.

THE CHEVALIER: I was twenty only three days ago, and I tell you, Araminthe, it is a terrible thing.

ARAMINTHE: You will accustom yourself to it, I assure you. And by the time you have done so it will not be terrible any longer.

THE CHEVALIER: Soon I will be old, Araminthe, and I have not yet even lived. You say you reached my age without loving. Does not your heart feel oppressed for having wasted your life?

ARAMINTHE: To be truthful with you, Monsieur le Chevalier, I still have hope.

THE CHEVALIER: And you are right. You are too pretty not to have hope. Do you know that if I was not in love with Cecile I would just die to kiss your hand. I trust you will forgive my speaking so informally. After all, you are like my sister.

ARAMINTHE (*withdrawing her hand*): Speak informally if it gives you pleasure, only I beg you to treat my hand with more formality.

THE CHEVALIER (*suddenly*): Do you know that I am desperate, Araminthe?

ARAMINTHE: Really! As much as yesterday?

THE CHEVALIER: Much more. I had it out with my father this morning and it was a stormy session. He forbade me to see Cecile again. He made me swear that I had entered this home for the last time.

ARAMINTHE: And you swore?

THE CHEVALIER: Yes . . . with all kinds of mental reservations. But you see I was forced to do so.

ARAMINTHE: Your father has no heart.

THE CHEVALIER: I believe more particularly that he has no money. And Cecile's dowry is meager. (You know, Araminthe, that fathers are the most extraordinary creatures I know. My father already had the most explicit information from her father's notary as to the amount of her dowry before I had kissed Cecile even once!) He says that he wants only my happiness, and I think he does. But he has my two older brothers whom he must first set up. Nothing will be left for me. I can choose between two things: Either wait until my uncle dies and then become a Knight of Malta—which leaves Cecile out of the picture since the order insists on celibacy—or else marry a crock of gold which equally leaves Cecile out of it.

ARAMINTHE: And has he found it?

THE CHEVALIER: What?

ARAMINTHE: The "crock"?

THE CHEVALIER: Yes. And it is overflowing. But she is like a skeleton, ugly as a witch, and old on top of all that. She will soon be twenty-five years old.

ARAMINTHE: So in two years I shall be old! You are not very gracious, Monsieur le Chevalier.

THE CHEVALIER (kissing her hands): You do not understand. Naturally, if it concerns you, Araminthe, age would not count . . . (He stops.) No . . . no, you see, even if it did concern you, I still love Cecile . . . And yet I like to kiss your hands. You know so much about life, Araminthe, tell me, do you believe that everything always remains so entangled in one's heart?

ARAMINTHE: Always.

THE CHEVALIER: In any case, you won't leave us if I marry Cecile, will you? You are like her sister somehow, and I want to marry you as well—like a sister.

ARAMINTHE: You ask for Cecile's hand, but you also want my two hands from time to time, don't you? Monsieur le Chevalier gets on quite well for someone who was twenty years old only three days ago. But I am afraid you are not going to have either. How can you possibly marry Cecile since her dowry is too small and you have absolutely nothing!

THE CHEVALIER: Ah? I haven't told you yet. But I have come to a decision.

ARAMINTHE: Yes?

THE CHEVALIER: I am eloping with her this very night. To see her again I am forced to do that since I swore never to set foot here any more. Naturally, I am taking you as well.

ARAMINTHE: I ought not to tell you but I believe Mademoiselle Cecile is crazy enough to follow you. However, I am here to dissuade her from it.

THE CHEVALIER: You would have the heart to prevent us from loving each other?

ARAMINTHE: To prevent you from doing something stupid? Why, of course. Have you even thought of the consequences of what you plan to do?

THE CHEVALIER: The consequences are quite simple. Thank heavens, Monsieur Rousseau has made it fashionable for fathers to be sympathetic. When Cecile and I are married, Araminthe, we will have to endure their scandalized reproofs—

just for custom's sake—and then they will have nothing left to do but give us their blessing.

ARAMINTHE: Perhaps they will agree to give you their blessing since it costs nothing. But they certainly won't give you a sou.

THE CHEVALIER: Don't you think that if my father had my three sisters become nuns he could find it possible to do some little thing for me?

ARAMINTHE: I am not familiar with your father's state of affairs but I do believe you decide your sisters' vocations a bit too easily!

THE CHEVALIER: Bah! They are ugly, Araminthe. They will never find a more indulgent husband than Jesus Christ. And then their eternal life would be assured. Everything passes so quickly here below! Look at yourself! You just said three years have hardly gone by since you were twenty and you are already disillusioned. We help them avoid I don't know how many opportunities for feeling bitter and how many temptations to sin in condemning them to heaven! And then, I love Cecile so much!

ARAMINTHE (*putting her finger on his chest*): This nice little heart, all brand new, which beats so violently for everything seems to me, Monsieur le Chevalier, to be a pretty little stone.

THE CHEVALIER: Do not deceive yourself. I am sensitive. I have often wept torrents of tears. But one cannot weep for the entire world. It is beyond human strength. One must choose.

ARAMINTHE: Never mind; leave your sisters. It is wicked to think as you do . . . And besides no good could come out of it. I am sure your father would not have the heart to sacrifice all three even if circumstances forced him to let you marry Cecile. You must weigh the consequences of your act. Are you willing to accept poverty?

THE CHEVALIER: What do you mean by that, Araminthe? All the same I would be able to have a new coat tailored from time to time, wouldn't I?

ARAMINTHE: Yes, I believe so. I am sure that no matter how poor Monsieur Orlas may be he would not let Cecile nor you go without ribbons. But you are a handsome man, Chevalier, and come from a very good family. Have you never dreamt of having a great fortune? Dreamt of life at court, festive occasions, the King's favor, and perhaps a famous regiment with you as commander?

THE CHEVALIER (*exclaiming miserably*): I have dreamt only of these things since I was fifteen! You know that very well! But I love Cecile. You are cruel, Araminthe. Why do you delight in putting salt on the wound?

ARAMINTHE: To see if I am able to give you my consent.

THE CHEVALIER: I would give everything in the world to lead my men on a horse and lead them to assault! The smell of gunpowder, the swords glimmering in the sun, death! . . . Ah! what a wonderful life!

ARAMINTHE: Well, my little horseman, you cannot take Cecile with you on your horse. You cannot lead an assault well when a woman you love rides with you. No, do not lower your head. Look at me. (*She raises his head.*)

THE CHEVALIER (*taking her hands and covering them with kisses*): Oh! your hands! your hands! I adore your hands, Araminthe!

ARAMINTHE: You adore my hands, you adore to lead an assault, you adore Cecile, but at bottom I am afraid that you only adore yourself. I refuse to give my consent, Monsieur. You will not elope with my pupil.

THE CHEVALIER: You are not serious, Araminthe? I would kill myself.

ARAMINTHE: My little finger told me no.

THE CHEVALIER: And you believe it? Show me your finger and I will give it a piece of my mind! (*He takes the little finger and kisses it.*)

MONSIEUR ORLAS (*entering*): Chevalier!

**THE CHEVALIER** (*greeting him*): I kiss your hands, Monsieur.

**MONSIEUR ORLAS**: Mine as well? Does it seem perfectly natural to you, Monsieur le Chevalier, that I cannot open a single door in this house without finding you kissing somebody?

**THE CHEVALIER**: I was merely greeting Araminthe.

**MONSIEUR ORLAS**: And in a moment you will merely be greeting my daughter. Well, you are a young man who greets too much. I have a great many things to do in this house. In the future behave in such a manner that I can open any door with peace of mind.

**THE CHEVALIER** (*bowing gravely*): I promise to see to that, Monsieur. (**MONSIEUR ORLAS** *exits.*) Have I spoken to him with sufficient respect? It seems to me that I have been perfect with him.

**ARAMINTHE**: Perfect. Only he has just caught you kissing the hands of a person he is courting, and you are going to elope with his daughter tonight.

**THE CHEVALIER**: What are you saying? Monsieur Orlas is courting you? I will not permit it!

**ARAMINTHE**: Really? And why not?

**THE CHEVALIER**: Have I not told you that you are my sister! I am going to find him at once and demand an explanation of his behavior. I tell you, Araminthe, that I will not allow anyone to bother you!

**ARAMINTHE**: How do you know that he bothers me? And as for demanding an explanation of his behavior, wait until tomorrow. He will have to demand an explanation from you then, and that way you can kill two birds with one stone.

**THE CHEVALIER**: It would be the height of absurdity to wait until tomorrow. He would clearly have the upper hand after what will take place tonight and I would be at a distinct disadvantage. I am going at once!

ARAMINTHE (*stopping him*): And if I should forbid you to go?

THE CHEVALIER: Ah, so you are flattered by his attentions! The attentions of a man almost forty who already has a foot in his grave? You appall me, Araminthe! . . . You do not know how to read your own heart. You cannot possibly love this old man!

ARAMINTHE: Who said that I loved him?

THE CHEVALIER: You love me, Araminthe. You love me like a brother because I love Cecile. But still, you love me.

ARAMINTHE: That is news to me!

CECILE (*entering, in a rage*): I have been waiting for you, Monsieur, at the appointed place for over an hour. I know you have been here a long time for I heard the front bell ring. And all this while you have been speaking to Araminthe!

THE CHEVALIER (*going to her*): Cecile, my love, I was simply arranging the final details with her for tonight. My father forced me to swear that I would never come here again. Things are coming to a point. Tonight I must elope with you.

CECILE: If you are in so little hurry, Monsieur, to see me when you come here, what will it be like when we are married and you can see me all the time? I must think this over again. I am not so sure I want to elope.

THE CHEVALIER (*trying to take her hands*): Cecile, my love!

CECILE: No, Monsieur. Tell these pretty words you say so well to others, Monsieur. Kiss their hands!

THE CHEVALIER: This is scandalous! Who dared tell you? Your father, was it not?

CECILE: I have not seen my father since lunch, and he told me nothing at all! But I know enough about men to have understood everything while I was waiting for you.

THE CHEVALIER: Who could have been wicked enough to have told you that, Cecile? It is true that I kissed Araminthe's hands, but I was only thanking her for helping our love . . .

CECILE: What are you saying, Monsieur? Do my ears deceive me? You kissed Araminthe's hands? No, it cannot be true . . .

THE CHEVALIER: But you have just said to me yourself that someone told you he had seen me!

CECILE: I told you that no one said anything to me, Monsieur! You took the responsibility of disclosing this deed yourself which at least is something in your favor. So then! You keep my esteem for this confession, as cruel as it may be, even if you have lost my love. Farewell, Monsieur. Keep the oath you made to your father. Never show your face here again. (*She exits.*)

THE CHEVALIER (*throwing himself at* ARAMINTHE'S *feet*): Araminthe, I perish before your eyes! Catch her! Tell her I love her! Tell her I don't love you! It is true your hands are like honey to my lips, but their sweetness is the fleeting pleasure of a moment. But as soon as Cecile leaves my side everything grows dark! Quickly, run after her and tell her I love only her, Araminthe, and I swear that I will always love you!

ARAMINTHE: All right, Monsieur. But now we do not have much time. I do not want to waste time pointing out your contradictions, and I am going to try and arrange your affairs. Have everything ready for tonight.

THE CHEVALIER: You agree then to my elopement?

ARAMINTHE: I will see when the moment comes if I can allow everything to take its course. At least, I agree to your making believe to elope. You are right. Perhaps it is a way to make your fathers come to some agreement.

THE CHEVALIER: Oh, thank you! I adore you, Araminthe! Let me kiss your hands!

ARAMINTHE: Monsieur, you are completely irresponsible.

THE CHEVALIER: Yes, it is true. I forgot. I shan't ask you any more. Or at least only after I have married Cecile, and will no longer risk losing her!

ARAMINTHE (*exits laughing*): You can be sure of it! Shrewd young man!

THE CHEVALIER (*alone*): Ah, how amusing life is! . . . I must go and warn my bodyguards. We may be forced to resort to violence tonight. I adore Cecile, I adore Araminthe, tonight I kidnap them both and only three days ago I was twenty years old! (*He exits.*)

*The stage remains empty for a moment. Perhaps some soft music is heard. Then* MONSIEUR ORLAS *and* CECILE *enter, returning from a walk.*

MONSIEUR ORLAS: Cecile, I must have a talk with you. I have wanted to for ever so long. Neither of us does so very much all during the day, and yet I simply haven't found the time. The problems in this house overwhelm me. You are very young, Cecile, and you will learn as you grow older that knowing how to live is quite a problem. "Ah, yes, Papa," you will tell me. "You merely have to get up in the morning and go to bed at night and with a little patience the day goes by . . . If only you enjoy the delicacies of a well-set table and have a friend or two come and chat with you during the afternoon, the trick is done! Then it is time to go back to bed and to forget everything!" But unfortunately the brain keeps ticking away.

CECILE: Yes, Papa.

MONSIEUR ORLAS: "Yes, Papa!" What kind of an answer is that? I don't want you to listen to me politely while you are thinking of something else, Cecile. I want you to make an effort to understand what I am saying to you. It is too easy to remain a child and think: "Fathers are stupid, and definitely narrow-minded. They live with the prejudices of their time. They know nothing of what is good. Listen to them respectfully since that is the custom. Yes, Papa. I promise indeed, Papa." . . . And then as soon as my back is turned you do whatever you like.

CECILE: No, Papa.

MONSIEUR ORLAS: "No, Papa!" It is the same thing. I demand a little less respect, Cecile, but instead a little gleam in your eye which proves to me you are listening. If I speak to you as a father and you listen as a young daughter, when we have finished you will make me a pretty curtsy and I will give you a little friendly pat on the cheek, but we won't have accomplished a thing! I would much prefer that you cast aside the privilege of your age and that you grant me for a brief moment the attention and consideration you would have for another child!

CECILE: You know that I always respectfully obey you in everything, Papa.

MONSIEUR ORLAS: Well! Now you are acting like a little fool. You know very well I do not ask you that. Still there is something in your glance that has betrayed you and I think you understand me. You are a lively little creature, cunning, with the wisdom of an old Chinese philosopher under your wild youthfulness. But century-old conventions have placed impenetrable barriers between us. Each of us thinks he must act the ready-made part just because I am your father and you are my daughter. Everything I want to tell you is already branded in your mind as banal, conventional, and boring. You are unjust, Cecile . . . Can't you imagine that I am not your father for a minute? And that I am a witty and charming man.

CECILE: Yes, Papa.

MONSIEUR ORLAS (bitterly): "Yes, Papa!" It is better if you do not answer at all! We will make headway more quickly. I want to confess something first, Cecile: I am just about as old as you! (He looks at her with satisfaction.) Well, at least I have managed to surprise you all the same! . . . But I see very well that you still do not trust me! You are thinking it is an unusual beginning. But let us be wary. All this will end as usual by lecturing. Everybody knows nothing else can come from a father's lips. Do you know what you look like this very moment, Cecile? Like a little prisoner being questioned by an enemy General Staff . . . However, you are grown-up and beautiful. In a year, in a month, who knows . . . perhaps even tomorrow you will have gone over to the other side. You as well: you will be a woman. Then we shall be able to understand each other, but perhaps it will be too late. I would have liked to find the way to your heart before.

CECILE: But my heart is yours, Papa.

MONSIEUR ORLAS: Like a little closed-up box whose key one has lost. I will never know what is inside.

CECILE (*after a moment*): I do not know what you mean, Monsieur.

MONSIEUR ORLAS: Ah, this time you did not say "Papa." We are making headway. Now I confess a second thing, Cecile: not only are we the same age, but you please me very much. We are lucky to have disentangled ourselves from conventions. I would never have tried to attract your attention had you been very ugly, bigoted, or stupid. But for the past ten minutes I have been making witty remarks to please you and I am not even sure that I have astonished you. It is really sad, Cecile. You will see when you are a bit older that there are not many interesting men in the world. You had one close at hand. It is a pity you paid no attention to him because he was your father.

CECILE (*after a pause*): You urge me too quickly, Monsieur. This is our first meeting. We must see each other again.

MONSIEUR ORLAS: Thank you, Cecile! You are a clever girl. Thank God, I was not mistaken! And you are wisdom itself. Indeed, I have rushed things a bit. One must be a terribly young man to believe you can push matters of the heart.

Well, we will take all the time that is necessary. You see
there are certain things you know much more about than
I do. Let me kiss your hand as I would a lady. I gather you
have promised me another rendezvous. Shall we say this
evening after dinner in the garden? We shall do as usual
and seem to go to our rooms and then when everyone is
asleep we will find each other here again, hmm? It is better
if no one knows anything about our meetings.

CECILE (*stammering bewilderedly*): Did you say this evening,
Monsieur?

MONSIEUR ORLAS: Yes. Does it seem too soon to you? Do you
want more time to think over matters?

CECILE *does not say a word.*

Well, answer me! What is wrong with you?

CECILE (*suddenly*): Since you demand that we speak frankly,
Monsieur . . . this evening I have a rendezvous.

MONSIEUR ORLAS (*slumping*): Have a rendezvous! After dinner?
What do you mean? I cannot have heard correctly!

CECILE: Oh, but you have! I have a rendezvous. I cannot tell you
more, Monsieur.

MONSIEUR ORLAS (*beside·himself*): You cannot tell me more,
Mademoiselle? Do you realize that you are making a fool
of me right now? And that I will not stand for it! With
whom do you have a rendezvous this evening? Hmm? Well,
answer!

CECILE *remains silent.*

Cecile, I am your father and I demand a reply! Now you
are going too far! "Monsieur, this evening I have a rendezvous!" To have the audacity even to say that in front of
me, her own father and only seventeen! Do you think of
making me the accomplice in your debauchery, wretched
child? What becomes of the respect you owe me in every

matter? Do you forget who I am and is it mandatory that I remind you? Ah, believe me, I regret my credulousness and my confidence: But from now on I will treat you as you deserve. Now go to your room, Mademoiselle.

CECILE *starts to speak.*

Not a word! I order you to stay there until you hear otherwise—and I assure you I shall do everything to prevent you from going out of your room tonight! Now go!

CECILE (*curtsies and goes toward the house. She turns at the door and in a pitiful voice says simply*): You see how difficult it is, Monsieur. (*She exits.*)

MONSIEUR ORLAS: "You see how difficult it is, Monsieur!" And to her own father! Ah, nothing is sacred any longer! (*To* ARAMINTHE, *who has just entered.*) Araminthe, I am beside myself!

ARAMINTHE: What has happened, Monsieur?

MONSIEUR ORLAS: I decided to have a heart-to-heart talk with Cecile. I did everything I could to inspire her with confidence, to make her understand that it was not the father but a friend who spoke to her. I thought I was on the point of solving the mystery of this little Sphinx and making myself understood for once! I proposed that we meet in the garden at night so that the moon and the stars might add a bit of romantic atmosphere to our conversation. I told her to be frank with me and forget who I was. And do you know what reply she made?

ARAMINTHE (*laughing*): That she would be unable to because she had another rendezvous this evening?

MONSIEUR ORLAS (*jumping*): Thunder and blazes, Mademoiselle! Does everyone make a fool of me in this house! Did you know all about it?

ARAMINTHE: You wanted Cecile to speak to you as a friend, Monsieur. I think the confidence she showed you terribly

moving. She simply told you the truth. It is true. She has
a rendezvous tonight.

MONSIEUR ORLAS: My daughter has a rendezvous tonight! And
her governess herself tells me so to my face! We are in an
insane asylum. Would it be indiscreet, Mademoiselle, to
inquire with whom my daughter has a rendezvous tonight?

ARAMINTHE: Yes, Monsieur. It would be most indiscreet. It is a
secret between the two of us.

MONSIEUR ORLAS: A secret between the two of you! That is really
incredible . . . I am deeply hurt, Araminthe. Cecile is only
a little child with a child's brain. But I did hope that you at
least would not make a fool of me. I am a very lonely man,
Araminthe. I may seem gay, but most of the time I am sunk
in despair. *You* all believe that I am working when I lock
myself in my study, don't you? Working at God only
knows what since I have never done anything in my life!
The entire household goes about on tiptoe so as not to disturb me. But do you know what I actually do in this
sanctuary of mine? I sit for hours in front of my desk and
look at the wall opposite me.

ARAMINTHE: You should come and speak to us, Monsieur. Your
daughter and I would be most happy to amuse you.

MONSIEUR ORLAS: I do not feel either of you trusts me. Something tells me that you always have some little secret which
belongs only to you both. You giggle over your tapestries
whispering Heaven only knows what in each other's ear. As
soon as I come you stop! One would really think that I turn
you into stone!

ARAMINTHE: It is the respect we both owe you, Monsieur, that
makes us pause. You are the master, you have serious problems. We believe that you have no time for our silly chatter.

MONSIEUR ORLAS: You are wrong. I have nothing to think of,
Araminthe, except my ennui. I have a modest income, but it
takes care of itself. And I have never had the good fortune

to take politics seriously as most men of my age. When I
was twenty, I lived as flippantly as you and time slipped
through my fingers. As I grew older, I believed I had to
strike an attitude to give myself importance. Yet each day
that goes by enchains me more and more to this ridiculous
prison where I am my own jailer. Why don't you free me,
Araminthe, by loving me? It would be a charitable act.

ARAMINTHE: I think the only reason one loves, Monsieur, is for
his own pleasure. But you are still young and handsome.
Why do you not take a mistress? That would keep you busy.

MONSIEUR ORLAS: A fine thing to come from your lips!

ARAMINTHE: I know at least two or three young and beautiful
women in the town who would be delighted to become
your mistress.

MONSIEUR ORLAS: I know them too. They do not appeal to me at
all.

ARAMINTHE: Still if you need them to cure you?

MONSIEUR ORLAS: But love is not a medicine! Once pleasure passes,
and it passes quickly—as you will learn one day, my child—I
shan't have anything to tell them and I will simply die of
boredom. I would rather sit in front of my wall. At least,
I don't feel compelled to speak to myself.

ARAMINTHE: Do you believe, Monsieur, in all frankness, that you
would have very much more to tell me if I left my door
ajar to you? Once pleasure passes—and it passes quickly as
you have just taught me—it would be exactly the same.

MONSIEUR ORLAS: With you?

ARAMINTHE: Yes, with me, Monsieur, for  you do not love me as I
want to be loved one day. You are bored: I am young and
fresh and I live here at your home. There is no more mystery
than that. You spoke to me of the baron a while ago. But tell
me honestly what man finding himself in your position would
not try—just for the sake of trying—to knock softly on my

door while going to bed at night? You simply conform to the most banal order of things, and for my part I do the same by not opening it. You can be sure that when I know that I love and am loved—I will hear. I have a sharp ear and I will hear, however softly one knocks.

MONSIEUR ORLAS (*severely*): And if this young man who kissed your hand a while ago would softly knock, Mademoiselle, would you hear him? I was not born yesterday, Araminthe. Other women were already playing this little game with me while you were still a child. So don't try to fool me! It isn't worthy of you—nor of me. My eyes are finally opening, you little schemer. Cecile is only a pretext which explains your entire attitude. This young fellow comes here to see you!

ARAMINTHE: And if it were so, Monsieur? I am single. I am free. Who could find anything wrong in that?

MONSIEUR ORLAS: I could, Heaven knows!

ARAMINTHE: You could? And by what right?

MONSIEUR ORLAS: By right of . . . Don't ask me so many questions! Your father entrusted you to me, Araminthe. The sacredness of your honor is in my hands. I am not a suspicious man—perhaps I should be more so—but woe to the one who trifles with me when it comes to honor. It will be my duty to warn your father if ever you are mad enough to open your door to this little puppy! And you can be sure he will be warned.

ARAMINTHE: And who would have warned my father then, had I opened it to you, Monsieur?

MONSIEUR ORLAS (*slightly embarrassed*): Well, in such a case . . . Oh, stop joking, Araminthe! You are the only one who laughs at your jokes!

ARAMINTHE: Then stop living in a dream world, Monsieur! The little Chevalier comes here to see Cecile and not me! Everybody knows it, and you as well. I will even tell you a secret if you swear not to repeat it. But first you must swear. I do not trust you completely, Monsieur. It is true you are a gentleman but still you have two or three personalities and sometimes you are unable to tell one from the other.

MONSIEUR ORLAS: Enough, enough. I swear. But heaven alone knows if I understand you.

ARAMINTHE: Swear on what is most precious to you, and swear that you will never tell anyone. Well, go on and swear! And everything must be according to rules. So spit as well!

MONSIEUR ORLAS: Araminthe, you are making fun of me. But there, I swear. (*He holds up his hand.*) And I spit!

ARAMINTHE: Well, Monsieur, the Chevalier thinks so little of me that he is eloping with your daughter tonight.

MONSIEUR ORLAS (*at first astounded, bursts out laughing*): Ah! Ah! That is a good one! Whom do you take me for? The stock father in a comedy? You think that I am going to masquerade in a dark cloak and catch a cold in the garden just to see if I don't find a hidden ladder, hmm? You are talking to the wrong person, Mademoiselle.

ARAMINTHE: I believe it would be most prudent, Monsieur. If Cecile told you she had a rendezvous tonight, it was not without reason.

MONSIEUR ORLAS: I will lock Cecile in her room, Mademoiselle, and save that unfortunate child from playing I don't know what scandalous part in this affair between you and your lover. And I shall sleep soundly tonight, have no fears! After all, it is no business of mine if you have decided to ruin yourself!

ARAMINTHE: And you are right! But if I were in your place, Monsieur, I would still keep a watch to see if anyone were kidnapped tonight.

MONSIEUR ORLAS: That's right, laugh at me. Now I see that you never loved me and never will love me. I am going to my study and think of ways not to suffer any more. I am too old now to yield to despair. Tomorrow I will tell you what I

have decided. Adieu, Araminthe! I am deeply wounded.
(*He takes a step and looks back.*) Yet, Araminthe, I want
to tell you something. It is true I knocked at your door. But
I never really insisted. And although God knows how much
I love making love, I was almost happy that your door re-
mained closed.

ARAMINTHE (*stammering, bewildered*): What do you mean, Monsieur?

MONSIEUR ORLAS (*continuing*): Yes, almost happy. You may already be the mistress of this boy, and I am making myself
ridiculous by speaking to you as I do. I am not easily respectful, Araminthe. There is something about a skirt floating
around a supple waist that does away with the sense of respect in my mind. And yet there are such strong contradictions in one's heart, that I was almost happy in my
bitterness to learn how to respect you before your silent
door. There it is. Ask that little man tonight if he understands anything of this! (*He exits.*)

ARAMINTHE (*smiling happily to herself and whispering*): It only
had to be said, Monsieur . . . You went through so much
trouble for nothing before! . . . And now without even
wanting to you have found the words which unlock a girl's
door . . . Poor little men! Poor little strutting peacocks!
They spread out their tails as conquerors almost as soon as
they are able to walk . . . And they could have such an easy
victory if they knew they only had to be a little wounded
and sad . . . But we are certainly not going to teach them
that! . . . I have no fears for this one! He will be in the
garden as soon as night falls, with a dark, concealing cloak,
pistols at his side, and a taste for blood in his mouth. He
may catch a cold there, or he may find love . . . Or perhaps even both. Well, we shall see! . . . I will tell you a
secret: The playwright himself doesn't know! . . . (*She exits
after a small curtsy.*)

*The stage remains empty and night begins to fall while a
mocking tune is being played. When night is fully established*

*—quickly enough for this time of year—a man appears wrapped in a dark cloak. He advances cautiously. He beckons to someone and two men also in dark cloaks come from a black corner of the garden and join him.*

THE MAN: Ssssh!

THE MEN: Ssssh!

*Still another figure in a dark cloak comes from the house, his face concealed in the folds of his cloak. It is* MONSIEUR ORLAS. *The man who first appeared motions his men to go away.* MONSIEUR ORLAS *and the other man cautiously survey each other before approaching.*

MONSIEUR ORLAS (*in a low voice*): Monsieur Damiens?

MONSIEUR DAMIENS (*in the same voice*): Monsieur Orlas?

MONSIEUR ORLAS: Yes. It is I.

*They greet each other.*

MONSIEUR DAMIENS: Many thanks, Monsieur, for warning me.

MONSIEUR ORLAS: Do not mention it, Monsieur. It was only my duty. I am a father like yourself, Monsieur. (*He motions to the two men who are waiting.*) Are these gentlemen with you?

MONSIEUR DAMIENS: Two bodyguards whom I thought worth while bringing. I thought that we might have to meet force with force.

MONSIEUR ORLAS: You did wisely, Monsieur. I myself am armed with pistols. (*He points to them under his cloak.*)

MONSIEUR DAMIENS: How can I ever thank you, Monsieur?

MONSIEUR ORLAS: It is the most natural thing in the world, Monsieur. You have entrusted Araminthe to my care. Her honor is as precious to me as to you. But why are you trembling? Have no fear.

MONSIEUR DAMIENS: I am a father, Monsieur. And I will also tell you without false shame that I am an old lawyer, Monsieur, and that I have little experience when it comes to battles.

MONSIEUR ORLAS: I have no more taste for fighting than you, Monsieur. But when my daughter's honor is concerned or your daughter's—you see I place them both on the same level—I am ready to take up arms. Besides, the law is on our side.

MONSIEUR DAMIENS: Yes, it is. Still I don't hide from you that I would have preferred a good lawsuit. I would have crushed my opponent with the situation I hold and such a flagrant offense as this! Alas! A lawsuit would have been too slow. Lovers work more quickly than we do, Monsieur. You are a father yourself. You know how difficult it is to protect your daughter!

MONSIEUR ORLAS: You're telling me, Monsieur! I had fears for my own daughter before seeing through their intrigue. These little young fellows no longer have respect for anything. It seems to me when we were their age we had more respect for family honor.

MONSIEUR DAMIENS: Oh, I don't know! We have also had our day. I can tell you a hundred stories in which I have been a little imprudent. I was hot-blooded when I was twenty.

MONSIEUR ORLAS: Yes, they were still speaking about it when I was old enough to understand. You were really hot-blooded, Monsieur!

MONSIEUR DAMIENS: He! He! Yes, I suppose I was!

MONSIEUR ORLAS: Plenty of the ladies in this part of the country know a thing or two! They blushed every time your name was mentioned.

MONSIEUR DAMIENS: He! He! Yes, I suppose they did!

MONSIEUR ORLAS: I was still only a boy, Monsieur, when I dreamt of following in your footsteps!

MONSIEUR DAMIENS: He! He! Yes, I suppose you were! You

flatter me, Monsieur. It is true that very few women treated
me cruelly under the late King. But if I am not mistaken,
Monsieur, I believe that you yourself have established some
reputation in our little town, haven't you?

MONSIEUR ORLAS: Well! I suppose I have broken several hearts,
but I was paid back in time. One has to make hay while the
sun shines!

MONSIEUR DAMIENS: And we made it, Monsieur. But with good
manners. We were not like these little young fellows . . .

MONSIEUR ORLAS: Who respect nothing, Monsieur!

MONSIEUR DAMIENS: We were satisfied with married women!
After all, what is the difference between one cuckold more
or less!

MONSIEUR ORLAS: Or even some servant, if need be! Or some
wayward peasant! Hmm? But when it comes to young ladies
of quality, Monsieur! . . .

MONSIEUR DAMIENS: Without caring for the father's honor! . . .

MONSIEUR ORLAS: We must be ruthless, Monsieur! Sssh! Be careful! Let us hide! I think I saw a shadow at the end of the
path by the linden trees. It must be our adventurer.

MONSIEUR DAMIENS: Do you think he is the kind of man who
draws his sword easily? These little Monsieurs of the Nobility
believe that everything is permitted them!

MONSIEUR ORLAS: The law is on our side, Monsieur. And besides there are four of us with your bodyguards.

MONSIEUR DAMIENS: Yes. But we should take care not to be
wounded. Let us hide far away. We will throw our men at
him at the proper time.

MONSIEUR ORLAS: Do not be afraid. We will shame that boy before he even thinks of drawing his sword.

THE CHEVALIER *enters dressed in a dark cloak as well. He goes toward the house, gives a signal.* ARAMINTHE *appears at the window.*

THE CHEVALIER: Is it you, Araminthe?

ARAMINTHE: Yes, it is. (*She appears at the door, wrapped in a cloak and goes to him.*)

THE CHEVALIER: And where is Cecile?

ARAMINTHE: She is coming. But there is a little difficulty I shall tell you about directly. You must hide here for a while. (*She leads him to the little Chinese pavilion and lets him in.*) Do not make a sound until I return, and no matter what you hear, do not make a move. (*She locks him inside.*)

THE CHEVALIER (*in the pavilion*): Why do you lock the door?

ARAMINTHE: To be sure I will find you here at the proper time. Sssh! Not a word! Everything will be all right. (*She returns to the house and gives a signal.*)

CECILE (*appears, hidden under a mantle*): Is it you, Araminthe?

ARAMINTHE: Yes. You can come now. Everything is going as we expected. I am going in to get our things. Wait for me there.

CECILE: Where is the Chevalier? You know very well that I am afraid in the dark.

ARAMINTHE: One must not be afraid the night one elopes, Mademoiselle! . . . The Chevalier will join you in a minute. (*She disappears into the house.*)

MONSIEUR ORLAS, *hidden under his cape, walks around* CECILE, *who grows obviously worried and is not sure that she recognizes him.*

MONSIEUR ORLAS (*in a whisper*): Is it you?

CECILE (*in the same tone*): Yes, it is. Is it you?

MONSIEUR ORLAS: Yes. (*To himself.*) Aha, the bird is caught. I shall make believe I am the Chevalier.

CECILE: I am a little afraid.

MONSIEUR ORLAS: Do not be afraid of anything, my child. I am here.

CECILE: Are you sure at least that you love me? Because if you don't there still is time.

MONSIEUR ORLAS: Do not doubt it, my sweet. I am yours forever.

CECILE: How strangely you speak! I do not recognize your voice.

MONSIEUR ORLAS: It is because I speak low so that no one will hear us . . .

CECILE: As soon as she comes we'll run away quickly. Are your horses and bodyguards at the little gate?

MONSIEUR ORLAS: As arranged. (*To himself.*) The scoundrels! They planned to take my daughter as well.

CECILE: What are you saying?

MONSIEUR ORLAS: I said: "She is very nice but why bother to take that child?" Would we not be better off without her?

CECILE: I may be mad, Monsieur, but I shall not elope without my chaperon.

MONSIEUR ORLAS: What! This infant your chaperon? And what will her father say?

CECILE: And what will mine say? You must put up with some little unpleasantness when you elope.

MONSIEUR ORLAS (*to himself*): "Some little unpleasantness!" Ah, how they dare trifle with serious matters!

CECILE: What are you always muttering about? I cannot see your face.

MONSIEUR ORLAS: I was simply telling myself that she would get in our way, and that we would have been much better alone, my beloved.

CECILE: She is my sister, Monsieur. I cannot do anything without her. But you must swear to me that you will never kiss her hands again.

MONSIEUR ORLAS (*to himself*): Ha! Ha! Now it comes out!

CECILE: You elope with us both, but I am the one you are marrying!

MONSIEUR ORLAS: And do you doubt it, my love? (*To himself.*) I was right! The rascal intended to play with them both! (*To* CECILE.) My attentions towards her were only a convenient mask to hide my real feelings for you. Besides why speak of marriage at all? Is not love, love alone, enough for us?

CECILS I love you, Monsieur, and it is indeed a sufficient reason to follow you. But must we not conform to law?

MONSIEUR ORLAS: What an ugly word in such a pretty mouth! What other law is there but the law of our hearts?

CECILE: But what about my father, Monsieur?

MONSIEUR ORLAS: What does that suspicious old man matter? We will travel, my love. We will be like those glamorous persons hated by weak-hearted ones who never dared give everything to love! We shall be lovers! Ah, lovers! Have you ever been able to hear that word without feeling disturbed? Have you, Araminthe?

CECILE (*draws back, murmuring*): Araminthe?

MONSIEUR ORLAS: Is it not better than a household with screaming children hanging on your apron strings, and servants with their pots and pans to order around? The drudge of daily life ruins the sense of love. But each morning will see our love blossom anew, ready to be defended and conquered anew. We will have frightful scenes, wound each other to the heart. Each of us will torment the other, and yet we won't ever be able to part. Each of us will be the slave and the tyrant of the other. Men, all men, will desire you at the sumptuous gatherings where we will spend our nights, and their desire will reveal you to yourself and you will make a game of torturing me. I will never know if you really love me nor what is concealed behind your smiles. And if one day you happen to be away from me for a single hour, anxiety will gnaw my heart away. Because you will always lie to me and you will always be an everlasting mystery to me . . . This is life, Araminthe! This is what it is to be a woman and to love!

CECILE (*who has recognized her father while he was speaking, has a little smile as she says*): Good Heavens, Monsieur, how mistaken you are! I have no desire ever to leave you—even for an hour. Nor have I any desire to lie to you. And how absurd to think I would torment you! Can't you see that the least little sadness in your eye makes me suffer so? I simply want to be yours and to know it will always be that way. You certainly are very young and you know nothing about women. Even the wildest among them, Monsieur, wish for nothing else.

MONSIEUR ORLAS: Have you not read the lives of famous mistresses? They only love themselves, my poor child. Men were clods of clay they molded according to their whims. Men were simply instruments of their own triumph like their splendid gowns and their luxurious jewels. Does it not tempt you to become one of these monstrous goddesses, and to ravage all the hearts about you?

CECILE: Not at all, Monsieur! Not in the least! How monotonous it must be to love only one's self. And do you believe that if any of those famous ladies had ever known real happiness with one man they would have had any desire to change? I never think of them, but if one day I should it would be to pity them for never having found love.

MONSIEUR ORLAS: Love! Love! What do you know about love at your age?

CECILE: Everything that cannot be taught, Monsieur. That is to say, almost everything.

MONSIEUR ORLAS (*drawing nearer to her*): Very well, then, I will teach you the rest . . .

CECILE (*drawing back*): Indeed, Monsieur, these are strange words coming from your mouth and they disturb me. Throw off your disguise now. You know that I recognized you in spite of the dark. What would your daughter who loves and respects you say if she knew that you speak this way to other girls at night?

MONSIEUR ORLAS (*at first surprised, taking off his disguise*): Very well! Off with my disguise! Araminthe! You have recognized me. I am the man who has desired you for so long a time. I wanted to prevent this ridiculous elopement, because I know better than you that you cannot love that little boy. And do not worry about Cecile. She is a child who doesn't know anything. Don't give her another thought. We shall put her in a convent or send her to her aunt's. And tonight you will follow no one but me. For I love you, Araminthe, you hear me, I love you, love you madly, and I cannot live without you any more!

CECILE (*in her true voice*): I have known for a long time that you love Araminthe, but if you love her as much as you say, why don't you marry her, Papa?

MONSIEUR ORLAS (*jumps and draws back, shouting*): Papa! Who are you then? Unfortunate child! How could you possibly make fun of your father in this way?

CECILE: Did I approach you, Monsieur? Did I take the initiative of beginning this strange conversation?

MONSIEUR ORLAS: Wretched little girl! Forget at once everything I said to you. Not a word of it was true.

CECILE (*softly*): But I have not heard a word, Monsieur.

MONSIEUR ORLAS: You must know that I recognized you myself and I only wanted to shame you.

CECILE: Then why all this comedy? It would have been so easy to tell Araminthe that you love her.

MONSIEUR ORLAS (*sternly*): Mademoiselle! It is your father's right to ask you questions and not yours! What were you doing in the garden so late at night, and in a traveling cloak as well? To whom did you think you were speaking before you recognized me?

ARAMINTHE (*appears smiling*): To the Chevalier, Monsieur, who loves her and wanted to elope with her this very night to marry her and make her happy. I warned you, remember?

MONSIEUR ORLAS: You dare show your face, Mademoiselle? You should know by now that there are laws in this country which protect a father's honor. It will rest with others to weigh your part in this escapade for I intend to notify the proper authority of all this! You were going to make yourself the accomplice of a villainous act, Mademoiselle! Let me tell you marriage is a sacred thing and it alone can sanctify love! You wanted my daughter to elope tonight, didn't you? You wanted to make her like one of those lost creatures who ruin themselves forever by placing love before duty, didn't you? Well, answer me!

ARAMINTHE: I was at the window, Monsieur, and I heard you when you thought you convinced me of the contrary a little while ago. You compromise yourself too much. You do better not to insist, and far better to leave your pistols alone. Your daughter and I have been able to keep our honor without you—and sometimes even in spite of you! Haven't we? Cecile has parried your wily thrusts as well as I could have done myself. Are you not willing to grant us a bit of respect and confidence now?

MONSIEUR ORLAS: Come into my arms, my charming girl! Cecile was right indeed. If I love you why not admit it and simply ask you to marry me! . . . I know now that you love me too.

CECILE: You may kiss her, Monsieur. I shan't look.

MONSIEUR ORLAS: Thank you, Cecile. But I shall do it with such tenderness that even you can be a witness.

MONSIEUR DAMIENS (*rushing in with his bodyguards*): Upon him, my brave men! We have him now!

*They throw themselves on* MONSIEUR ORLAS.

Caught in the very act, Monsieur! Kissing my daughter! And eloping! You will surely be condemned to the galleys! (*He recognizes* MONSIEUR ORLAS.) But what is this? A betrayal? To find you, Monsieur, kissing my daughter in the dark?

MONSIEUR ORLAS: I can explain everything, Monsieur . . .

MONSIEUR DAMIENS: I thought you were a father, Monsieur, but you are only a vile seducer! Did you not swear a while ago with pistols in your hands that you would protect the honor of your ladies . . . or was I dreaming?

MONSIEUR ORLAS (*beginning to explain with embarrassment*): Love, Monsieur, is my only excuse. This feeling is stronger than anything and . . .

MONSIEUR DAMIENS: To whom do you think you are talking, Monsieur? I was not born yesterday! Do you bandy the most sacred things so lightly, Monsieur? Are you one of these thoughtless men who ruin ladies' reputations?

MONSIEUR ORLAS: No, Monsieur. But sometimes there are occasions where love . . .

MONSIEUR DAMIENS: Idle talk! Take care, Monsieur, you are speaking to a father! Love is a word they do not understand! I was greatly mistaken, Monsieur, to put so much confidence in you! You are nothing but a young puppy!

MONSIEUR ORLAS: But Monsieur . . .

MONSIEUR DAMIENS: Have respect for my age, Monsieur! I am old enough to be your father, Monsieur!

ARAMINTHE (*in the arms of* MONSIEUR ORLAS): Thank you, Papa, for this charming phrase! Now I know I can love him!

MONSIEUR DAMIENS: Love! Love! Don't any of you know any

other word? Am I the only one too old to use it? I shall make you young people pay for it, and dearly too!

MONSIEUR ORLAS: You are unfair, Monsieur. You have known love yourself. You confessed as much a little while ago. There is in love a force which triumphs over everything and it is why . . . (*He sees* CECILE *being kissed by* THE CHEVALIER *whom* CECILE *has freed with* ARAMINTHE's *key*.) One minute, Monsieur. Here is our young rascal! (*He approaches them with indignation*.) Monsieur! Am I dreaming? Do you dare kiss my daughter, in my own garden at night and before my very eyes?

THE CHEVALIER: I love her, Monsieur!

MONSIEUR ORLAS: A good excuse, Monsieur!

THE CHEVALIER: But you just said yourself, Monsieur, that love . . .

MONSIEUR ORLAS: It is too easy a word for you to use, young man. It has an entirely different meaning in my mouth! Yes, my young libertine, I know what dark designs you were contriving. But God be praised, I came in time. The law will take care of you! And do you know the price you will pay? Hmm? The galleys, Monsieur, the galleys! . . .

THE CHEVALIER: But, Monsieur, you would not have the heart to . . .

MONSIEUR ORLAS: You are speaking to a father, Monsieur, the protector of his daughter's honor. A father, do you hear? There is something in the majesty of the word "father" which should have made you pause!

MONSIEUR DAMIENS (*taking hold of him*): A fine thing for you to be saying! What about me, Monsieur? I am also a father, Monsieur! Do not try to change the issue by talking of your daughter's honor! I want you to account for my own daughter's honor, Monsieur!

MONSIEUR ORLAS: But since I tell you that I love her, Monsieur! . . .

THE CHEVALIER (*to* MONSIEUR ORLAS): But since I tell you that I love her! . . .

ARAMINTHE (*coming forward*): This little comedy is beginning to be too long. Don't you think we have all spoken enough? Papa, Monsieur Orlas is marrying me. (*To* MONSIEUR ORLAS.) The Chevalier, Monsieur, has the honor to ask for your daughter's hand. Don't you think we can set our dark cloaks aside and continue this discussion in another place than the garden? The night is cool, we risk catching a cold, and besides I have had a midnight table laid for us. (*She claps her hands.*)

*Two footmen appear with candelabras. Other candles are lit inside the house.*

If you only take the trouble to enter the house, you will find everything ready . . . I even had musicians come secretly, and had an enormous engagement cake made for dessert with our four names engraved in silver icing.

MONSIEUR ORLAS: Did you know then that everything would end this way, precious girl?

ARAMINTHE: I was in on the secret of this comedy, Monsieur. And there must always be a happy ending for this kind of play.

MONSIEUR ORLAS (*taking* MONSIEUR DAMIENS's *arm*): Come, Monsieur Damiens, let us go and dine! Everything ends this way in France. Everything! Weddings, christenings, duels, burials, swindlings, diplomatic affairs . . . everything is a pretext to a good dinner. Besides my cook is a genius! She would be reason enough, Monsieur, for your entering my family . . . You may as well tell your bodyguards to go and have a drink in the kitchen. (*To* THE CHEVALIER.) Tell yours as well, Monsieur, who it seems are waiting at the little gate.

THE CHEVALIER: A thousand thanks, Monsieur! But it so happens that we have the same bodyguards!

MONSIEUR DAMIENS: What do you mean, "the same"! I shall have them hanged!

MONSIEUR ORLAS (*drawing him towards the house*): Forgive them, Monsieur. We only have two bodyguards in our little town and work is so scarce.

*They go in a procession into the now illuminated house. One can hear music playing.* CECILE *remains behind, and appears to be sulking.*

THE CHEVALIER (*going to her*): Well, Cecile, here you stand sulking while happiness stares you in the face. What are you waiting for?

CECILE: I am making a very important decision, Monsieur.

THE CHEVALIER: I swear to you, my love, that I will never kiss Araminthe's hands any more. Never!

CECILE: I should hope so, Monsieur. But I have been thinking about everything my father has just told me . . . How really naïve I was . . . When all is said and done, Monsieur, I think that I will make you suffer. (*She enters the house, the worried* CHEVALIER *following her.*)

*The music grows clear and brisk as the curtain falls.*

CURTAIN

# This Music Crept by Me Upon the Waters

by Archibald MacLeish

CHUCK STONE

ELIZABETH, *his wife*

OLIVER OREN

ALICE LIAM

COLONEL HARRY KEOGH

SALLY, *his wife*

J.B. HALSEY

HELEN, *his wife*

PETER BOLT

ANN, *his wife*

*Scene: The Antilles. A garden above the sea. Evening. Across the back of the stage and to the audience's left, the two wings of a small but elegant one-storey house: to the right, palm trees and a low wall along a cliff's edge, the sea beyond. An archway to the road outside pierces the left wall of the house. An entrance door leading to the living-room opens in the middle of the rear wall. The garden is dark except for the light of four enormous candles in hurricane lamps.* CHUCK STONE, *his wife,* ELIZABETH, OLIVER OREN, *and* ALICE LIAM *sit in long chairs half facing the low wall and the sea.* OLIVER *is an Englishman in his late forties, the rest Americans:* ALICE *about* OLIVER's *age, the* STONES *perhaps ten years younger. They are dressed for dinner in the Caribbean fashion: the men in loose white coats, the women in cotton dinner dresses. The conversation which has been going on for some time has pretty well run out. There are empty glasses on the little tables beside the chairs.*

ALICE: Who else?

ELIZABETH:　　　Else?

217

ALICE:                    Who else is coming?

ELIZABETH *does not answer: she is looking off toward the sea.*

Darling Elizabeth, have you forgotten?
Your dinner guests! You said the Halseys.

ELIZABETH: Yes, the Halseys.

ALICE:                         And who else?

OLIVER: Of course the girl's forgotten. Why shouldn't she?—
Waiting all these mortal hours!

ALICE: Who else besides the Halseys?

CHUCK:                    Don't
Bother, Alice! She can't hear you.
God knows what she listens to:
Not me at least. Not on this island.

ELIZABETH: I always listen, Chuck. I hear
The sea too, that's all . . . and the wind.

ALICE: You love your island, darling, don't you?

CHUCK: Sometimes I think she hates it.

ELIZABETH:                    No!
Not the island.

CHUCK:             Well, the people.

ELIZABETH: Not the island people.

CHUCK:                    No,
Not the island people! Our kind!

ELIZABETH: It isn't true I hate the island.

CHUCK: All right! You love it then!

ELIZABETH:                    I live in it.

*There is a moment's silence.*

OLIVER: God, will they never come? I'm starving.
    It must be going on for nine.

CHUCK: It's eight.

OLIVER:             Not by the belt I buckle.

ALICE: People don't keep clocks in Paradise?

OLIVER: What Negro ever kept a spring
    Wound in a metal box to chirp at him?
    That's the white man's privilege.

CHUCK:                      Privilege!
    You tell by constellations in your coconuts—
    Or by your gullet if you've got one.
    Drink, Oliver?

OLIVER:          No, no more:
    Not on yesterday's stomach, thank you.

CHUCK: I've known the whole American community
    Fifty minutes out by clock time.

OLIVER: Have you? Extraordinary. Quite like natives.

ELIZABETH: Not the least like!

CHUCK:                      Fifty! Think of it!

ELIZABETH: Not the least like natives, Oliver.
    *They* have no time to lose. They live
    Now. Not late, not soon, but now.
    They can't lose now. They live there.

OLIVER:                             Only the
    Trees have found that fabulous country.

ELIZABETH: Every paradise is laid in it.
    Here and now must meet each other
    Like two impossible rivers joining
    Just where Jerusalem begins . . .
    No matter which Jerusalem.

OLIVER: The unattainable, unvisited now
   That's never here when we are.

ELIZABETH (*violently*):                    No!
   Now and here together in one gulp
   To burn the heart out with its happiness!

CHUCK: Elizabeth!

ELIZABETH:          I'm sorry.

OLIVER:                    Why be sorry?
   Only those who've been there know it.

ALICE: And most of them won't tell.

ELIZABETH:                    Sorry
   Because I've never been there, then.

OLIVER: I wish your guests were now . . . *and* here.
   Are you quite sure you asked them, darling?

CHUCK: *I'm* sure!

OLIVER:          Ah, it's Chuck that did it.

CHUCK: The Englishman and his stomach, Oliver!

OLIVER: Why shouldn't I be hungry? Lunch—
   Alice's and mine—was sandwiches
   Seven thousand feet above
   The empty earth—and that was water.

ALICE: Cheese what's more.

OLIVER:                    What's less!

ELIZABETH:                    Look!
   It's brightening!

ALICE:          The moon?

ELIZABETH:               The moon.

OLIVER:                         For God's sake
   Don't divert me when I'm miserable.

CHUCK: Watch these palm trees on the cliff now . . .

ALICE: You're like a hen in thunder, Oliver,
Brooding your addled eggs.

CHUCK:                    . . . I planted them.
The moon, from where you're sitting, both of you,
Rises—ought to rise—just there.
I worked it out myself with almanacs.
The February moon should rise
Just in that frame of fronds precisely . . .
Some day this garden will be wonderful.
You wait! Another year. Two years.

ELIZABETH: Why wait? Why not delight in it now?

OLIVER: He can't. Nor you. Nor any of us.
Who was it said his whole life seemed
A preparation for what never happened? . . .
Like your dinner, dear Elizabeth:
A preparation for who never comes.

ALICE: How smooth the wind is. Like a river.

ELIZABETH: The always flowing of the wind . . .

CHUCK: They never fail, the Trades.

ALICE:                    It feels—
The air against my face—as though
The air were still and the earth turning.

ELIZABETH: I know. You feel the turning earth here.

ALICE: Bodies should go naked in it.

OLIVER: Not some that I can think of.

ALICE:                    All!
All should go beautiful in Paradise!

OLIVER: The Island Paradise! Who called it that?

CHUCK: Columbus. On the second voyage.

OLIVER: The Admiral was not precisely

Reticent was he? I remember
One of his discoveries he called
La Desirada.

CHUCK:                    La Désirade.
It's French now.

OLIVER:                    And it takes the consequences?

ELIZABETH: Quand bleuirat sur l'horizon la Désirade . . .

OLIVER: What's that?

ELIZABETH:                    Apollinaire I think:
When will the desired land-fall
Loom—grow blue—on the horizon . . .

OLIVER: Another of Chuck's sort, Elizabeth—
Apollinaire. The sort for whom
No voyages ever come to shore
However the sad heart prepares for it.
That's the modern poet for you!
Journeys end in no one's meeting . . .
But Paradise! How did he know?

CHUCK:                                        Know what?

OLIVER: The place was Paradise?

ALICE:                              The Admiral?

OLIVER:                                        The Admiral.
How did he know? It must have looked
An island much like any island.

ALICE: Maybe the Indians told him.

ELIZABETH:                            They might have.
Those Arawaks were cheerful creatures,
Pretty and gentle and so gay . . .

CHUCK: Before the Caribs ate them and the Spaniards
Relieved them of their sinful flesh
With whips and salt mines!

ELIZABETH: Old philosophers
Took them for witnesses of human innocence:
The primitive happiness of mankind.

CHUCK: What Elizabeth means—the books latched onto them.
Rousseau's Noble Savage was an Arawak.

OLIVER: Ah, that explains it all! Columbus,
Seeing those laughing, splashing Indians
Naked as jays and beautiful as children
Knew at once what latitudes he sailed in.
The place was Paradise! That settled it!
Had he no eyes at all for reefs
Or shark fins or the green volcanoes
Lurking in this smile of trees?

ALICE: They were the angels at the gate.

ELIZABETH (*excitedly*):
I think he saw it all. And knew.
This was no island in the sea.
This was another kind of island—
A shoal in time where happiness was possible:
More perhaps than possible—inevitable.

OLIVER: Inevitable? Happiness?

ELIZABETH: Yes. Inevitable . . .
For those who found his island.

OLIVER: Found it!
Thousands of wanderers must have found it—
Indians, Spaniards, Negroes, Frenchmen—
Even Americans! And were they happy?
Are they? All of them? Those Negroes
Swinking half-naked in the cane?
Americans stark naked on the beaches?

ELIZABETH: Few of them have found *his* island.

OLIVER: Yes, and fewer ever will,
And fewer still return to tell of it.
Perhaps some bronze brown African woman

Lying like summer in the sun,
Languid with her mute desire,
Might turn her head and be there—might!
But who else? Your American neighbors?
If one American should see this Paradise,
Even from far off in his grog,
The way you think the Admiral saw it,
His mind would fail him! Don't deceive yourself.
We're all sleep-walkers here, Elizabeth.
You are. I am. Chuck there. Alice.
If we should find ourselves awake
Where "now" was truly now, and "here"
Just here, and nothing left to hide us,
We'd huddle shivering in our souls
Like those who waken in cathedrals, naked.
Oh, we'd sweat I tell you. We'd be miserable.

ELIZABETH: Some would. Some would laugh—or try to.
One or two would change their lives.

OLIVER: Would they, Elizabeth? Change? You think so?

ELIZABETH: Peter would go back to sleep.

ALICE: Peter! Peter Bolt you mean?
Is he here? On this island? Peter?
Followed you all this way?

CHUCK:                                    *Followed* us!

ALICE: Oh, not you, Chuck.

ELIZABETH:                        Peter Bolt.
It's never now or here with Peter.
It's always somewhere else and afterward:
Afterward when the work is finished,
The fame won.

CHUCK:                        You think that's strange?
You think, because I quit and came here
Looking for—what you haven't found—
It isn't so with me too? All of us?

ALICE: What is it that you haven't found?—

ELIZABETH: What's all around us.

CHUCK:                           Is it? Is it?

OLIVER: But this not quite impetuous Peter? . . .

CHUCK: Lawyer. One of the best they tell me.
      Young too. Must have heard his name.
      He has a house here. God knows why:
      He's never in it. One week. Two weeks.

OLIVER: Here now?

CHUCK:             They're dining with us.

OLIVER:                           *They!*

CHUCK: He has a wife of course.

OLIVER:                   "Of course"?
      That kind of wife? . . . Well? Isn't she?

ALICE: Elizabeth is our authority.

ELIZABETH:                   Authority?
      Years ago I used to know him.
      We haven't really talked for years.

CHUCK: Ann, my love! Not Peter: *Ann.*

ELIZABETH: No one can speak for Ann.

ALICE:                           Not even
      Ann.

OLIVER (*to* ALICE):
      You know her?

ALICE:             Yes. She's beautiful.

ELIZABETH: She's everything a woman should be.

ALICE: There's nothing Ann can't do . . .

OLIVER:                           But? . . .

ELIZABETH:                                       Feel.

ALICE: Or know she feels at least.

ELIZABETH:                              Or show it.

OLIVER: Patently, she's mad about him.

ALICE:                                         Mad!
You haven't seen that smooth brown hair!

OLIVER: And he? Does he deserve her?

ALICE:                                 Dotes on her!
Thinks of her morning noon and night!
Where is she? Is she well? Safe? Comfortable?

ELIZABETH: You think anxiety is proof of love?
It may be proof of love's disaster:
Duty doubling duty's care
Because the passionate carefulness of the heart
No longer rushes breathless . . .

OLIVER *flings out of his chair, paces the garden.*

OLIVER:                                     God!
I'm famishing. Where are these pretty people?
Do they exist? Or did Elizabeth
Dream them in that elegant head
To populate her Paradise, her island?

ALICE: Oh, they're real enough. I'd call
The J.B. Halseys real. Thick as
Porterhouses, both of them.

CHUCK:                                 The Keoghs.

ALICE: Oliver wouldn't know the Keoghs:
They're just simple, decent people!

CHUCK: From Milwaukee.

ALICE:                           From Milwaukee.

OLIVER: They must be something more than simple.

CHUCK: Why?

OLIVER:         To live here.

CHUCK:                   Why, to live here?

OLIVER: Live in this Paradise of Elizabeth's?

CHUCK: What's wrong with Paradise?

OLIVER:                      For saints,
     Nothing.

CHUCK:     For simple, decent people.
     Even the decent have a right to happiness.

OLIVER: Oh, a right! You Americans
     Guarantee it somewhere, don't you?
     All men have a right to happiness—
     You, the Keoghs, everybody.
     What if happiness laid claim to them?
     It might, in Paradise, you know—
     People who all their lives have lived
     Pursuing happiness, pursuing something
     More or farther off or brighter.
     In Paradise there's nothing more.
     Everything that will be, is.

ELIZABETH: Is, and is everything!

OLIVER:                      They'd go mad.
     We all would—all of us. We're all the same:
     We live by what's still left to live for:
     Something in another life,
     Another love, another country,
     Even in another world,
     At least some other day. In Paradise
     Everything is here, is this:
     The ordinary heart can't bear it.
     Suffering, yes: suffering we endure.
     But happiness! Happiness is long ago
     Or far away or not yet come to.
     Only a child or those like children,

Meeting happiness in a summer's door
Can take it by the hand and run with it.
The rest walk past it and remember.

ELIZABETH: Some walk past it and forget.

OLIVER: Your island, dear Elizabeth! Your island!
It's Shakespeare's parable all over.
Enchanting music draws us through the sea,
We glimpse an inexpressible happiness,
We turn into the things we were—
A duke, his daughter, attendants, gentlemen

ALICE: Oliver'd turn us into saints.

OLIVER: Saints of a far more rigorous discipline
Than any the meek church acknowledges.
Mexican Indians. Chinese poets.
No ordinary saint can sit
In sunlight at a door, like those
Old Negro women of Elizabeth's.
Watch your compatriots at play or mine!
Look at the Riviera! Strewn with them!
The wreckage of the right to happiness
In painted shirts and canvas trousers
Drinking Pernod before breakfast,
The possibility of Paradise so terrifies them!

ALICE: And our compatriots here?

CHUCK:                                   They drink.
A little.

ALICE:        Chuck!

CHUCK:              All right! They drink!
Why not? It passes time.

OLIVER:                     Does it?
Not if the place is what he called it.
Time in Paradise never passes.
The blessed live their lives awake.

ELIZABETH: Each minute like the last that will be:
    Each like the first that ever was.

OLIVER: How wise the child is all at once.

ALICE: She's had her glimpses of the garden:
    Who hasn't?

*The brightening of the sky above the sea increases.* OLIVER
*stands with his back to it. They are silent.*

OLIVER:           Happiness is difficult.
    It takes a kind of courage most men
    Never are masters of, a kind of
    Innocent ruthlessness that lives
    Like leaves in the instant of the air:
    The courage just to be—to trust
    The wind that blows you.

ELIZABETH:           Look! The moon!
    It's rising!

OLIVER:      Do you think that fact,
    Elizabeth, deserves remark
    Just at this juncture of my discourse?

ALICE: How slow it lifts into the sky!
    Look at it, Oliver! It's marvellous.

OLIVER: Dear girl, we have a moon in England.

CHUCK: Only you never see it.

OLIVER:           Don't we!
    Demure among her clouds. not strutting
    Naked like that tropical piece.
    Shameless the way she stares at us!

ELIZABETH:           They say
    The moon feeds on our eyes. I think
    I never saw a moon more gluttonous . . .
    I know I never saw one stranger:
    So still! Silver and intent and still!
    It burns like silence in a mirror.

CHUCK: Because the wind has fallen. Listen!
The Trade Wind almost never falls
Night or day—not at this season.

ALICE: I hear a kind of murmuring in the sea—
Between the slidings of the sea a syllable.

ELIZABETH: So still! So still!

ALICE:                          I've never known
The world—the sea, the sky, the air—
So still.

ELIZABETH: Nor I

ALICE:               The palm leaves fill
And fall as though not air but moonlight
Gathered them and let them go.
You know, it could be Paradise, it could be—
This moment anyway.

ELIZABETH:                    It is!
If only we ourselves awoke
And trusted it, it could be. Even for
Us! If we could take it . . . Dared to . . .

CHUCK: Take what?

ELIZABETH:              Our lives! Our lives! Our lives!

   ELIZABETH *crosses to the cliff's edge, stands there looking out
   to sea.*

ALICE: Turn your face up! Close your eyes!
Feel the almost imperceptible movement
Of cool and warm across your lids
The moon makes touching you—the sliding moon.
Something unimaginably beautiful
Seems no farther from me than my hand
Could reach, if I should lift one finger.

OLIVER: Alice is giddy from her fast.

ALICE: Jeer if you please. You feel it too.
I know you, Oliver.

OLIVER:                    All right, I'm giddy.
Why not? If the moon is risen
It must be—God knows what it must be—
Ten?

CHUCK:   It's half past eight.

OLIVER:                    Great God!
And not a sign of them. No message.
You don't suppose this settlement of yours
Has vanished at the clap of moonlight?
Strange things happen in the wilderness.
Remember Raleigh's settlement at Jamestown?
Gone—just gone—the table set,
Food in the kitchens, and the place
Deserted. Not a soul. Perhaps
It wasn't Raleigh. Even Jamestown.

ELIZABETH: Be quiet! Listen to the sky!

OLIVER: Or those deserted ships at sea
Discovered drifting with their sails set, everything
Neat, everything in order—a child's
Toy, the captain's toddy, biscuits—
Even the cat's milk sweet and not
One single soul aboard—no explanation—
Nothing but the slapping sails,
The groaning timbers . . .

ALICE:                    And the little girl
Crunching popcorn in the row behind you!

CHUCK: My guess would be they stopped at Peter's
Meaning to have one drink and had
Another and, just possibly, another.

OLIVER: It isn't conceivable. I won't believe you.
People don't sit down and drink
While others hunger. No, they're gone.
Something—who knows what?—has tempted them
Past the familiar safe stockade

To those dark forests off beyond it—
God have mercy on their souls!—
Leaving the settlement uninhabited
Save for ourselves: we few remaining.

ELIZABETH: What makes you think we're safe inside,
We others? That blazing moon could burn
The whole stockade of certainty and leave us
Ignorant in the wilderness, no matter
How we'd built it out of words from home.
Where would we hide our hunger then?

CHUCK: Oh, for God's sake, no, Elizabeth.
I hate those games: You know I hate them.
Elizabeth is always asking
Where? . . . When? . . .

OLIVER:                          And you reply?

CHUCK: That's it: I don't . . .

ALICE:                          Listen! . . . Listen! . . .
Chuck, there's something . . . not the sea . . .

CHUCK: It's them! They're coming!

OLIVER:                          Ah, they're coming!
How shall we welcome them, Elizabeth?—
Sit here as though we'd finished dinner,
Smoking our cigars, and rise,
Polite in our restrained astonishment,
And wait until the boldest chirps:
"It *was* tonight, dear, wasn't it?"
And answer awfully: "It *was*!"?

ALICE: Oliver! He would! You know he would.
Don't encourage him Elizabeth.

OLIVER: You call that look encouragement?
She hasn't heard a word I've said.

*Headlights swing across the arch: engines are cut off: voices.*

CHUCK: Anything you want to bet
   They feel no pain.

OLIVER:                     Those tell-tale voices!
   How hideously rum reveals
   The insipidity of its origins!
   Liquid sugar! Listen to them!

   KEOGH *opens the gateway in the arch: his wife* SALLY *pushes past him.*

KEOGH: God, boy, do I need a drink!

SALLY: What he means he needs another . . .

KEOGH: OK!

SALLY:         . . . little drink. He's beautiful!
   The way he wears that shirt, he's beautiful!
   Isn't he beautiful, Elizabeth?

KEOGH: Boy, what I've been through!

SALLY:                              Just beautiful!

KEOGH: Watching these goddam goofy idiots
   Gawk by the water while the moon
   Came up and gawked at them, for Chri'sake!

   HELEN HALSEY *comes through the arch: then her husband.*

HELEN: Dear Elizabeth, forgive us!
   We must be very, very late.
   Peter's just behind. And Annie.

KEOGH: Behind! He hasn't left that beach.
   Poor bastard's stuck there staring at it
   Stiff as a jacked fish. Stiffer.

SALLY:                              Just
   Staring at it.

CHUCK:         Staring where?
   What's he staring at?

SALLY:                     Just staring.

HELEN: Standing staring.

KEOGH:                          Wouldn't let me
   Speak not even.

SALLY:                 Imagine that!
   Not even Harry even speak!
   Each of us just stood there staring.

CHUCK: Where? At what?

KEOGH:                          Beside the road there.

HALSEY: Where the road runs by the beach.

HELEN: The moon. We watched it rising.

KEOGH:                                   *She* did!
   Stopped us all beside the dune.

HELEN: No one knows how long we stood there.

KEOGH: *I* do. *I* know. Ask me darling.

HELEN: All of us had silver glasses.

CHUCK: Glasses?

SALLY:          Silver in the moon.
   Peter gave us silver glasses.

KEOGH: Keeps his cocktails in his car,
   The thoughtful bastard.

HELLN:                      All of silver

   Oh, it was wonderful, Elizabeth.

ELIZABETH: It sounds so. Do you know each other?
   This is Alice Liam, Sally:
   You know Alice, Sally, don't you?
   Sally Keogh, Harry Keogh . . .
   Oliver, do you know the Halseys?
   This is Oliver Oren, Helen.
   Mr. and Mrs. Keogh, Oliver.

KEOGH: Colonel Keogh!

ELIZABETH:                 Oh, I'm sorry.
Colonel Keogh.

KEOGH:                 Not at all . . .
Natural error. When the wars are ended
Who remembers the poor soldiers?

HALSEY: The poor soldiers seem to, Colonel.

SALLY: Particularly colonels.

CHUCK:                 Oh
Generals remember pretty well:
Generals remember all the generals.

KEOGH: You can go to Hell, the lot of you.

ELIZABETH: Why did he stay there, Harry?

KEOGH:                                         Who?

ELIZABETH: Peter.

KEOGH:                 The beauty of the night!
Imagine that! At his age! Stuck there
Staring at the island in the moon
As though he'd never seen it till that moment!

OLIVER: Had he?

KEOGH:                 This is his seventh year!
It wasn't only Peter either.
Know what Halsey here was saying?

HALSEY: Forget it!

KEOGH:                 Don't you wish I would?
Don't you? Halsey here was saying:
"Yes!" Like that . . . "Yes!" . . . "Yes" . . .
Staring at the moon-rise: "Yes!" . . .

HELEN: It's true. I never saw him look so—
Not even at Hyannisport that summer.
I don't know what he meant.

KEOGH:                              Nor him:
   He doesn't either.

HALSEY:                    No! Forget it.

HELEN: I wish he'd looked at me like that:
   Just once.

SALLY:           Like what?

HELEN:                     Oh, like a man . . .
   Who sees the whole of his desire.

HALSEY: You don't know what you're saying, Helen.

HELEN: A man who saw his whole desire,
   Near as the world was in that moon,
   Might get it.

OLIVER:           Yes. And where would he be?

ELIZABETH: Here.

OLIVER:         Or his desire?

ELIZABETH:                      Here.

KEOGH: They're tight as mountain ticks, the lot of them.

SALLY: They're crazy, everybody's crazy,
   Craziest night I ever saw,
   Like Paris, who was that was saying
   Let's go crazy, dear, in Paris?
   Who? We did too, we went crazy,
   Just like Paris only rum,
   I like rum, want to know what *I* did?
   Want to know what little Sally
   Did?

KEOGH:    Quiet! You're a big girl now:
   You're forty-seven.

SALLY:                    I kept saying,
   I'm beautiful! I'm beautiful!

KEOGH: Shut up, I said. I meant it!

SALLY:                              Oh,
I stood there naked by the water . . .
I mean . . .
          I stood there . . .

*Silence.*

KEOGH:                    What she means
She's had one coke too many.

ELIZABETH:                    Does she?
I think she means that she was beautiful!

SALLY: Elizabeth, you flatterer!

ELIZABETH:                    It isn't flattery.
Why are you frightened to remember?

SALLY: I'm not!

ELIZABETH:     You are. You'd rather think
What Harry thinks—that you were drunk—
Than know what you knew then.

SALLY:                              Elizabeth!
I don't know what you mean.

ELIZABETH:                    I think you
Do . . . or did.

*There is an awkward silence.*

CHUCK:          Let's go indoors:
The Bolts will be along. We'll have
That drink the Colonel needs indoors.

KEOGH: And how he needs it!

OLIVER:                    Poor dear Alice,
Tottering for lack of food.

ALICE:                              I thought
You'd fainted, Oliver. I couldn't hear you.

SALLY: I want Elizabeth to answer me.

Elizabeth has made me cry . . .
I don't know why she did.

ELIZABETH:                        It isn't
You. It's all of us. We face our lives
Like young girls in a gallery of mirrors.
Some glittering, unexpected moment
Shows us our images and we shriek
With childish, hysterical laughter, caught
Naked in the simplicity of ourselves . . .
You needn't stare at me. You know it—all of you.

HELEN: Dear Elizabeth! It's the island!
People say things on an island—
Things they never meant to say:
They feel so far off . . .

ELIZABETH:                        Yes, and see
Things they never meant to see
And tell themselves they've never seen them!
We shouldn't live here, any of us.
We're out of place in so much light!
The green volcano in those hills
Could drown us in a flood of fire
And we'd go under giggling.

CHUCK:                                Sweet
Love! How violent you are!

ELIZABETH: Go in. I'll follow you. Please go.
Forgive me.

CHUCK:            Come and get it!
(*From the door.*)
                                Ice
Cold! Coals of ice!

*They straggle in, awkwardly and rather self-consciously.*
ELIZABETH *walks to the cliff's edge over the sea and stands
leaning against a palm trunk. The headlights of a car sweep
the archway against the moon and are switched off. Snatches*

*of phonograph music drift out over the sound of the sea, and,*
*occasionally, voices.*

KEOGH (*off*):
God that's good! What did he call it?

HALSEY (*off*):
Coals of ice.

ALICE (*off*):     Elizabeth's volcano.

SALLY (*off*):
Elizabeth's volcano!

CHUCK (*off*):
                    Right! Where is she?
Elizabeth!
(*He comes to the door calling.*)
          Elizabeth!

HELEN:              Don't pester her.
(*In the door beside him.*)
Even hostesses must have their moments.

CHUCK: What a woman of the world you are.

HELEN: Your world, Chuck?

CHUCK:                    And what a woman.
You smell like almonds. Only warmer.

HELEN: Don't! Please don't! Oh, I know
It's nothing to us—either of us:
Just the usual salute. It isn't
That . . .

CHUCK:     What is it, then?

HELEN:                    It's me:
I don't know who I am. I don't
Know!

CHUCK:   You want a man should show you?

HELEN: Please! I mean it Chuck. I heard

Something that frightened me beside the water.
There wasn't any sound at all—
No sound at all and yet I heard
Ravishing laughter on the sea
Like negresses: in love they say
They shriek with laughter . . . it was horrible!
I stood there staring at the moon and heard
Ravishing laughter on the water . . .
I don't know what I am, I don't know . . .

HALSEY (off):
Pull the door shut, will you?

HELEN:                                                    . . . anything.

HALSEY: The Colonel hates the moon . . .

CHUCK *and* HELEN *turn back into the room pulling the door to.* PETER *and* ANN BOLT *enter through the archway.* PETER *stops in the blazing moonlight in the garden turning away from the door and the chatter of voices.*

ANN: Peter, we're terribly late. Please come.

PETER: You go, I need time . . . It takes
Time.

ANN:          What does? What takes time?
I don't understand you, Peter.
What takes time? You've changed so.

PETER:                                                  Have I?
I wish I knew I had.

ANN:                          Peter!
You don't—can't—mean that, Peter!

PETER: Changed into something that can live.

ANN: Live!

PETER:          Live here. Live in this island.

ANN: You couldn't bear it. Not the island.
Not a night like this. I know you:

Oh, my dear, how well I know you.
You need to earn your life to live in it
Even though the earning cost you
All your lifetime and yourself.
I know those obstinate hounds you ride to.
I hear them whimpering in your sleep
Night after night.

PETER: For Christ's sake, Annie!
I said—if there were words to say it . . .

ANN: Tell me. Try to tell me, Peter.

PETER: I said that what I suddenly understood
There in the moonlight, on the beach, was—
This is what it *is!* Just this!—
Not something afterward or elsewhere.
You live it or you don't, but what you
Live or don't live is just this:
This, this moment now, this moon now . . .
This man here on an island watching.

(*He turns away from her.*)

I understood it as you understand
A knife blade driven in your side:
The way you understand in dreams
That waken in a giddiness of certainty.

ANN: That passes when you waken.

PETER: Yes!
Yes! God, Annie, you're so sensible!

ANN: I saw the moon too, rising.

PETER: You? . . .
All my life I've lived tomorrow
Waiting for my life to come:
Promises to come true tomorrow,
Journeys to begin tomorrow,
Mornings in the sun tomorrow,
Books read, words written,

All tomorrow. Cities visited.
Even this fever of the sleepless heart
Slept away tomorrow . . . all of it.

ANN: Truth to be told at last . . . tomorrow.

PETER: We cling so to the skirts of suffering
Like children to their mothers—hold
The hand that hurts our hand for fear
We'll lose ourselves unless it hurts us!—
Making a virtue of our cowardice:
Pretending that a sense of sin and shame
Is holier than the happiness we fumble.

ANN: What is it that you have to do?

PETER: To do?

ANN:          What is it?

PETER:                    I don't know.

ANN: And so there is . . . is something, Peter?

PETER: I need to know the thing I know.
I need to think a little.

ANN:                    Yes.
I'll go. Come when you can.

PETER:                    I promise.

ANN: Promise! If we only could . . .

(ANN *opens the door of the house, there is a burst of voices.*)

CHUCK (*off*):
    *There* they are!

SALLY: (*off*):          There *she* is!

KEOGH (*off*):                    Where's
Peter for the love of God?

ANN (*going in*):

                    Coming.

He's coming. Do forgive us, Chuck . . .
Elizabeth . . . Where is she? . . . all of you.

*The door closes.* ELIZABETH *comes into the moonlight.*

PETER: Elizabeth!

ELIZABETH: I didn't mean to startle you.
The rest of them went in. I couldn't.

PETER: We're dreadfully late. It's all my fault.
I'm sorry.

ELIZABETH: Don't be. Island chickens
Cook forever without noticing:
All you need to do is baste them.
Island diners baste themselves.

PETER: You heard?

ELIZABETH: I couldn't help it.

PETER: When the wind
Fell and that sudden silence of the moon
Touched everything . . .

ELIZABETH: With silver . . .

PETER: Yes,
With silver . . . where were you?

ELIZABETH: Beside
The palms there at the little table—
Alice and Oliver and Chuck and I.

PETER: I was on that beach beside the water
Drinking—I don't know—making drinks,
Talking the usual idiotic nonsense,
Thinking nothing at all: certainly
Nothing that would change a life . . .
And you? You too? Beside that palm tree?

ELIZABETH: As though I'd started out of sleep.

PETER: Yes. As one would start from sleep.

I stood and I was *there!* As though
I'd turned a corner suddenly and come—
I don't know where but come there. Oh,
As though I'd ended and begun.

ELIZABETH:                              I know.

PETER: Even the glass between my fingers
Glittered in that fiery silent moon
And such a surge of happiness went over me
Everything was possible.

ELIZABETH:                    I thought of
You.

PETER:    Only when I thought of you—
Only then did that inexplicable happiness
Take form and meaning and grow capable. . .

ELIZABETH:                                          Of breath.

PETER: Of breath.

ELIZABETH:     It's strange.

PETER:                    It's very strange
After all these years of silence.

ELIZABETH: Perhaps we've known too long in silence
Ever to find voices now.
We've kept our questions in the dark so deep
Like prisoners that they have no voices.

PETER: And yet they've learned to speak.

ELIZABETH:                              But how?

PETER: Who knows? The moon rose and the time was
Now.

ELIZABETH: Happiness was always now.
Happiness is real—the only
Real reality that any of us
Ever have glimpses of. The rest—

> The hurt, the misery—all vanishes,
> Only the blinding instant left us.

PETER: Why does it take so long to know?
We tell our miserable creeping hearts
Men aren't made for happiness.

ELIZABETH:                                    The world is.

PETER: I never knew it till tonight.

ELIZABETH: This world is. And we two in it.

PETER: Answerable to the loveliness of our lives:
To nothing else.

ELIZABETH:                    To nothing else.

*They touch each other.*

PETER: Removed by some enchantment not of change
To this . . . this instant . . . this forever . . .
Never to go back.

ELIZABETH:                    No! Never!

PETER:                                    Promise me.

ELIZABETH: I promise you . . . If we should turn
Even our hearts to look behind us. . .

PETER: Even our hearts would turn to salt.
Come!

ELIZABETH: Where?

PETER:                    No matter where.
Anywhere but through that door . . .

ELIZABETH: And back.

PETER:                    And back.

*They cross to the archway.* ELIZABETH *stops in the gate.*

ELIZABETH:                                    There's wind again.
Look! The clouds have crossed the moon.

PETER: Hurry! Hurry!

*The house door blows open in a gust of wind. The voices rise.*

CHUCK (*off, shouting*):

                Soup's on! Soup's on!

KEOGH (*off, singing*):
Dinner's over: supper's cookin'
Old Dan Tucker just stand there lookin' . . .

PETER: That's my car there. Can you see?
Wait, I'll pull the gate shut.

ELIZABETH (*off*):            Come!

HELEN (*in the door*):
Elizabeth was in the garden, wasn't she?
There they are. There's Peter anyway.
Where's your Annie, Peter?

SALLY (*in the door*):        Where's
Annie?

HELEN:    Can't you hear me, Peter?

KEOGH (*in the door*):
Old Dan Tucker just stand there lookin'

SALLY: The wind is up. He doesn't hear us.
Peter, Peter. Where's Annie, Peter?

PETER (*the gate still open*):
She's in the house.

HELEN:           She isn't though.
She came and looked and vanished.

SALLY:               Looked!
She didn't even look. She stood there
Smiling at the floor—just smiling.
When I spoke to her she was gone.

OLIVER, ALICE, HALSEY, *and* KEOGH *come out into the garden.*

OLIVER: A miracle, my friends, has happened.
Dinner has been announced. It may be,
After such protracted suffering,
The word conveys no meaning. Dinner!

SALLY: Peter, they saw her on the cliff.

PETER: The cliff?

HELEN: She's not there now.

PETER: What cliff?

SALLY: Outside that window of Elizabeth's
Where everything pitches off into the sea.
There's not five feet of level rock
Between the window sill and . . .

KEOGH: Listen!
What are you telling the poor guy!
Ann's all right. She always will be.

HALSEY: Of all the women in God's world
Ann would be the last to . . .

SALLY: What?
Go on and say it!

KEOGH: You goddam girls!
You make my tooth ache where it shouldn't.
You're acting like a pair of mischievous,
Wild, half-witted, crazy children
Trying to terrify yourselves
By scaring all of us.

SALLY: Drop dead!
And not from any cliff top either:
Just drop!

HALSEY: Sally!

SALLY: All right!
"Sally!" What's got into everybody?
You know the cliff as well as I do.
There's one way out: it's through the room.

OLIVER: She might have come and we not noticed.

Those coals of ice of Chuck's demand
The most meticulous concentration.

SALLY: I leaned across the cliff's edge, looking.
There wasn't anything at all—not anything.
Only the moonlight on those black
Enormous surges when they shattered:
They say they come from Africa, those surges.

KEOGH: I swear to God I'll beat you, Sally.

PETER *turns toward the door of the house, walks a few steps,
runs. The door swings in the wind after him.*

HELEN: He doesn't believe you, gentlemen.

SALLY:                                        Why should he?
Some things you have to see yourself.

KEOGH: You mean the things that haven't happened!

ELIZABETH *has come back through the gate. They do not see
her.*

HELEN: How can you know they haven't happened?

HALSEY: Not by looking in the sea
For dead girls' bodies!

HELEN:                    I think you're heartless,
Both of you! Heartless! Heartless!

ELIZABETH:                            Helen!
What is it, Helen?

HELEN:           Oh, Elizabeth:
It's Annie . . .

SALLY:        Annie's gone. She's gone.

HELEN: They saw her on the cliff . . .

HALSEY:                              Be quiet!
Will you be quiet, both of you?

ELIZABETH:                        Where's Peter?

SALLY: He's gone to look for her.

ELIZABETH:                        Gone back?

SALLY:                                Back?

ELIZABETH: It doesn't matter. Gone.

KEOGH:                       The whole thing's
Nonsense! Peter knows its nonsense.

PETER *comes slowly out of the door of the house.*

SALLY: All right—Ask him! There he is.

PETER: She's in the kitchen. Cooking.

OLIVER:                        Bless her!

PETER: Something went wrong with the potatoes.

KEOGH: There you have it, Sal, God damn you!

SALLY: Kiss me, I forgive you, darling.

OLIVER: Bless the woman! The potatoes!

ELIZABETH *has begun to laugh, a high, clear, sudden peal that turns into an hysterical sobbing sound and breaks off.* PETER *crosses to the wall above the sea.*

HELEN: Nothing has happened. It's all right.

ELIZABETH: I know.

HELEN:              Nothing. Nothing at all.

*The door opens.* CHUCK *is standing there with a cocktail shaker in his hand.*

CHUCK: Supper's over: breakfast's cooking.

OLIVER: Shall we break bread?

ELIZABETH:                   At least there's bread—
And salt.

OLIVER:        And Ann's potatoes.

ELIZABETH:                        Yes,
And Ann's potatoes. Are you coming, Peter?

*They go in. The door is pulled shut. There is the same chatter of indistinguishable voices over the playing of the phonograph. The moon, clear of the rushing clouds, shines white and still on the house front and the garden.*

**C U R T A I N**

# A Memory of
# Two Mondays

by Arthur Miller

*Scene: The shipping room of a large auto-parts warehouse. This is but the back of a large loft in an industrial section of New York. The front of the loft, where we cannot see, is filled with office machinery, records, the telephone switchboard, and the counter where customers may come who do not order by letter or phone.*

*The two basic structures are the long packing table which curves upstage at the left, and the factory-type windows which reach from floor to ceiling and are encrusted with the hard dirt of years. These windows are the background and seem to surround the entire stage.*

*At the back, near the center, is a door to the toilet; on it are hooks for clothing. The back wall is bare but for a large spindle on which orders are impaled every morning and taken off and filled by the workers all day long. At center there is an ancient desk and chair. Downstage right is a small bench. Boxes, a roll of packing paper on the table, and general untidiness. This place is rarely swept.*

*The right and left walls are composed of corridor openings, a louverlike effect, leading out into the alleys which are lined with bins reaching to the ceiling. Downstage center there is a large cast-iron floor scale with weights and balance exposed.*

*The nature of the work is simple. The men take orders off the hook, go out into the bin-lined alleys, fill the orders, bring the merchandise back to the table, where* KENNETH *packs and addresses everything. The desk is used by* GUS *and/or* TOM KELLY *to figure postage or express rates on, to eat on, to lean on, or to hide things in. It is just home base, generally.*

*A warning: The place must seem dirty and unmanageably chaotic, but since it is seen in this play with two separate visions it is also romantic. It is a little world, a home to which, unbelievably perhaps, these people like to come every Monday morning, despite what they say.*
*It is a hot Monday morning in summer, just before nine.*

*The stage is empty for a moment; then* BERT *enters. He is eighteen. His trousers are worn at the knees but not unrespectable; he has rolled-up sleeves and is tieless. He carries a thick book, a large lunch in a brown paper bag, and a New York Times. He stores the lunch behind the packing table, clears a place on the table, sits and opens the paper, reads.*

*Enter* RAYMOND RYAN, *the manager. He wears a tie, white shirt, pressed pants, carries a clean towel, a tabloid, and in the other hand a sheaf of orders.*

RAYMOND *is forty, weighed down by responsibilities, afraid to be kind, quite able to be tough. He walks with the suggestion of a stoop.*

*He goes directly to a large hook set in the back wall and impales the orders.* BERT *sees him but, getting no greeting, re-*

*turns to his paper. Preoccupied,* RAYMOND *walks past* BERT *toward the toilet, then halts in thought, turns back to* BERT.

RAYMOND: Tommy Kelly get in yet?

BERT: I haven't seen him, but I just got here myself.

*Raymond nods slightly, worried.*

He'll probably make it all right.

RAYMOND: What are you doing in so early?

BERT: I wanted to get a seat on the subway for once. Boy, it's nice to walk around in the streets before the crowds get out . . .

RAYMOND (*he has never paid much attention to Bert, is now curious, has time for it*): How do you get time to read that paper?

BERT: Well, I've got an hour and ten minutes on the subway. I don't read it all, though. Just reading about Hitler.

RAYMOND: Who's that?

BERT: He took over the German government last week.

RAYMOND (*nodding, uninterested*): Listen, I want you to sweep up that excelsior laying around the freight elevator.

BERT: Okay. I had a lot of orders on Saturday, so I didn't get to it.

RAYMOND (*self-consciously; thus almost in mockery*): I hear you're going to go to college. Is that true?

BERT (*embarrassed*): Oh, I don't know, Mr. Ryan. They may not even let me in, I got such bad marks in high school.

RAYMOND: *You* did?

BERT: Oh, yeah. I just played ball and fooled around, that's all. I think I wasn't listening, y'know?

RAYMOND: How much it going to cost you?

BERT: I guess about four, five hundred for the first year. So I'll be here a long time—if I ever do go. You ever go to college?

RAYMOND (*shaking his head negatively*): My kid brother went to pharmacy though. What are you going to take up?

BERT: I really don't know. You look through that catalogue—boy, you feel like taking it all, you know?

RAYMOND: This the same book you been reading?

BERT: Well, it's pretty long, and I fall asleep right after supper.

RAYMOND (*turning the book up*): "War and Peace"?

BERT: Yeah, he's supposed to be a great writer.

RAYMOND: How long it take you to read a book like this?

BERT: Oh, probably about three, four months, I guess. It's hard on the subway, with all those Russian names.

RAYMOND (*putting the book down*): What do you get out of a book like that?

BERT: Well, it's—it's literature.

RAYMOND (*nodding, mystified*): Be sure to open those three crates of axles that came in Saturday, will you? (*He starts to go toward the toilet.*)

BERT: I'll get to it this morning.

RAYMOND: And let me know when you decide to leave. I'll have to get somebody—

BERT: Oh, that'll be another year. Don't worry about it. I've got to save it all up first. I'm probably just dreaming anyway.

RAYMOND: How much do you save?

BERT: About eleven or twelve a week.

RAYMOND: Out of fifteen?

BERT: Well, I don't buy much. And my mother gives me my lunch.

RAYMOND: Well, sweep up around the elevator, will you?

RAYMOND *starts for the toilet as* AGNES *enters. She is a spinster in her late forties, always on the verge of laughter.*

AGNES: Morning, Ray!

RAYMOND: Morning, Agnes. (*He exits into the toilet.*)

AGNES (*to* BERT): Bet you wish you could go swimming, heh?

BERT: Boy, I wouldn't mind. It's starting to boil already.

AGNES: You ought to meet my nephew sometime, Bert. He's a wonderful swimmer. Really, you'd like him. He's very serious.

BERT: How old is he now?

AGNES: He's only thirteen, but he reads the *New York Times* too.

BERT: Yeah?

AGNES (*noticing the book*): You still reading that book?

BERT (*embarrassed*): Well, I only get time on the subway, Agnes—

AGNES: Don't let any of them kid you, Bert. You go ahead. You read the *New York Times* and all that. What happened today?

BERT: Hitler took over the German government.

AGNES: Oh, yes; my nephew knows about him. He loves civics. Last week one night he made a regular speech to all of us in the living room, and I realized that everything Roosevelt has done is absolutely illegal. Did you know that? Even my brother-in-law had to admit it, and he's a Democrat.

*Enter* PATRICIA *on her way to the toilet. She is twenty-three, blankly pretty, dressed just a little too tightly. She is not quite sure who she is yet.*

PATRICIA: Morning!

AGNES: Morning, Patricia! Where did you get that pin?

PATRICIA: It was given. (*She glances at Bert, who blushes.*)

AGNES: Oh, Patricia! Which one is he?

PATRICIA: Oh, somebody.

*She starts past for the toilet;* BERT *utters a warning "Ugh,"
and she remains.*

AGNES (*she tends to laugh constantly, softly*): Did you go to the
dance Saturday night?

PATRICIA (*fixing her clothing*): Well, they're always ending up
with six guys in the hospital at that dance, and like that, so
we went bowling.

AGNES: Did he give you that pin?

PATRICIA: No, I had a date after him.

AGNES (*laughing, titillated*): Pat!

PATRICIA: Well, I forgot all about him. So when I got home he
was still sitting in front of the house in his car. I thought he
was going to murder me. But isn't it an unusual pin? (*To*
BERT, *who has moved off:*) What are you always running
away for?

BERT (*embarrassed*): I was just getting ready to work, that's all.

*Enter* GUS. *He is sixty-eight, a barrel-bellied man, totally
bald, with a long, fierce, gray mustache that droops on the
right side. He wears a bowler, and his pants are a little too
short. He has a ready-made clip-on tie. He wears winter un-
derwear all summer long, changes once a week. There is
something neat and dusty about him—a rolling gait, bandy
legs, a belly hard as a rock and full of beer. He speaks with
a gruff Slavic accent.*

PATRICIA: Oh, God, here's King Kong. (*She goes out up one of
the corridors.*)

GUS (*calling after her halfheartedly—he is not completely sober,
not bright yet*): You let me get my hands on you I give you
King Kong!

AGNES (*laughing*): Oh, Gus, don't say those things!

GUS (*going for her*): Aggie, you make me crazy for you!

AGNES (*laughing and running from him toward the toilet door*): Gus!

GUS: Agnes, let's go Atlantic City!

*AGNES starts to open the toilet door. RAYMOND emerges from it.*

AGNES (*surprised by* RAYMOND): Oh!

RAYMOND (*with plaintive anger*): Gus! Why don't you cut it out, heh?

GUS: Oh, I'm sick and tired, Raymond.

*Agnes goes into the toilet.*

RAYMOND: How about getting all the orders shipped out by to-night, heh, Gus—for once?

GUS: What I did? I did something?

RAYMOND: Where's Jim?

GUS: How do I know where's Jim? Jim is my brother?

*JIM enters, stiff. He is in his mid-seventies, wears bent eye-glasses; has a full head of hair; pads about with careful tread.*

JIM (*dimly*): Morning, Raymond.

*He walks as though he will fall forward. All watch as* JIM *aims his jacket for a hook, then, with a sudden motion, makes it. But he never really sways.*

GUS: Attaboy, Jim! (*To* RAYMOND:) What you criticize Jim? Look at that!

JIM (*turning to* RAYMOND *with an apologetic smile*): Morning, Raymond. Hot day today. (*He goes to the spike and takes orders off it.*)

RAYMOND: Now look, Gus, Mr. Eagle is probably going to come today, so let's have everything going good, huh?

GUS: You can take Mr. Eagle and you shove him!

*AGNES enters from the toilet.*

RAYMOND: What's the matter with you? I don't want that language around here any more. I'm not kidding, either. It's getting worse and worse, and we've got orders left over every night. Let's get straightened out here, will you? It's the same circus every Monday morning. (*He goes out.*)

AGNES: How's Lilly? Feeling better?

GUS: She's all the time sick, Agnes. I think she gonna die.

AGNES: Oh, don't say that. Pray to God, Gus.

GUS (*routinely*): Aggie, come with me Atlantic City. (*He starts taking off his shirt.*)

AGNES (*going from him*): Oh, how you smell!

GUS (*loudly*): I stink, Aggie!

AGNES (*closing her ears, laughing*): Oh, Gus, you're so terrible! (*She rushes out.*)

GUS (*laughs loudly, tauntingly, and turns to* BERT): What are you doin'? It's nine o'clock.

BERT: Oh. (*He gets off the bench.*) I've got five to. Is your wife really sick? (*He gets an order from the hook.*)

GUS: You don't see Jim wait till nine o'clock! (*He goes to* JIM, *who is looking through the orders, and puts an arm around him.*) Goddam Raymond. You hear what he says to me?

JIM: Ssh, Gus, it's all right. Maybe better call Lilly.

GUS (*grasping* JIM's *arm*): Wanna beer?

JIM (*trying to disengage himself*): No, Gus, let's behave ourselves. Come on.

GUS (*looking around*): Oh, boy. Oh, goddam boy. Monday morning. Ach.

JIM (*to* BERT, *as he starts out*): Did you unpack those axles yet?

GUS (*taking the order out of* JIM's *hand*): What are you doing with axles? Man your age! (*He gives* BERT JIM's *order.*)

Bert! Here! You let him pick up heavy stuff I show you something! Go!

BERT: I always take Jim's heavy orders, Gus. (*He goes out with the orders.*)

GUS: Nice girls, heh, Jim?

JIM: Oh, darn nice. Darn nice girls, Gus.

GUS: I keep my promise, hah, Jim?

JIM: You did, Gus. I enjoyed myself. But maybe you ought to call up your wife. She might be wonderin' about you. You been missin' since Saturday, Gus.

GUS (*asking for a reminder*): Where we was yesterday?

JIM: That's when we went to Staten Island, I think. On the ferry? Remember? With the girls? I think we was on a ferry. So it must've been to Staten Island. You better call her.

GUS: Ach—She don't hear nothing, Jim.

JIM: But if the phone rings, Gus, she'll know you're all right.

GUS: All right, I ring the phone.

*He goes and dials.* JIM *leaves with his orders.*

PATRICIA *enters.*

PATRICIA: Morning, Kong!

GUS: Shatap.

*She goes into the toilet as* GUS *listens on the phone. Then he roars:*

Hallo! *Hallo!* Lilly! Gus! *Gus!* How you feel? *Gus!* Working! Ya! Ya! *Gus!* Oh, shatap!

*He hangs up the phone angrily, confused.* JIM *enters with a few small boxes, which he sets in a pile on the table.*

JIM: You call her?

GUS: Oh, Jim, she don't hear nothing.

*He goes idly to the toilet, opens the door.* PATRICIA *screams within, and* GUS *stands there in the open doorway, screaming with her in parody, then lets the door shut.*

*JIM starts out, examining his order, a pencil in his hand, as* KENNETH *enters, lunch in hand.* KENNETH *is twenty-six, a strapping, fair-skinned man, with thinning hair, delicately shy, very strong. He has only recently come to the country.*

JIM: Morning, Kenneth.

KENNETH: And how are you this fine exemplary morning, James?

JIM: Oh, comin' along. Goin' to be hot today. (*He goes out.*)

KENNETH *hangs up his jacket and stores his lunch.* GUS *is standing in thought, picking his ear with a pencil.*

KENNETH: Havin' yourself a thought this morning, Gus?

GUS *just looks at him, then goes back to his thought and his excavation.*

Gus, don't you think something could be done about the dust constantly fallin' through the air of this place? Don't you imagine a thing or two could be done about that?

GUS: Because it's dusty, that's why. (*He goes to the desk, sits.*)

KENNETH: That's what I was sayin'—it's dusty. Tommy Kelly get in?

GUS: No.

KENNETH: Oh, poor Tommy Kelly. (BERT *enters.*) Good morning to you, Bert. Have you finished your book yet?

BERT (*setting two heavy axles on the bench*): Not yet, Kenneth.

KENNETH (*his jacket in his hand*): Well, don't lose heart. (*He orates:*)

> "Courage, brother! do not stumble
>     Though thy path be dark as night;
> There's a star to guide the humble;
>     Trust in God, and do the Right."

By Norman Macleod.

BERT (*with wonder, respect*): How'd you learn all that poetry?

KENNETH (*hanging up his jacket*): Why, in Ireland, Bert; there's all kinds of useless occupations in Ireland. "When lilacs last in the dooryard bloom'd . . ."

GUS (*from the desk*): What the hell you doin'?

BERT *goes to order hook.*

KENNETH: Why, it's the poetry hour, Gus, don't you know that? This is the hour all men rise to thank God for the blue of the sky, the roundness of the everlasting globe, and the cheerful cleanliness of the subway system. And here we have some axles. Oh, Bert, I never thought I would end me life wrappin' brown paper around strange axles. (*He wraps.*) And what's the latest in the *New York Times* this morning?

BERT (*looking through orders on the hook*): Hitler took over the German government.

KENNETH: Oh, did he! Strange, isn't it, about the Germans? A great people they are for mustaches. You take Bismarck, now, or you take Frederick the Great, or even take Gus over here—

GUS: I'm no Heinie.

KENNETH: Why, I always thought you were, Gus. What are you, then?

GUS: American.

KENNETH: I know that, but what *are* you?

GUS: I fought in submarine.

KENNETH: Did you, now? An American submarine?

GUS: What the hell kind of submarine I fight in, Hungarian? (*He turns back to his desk.*)

KENNETH: Well, don't take offense, Gus. There's all kinds of submarines, y'know.

BERT *starts out, examining his order.*

How's this to be wrapped, Bert? Express?

BERT: I think that goes parcel post. It's for Skaneateles.

GUS (*erupting at his desk*): Axles parcel post? You crazy? You know how much gonna cost axles parcel post?

BERT: That's right. I guess it goes express.

GUS: And you gonna go college? Barber college you gonna go!

BERT: Well, I forgot it was axles, Gus.

GUS (*muttering over his desk*): Stupid.

KENNETH: I've never been to Skaneateles. Where would that be?

BERT: It's a little town upstate. It's supposed to be pretty there.

KENNETH: That a sweet thought? Sendin' these two grimy axles out into the green countryside? I spent yesterday in the park. What did you do, Bert? Go swimmin' again, I suppose?

GUS (*turning*): You gonna talk all day?

BERT: We're working.

*He goes out.* KENNETH *wraps.*

KENNETH: You're rubbin' that poor kid pretty hard, Gus; he's got other things on his mind than parcel post and—

GUS: What the hell I care what he got on his mind? Axles he gonna send parcel post! (*He returns to his work on the desk.*)

KENNETH (*wraps, then*): Can you feel the heat rising in this building! If only some of it could be saved for the winter. (*Pause. He is wrapping.*) The fiery furnace. Nebuchadnezzar was the architect. (*Pause.*) What do you suppose would happen, Gus, if a man took it into his head to wash these windows? They'd snatch him off to the nuthouse, heh? (*Pause.*) I wonder if he's only kiddin'—Bert. About goin' to college someday.

GUS (*not turning from his desk*): Barber college he gonna go.

KENNETH (*he works, thinking*): He must have a wealthy family. Still and all, he don't spend much. I suppose he's just got some strong idea in his mind. That's the thing, y'know. I often conceive them myself, but I'm all the time losin' them, though. It's the holdin' on—that's what does it. You can almost see it in him, y'know? He's holdin' on to somethin'. (*He shakes his head in wonder, then sings:*)

> Oh, the heat of the summer,
> The cool of the fall.
> The lady went swimming
> With nothing at all.

Ah, that's a filthy song, isn't it! (*Pause. He wraps.*) Gus, you suppose Mr. Roosevelt'll be makin' it any better than it is? (*He sings:*)

> The minstrel boy to the war has gone,
> In the ranks of death . . .

PATRICIA *enters from the toilet.*

PATRICIA: Was that an Irish song?

KENNETH (*shyly*): All Irish here and none of yiz knows an Irish song.

PATRICIA: You have a terrific voice, Kenneth.

GUS (*to* PATRICIA): Why don't you make date with him?

KENNETH (*stamping his foot*): Oh, that's a nasty thing to say in front of a girl, Gus!

GUS *rises.*

PATRICIA (*backing away from* GUS): Now don't start with me, kid, because—

GUS *lunges for her. She turns to run, and he squeezes her buttocks mercilessly as she runs out and almost collides with* LARRY, *who is entering.* LARRY *is thirty-nine, a troubled but phlegmatic man, good-looking. He is carrying a container of coffee and a lighted cigarette. On the collision he spills a little coffee.*

LARRY (*with a slight humor*): Hey! Take it easy.

PATRICIA (*quite suddenly all concerned for* LARRY, *to* GUS): Look what you did, you big horse!

*LARRY sets the coffee on the table.*

LARRY: Jesus, Gus.

GUS: Tell her stop makin' all the men crazy! (*He returns to his desk.*)

PATRICIA: I'm sorry, Larry.

*She is alone, in effect, with* LARRY. *Both of them wipe the spot on his shirt.*

Did you buy it?

LARRY (*embarrassed but courageous, as though inwardly flaunting his own fears*): Yeah, I got it yesterday.

PATRICIA: Gee, I'd love to see it. You ever going to bring it to work?

LARRY (*now he meets her eyes*): I might. On a Saturday, maybe.

PATRICIA: 'Cause I love those Auburns, y'know?

LARRY: Yeah, they got nice valves. Maybe I'll drive you home some night. For the ride.

PATRICIA (*the news stuns her*): Oh, boy! Well—I'll see ya. (*She goes.*)

GUS: You crazy? Buy Auburn?

LARRY (*with depth—a profound conclusion*): I like the valves, Gus.

GUS: Yeah, but when you gonna go sell it who gonna buy an Auburn?

LARRY: Didn't you ever get to where you don't care about that? I *always* liked those valves, and I decided, that's all.

GUS: Yeah, but when you gonna go sell it—

LARRY: I don't care.

GUS: You don't care!

LARRY: I'm sick of dreaming about things. They've got the most beautifully laid-out valves in the country on that car, and I want it, that's all.

KENNETH *is weighing a package on the scales.*

GUS: Yeah, but when you gonna go sell it—

LARRY: I just don't care, Gus. Can't you understand that? (*He stares away, inhaling his cigarette.*)

KENNETH (*stooped over, sliding the scale weights*): There's a remarkable circumstance, Larry. Raymond's got twins, and now you with the triplets. And both in the same corporation. We ought to send that to the *Daily News* or something. I think they give you a dollar for an item like that.

BERT *enters, puts goods on the table.*

BERT: Gee, I'm getting hungry. Want a sandwich, Kenneth? (*He reaches behind the packing table for his lunch bag.*)

KENNETH: Thank you, Bert. I might take one later.

GUS (*turning from the desk to* BERT): Lunch you gonna eat nine o'clock?

BERT: I got up too early this morning. You want some?

KENNETH: He's only a growing boy, Gus—and by the way, if you care to bend down, Gus—(*Indicating under the scale platform.*)—there's more mice than ever under here.

GUS (*without turning*): Leave them mice alone.

KENNETH: Well, you're always complainin' the number of crayons I'm using, and I'm only tellin' you they're the ones is eatin' them up. (*He turns to* LARRY.) It's a feast of crayons goin' on here every night, Larry.

*Enter* JIM *with goods, padding along.*

JIM: Goin' to be hot today, Gus.

GUS: Take easy, what you running for?

JIM *stops to light his cigar butt.*

KENNETH (*reading off the scale weights*): Eighty-one pounds, Gus. For Skaneateles, in the green countryside of upper New York State.

GUS: What? What you want?

KENNETH: I want the express order—eighty-one pounds to Skaneateles, New York.

GUS: Then why don't you say that, goddam Irishman? You talk so much. When you gonna stop talkin'? (*He proceeds to make out the slip.*)

KENNETH: Oh, when I'm rich, Gus, I'll have very little more to say.

GUS *is busy making out the slip;* KENNETH *turns to* LARRY.

No sign yet of Tommy Kelly in the place, Larry.

LARRY: What'd you, cut a hole in your shoe?

KENNETH: A breath of air for me little toe. I only paid a quarter for them, y'know; feller was sellin' them in Bryant Park. Slightly used, but they're a fine pair of shoes, you can see that.

LARRY: They look small for you.

KENNETH: They are at that. But you can't complain for a quarter, I guess.

GUS: Here.

GUS *hands* KENNETH *an express slip, which* KENNETH *now proceeds to attach to the package on the table. Meanwhile* JIM *has been leafing through the orders on the hook and is now leaving with two in his hand.*

KENNETH: How do you keep up your strength, Jim? I'm always exhausted. You never stop movin', do ya?

JIM *just shakes his head with a "Heh, heh."*

I bet it's because you never got married, eh?

JIM: No, I guess I done everything there is but that.

LARRY: How come you never did get married, Jim?

JIM: Well, I was out West so long, you know, Larry. Out West.

*He starts to go again.*

KENNETH: Oh, don't they get married much out there?

JIM: Well, the cavalry was amongst the Indians most of the time.

BERT: How old are you now, Jim? No kidding.

KENNETH: I'll bet he's a hundred.

JIM: Me? No. I ain't no hunderd. I ain't near a hunderd. You don't have to be a hunderd to've fought the Indians. They was more Indians was fought than they tells in the schoolbooks, y'know. They was a hell of a lot of fightin' up to McKinley and all in there. I ain't no hunderd. (*He starts out.*)

KENNETH: Well, how old would you say you are, Jim?

JIM: Oh, I'm seventy-four, seventy-five, seventy-six—around in there. But I ain't no hunderd.

*He exits, and* KENNETH *sneezes.*

BERT (*he has put his lunch bag away and is about to leave*): Boy, I was hungry!

KENNETH (*irritated*): Larry, don't you suppose a word might be passed to Mr. Eagle about the dust? It's rainin' dust from the ceiling!

*BERT goes out.*

GUS: What the hell Mr. Eagle gonna do about the dust?

KENNETH: Why, he's supposed to be a brilliant man, isn't he? Dartmouth College graduate and all? I've been five and a half months in this country, and I never sneezed so much in my entire life before. My nose is all—

*Enter* FRANK, *the truckdriver, an impassive, burly man in his thirties.*

FRANK: Anything for the West Bronx?

KENNETH: Nothin' yet, Frank. I've only started, though.

JIM *enters with little boxes, which he adds to the pile on the bench.*

FRANK: You got anything for West Bronx, Jim? I've got the truck on the elevator.

GUS: What's the hurry?

FRANK: I got the truck on the elevator.

GUS: Well, take it off the elevator! You got one little box of bearings for the West Bronx. You can't go West Bronx with one little box.

FRANK: Well, I gotta go.

GUS: You got a little pussy in the West Bronx.

FRANK: Yeah, I gotta make it before lunch.

JIM (*riffling through his orders*): I think I got something for the East Bronx.

FRANK: No, West Bronx.

JIM (*removing one order from his batch*): How about Brooklyn?

FRANK: What part? (*He takes* JIM's *order, reads the address, looks up, thinking.*)

JIM: Didn't you have a girl around Williamsburg?

FRANK: I'll have to make a call. I'll be right back.

GUS: You gonna deliver only where you got a woman?

FRANK: No, Gus, I go any place you tell me. But as long as I'm goin' someplace I might as well—you know. (*He starts out.*)

GUS: You some truckdriver.

FRANK: You said it, Gus. (*He goes out.*)

GUS: Why don't you go with him sometime, Kenneth? Get yourself nice piece ding-a-ling—

KENNETH: Oh, don't be nasty now, Gus. You're only tryin' to be nasty to taunt me.

RAYMOND *enters.*

RAYMOND: Didn't Tommy Kelly get here?

GUS: Don't worry for Tommy. Tommy going to be all right.

LARRY: Can I see you a minute, Ray?

*He moves with* RAYMOND *over to the left.*

RAYMOND: Eagle's coming today, and if he sees him drunk again I don't know what I'm going to do.

LARRY: Ray, I'd like you to ask Eagle something for me.

RAYMOND: What?

LARRY: I've got to have more money.

RAYMOND: You and me both, boy.

LARRY: No, I can't make it any more, Ray. I mean it. The car put me a hundred and thirty bucks in the hole. If one of the kids gets sick I'll be strapped.

RAYMOND: Well, what'd you buy the car for?

LARRY: I'm almost forty, Ray. What am I going to be careful for?

RAYMOND: See, the problem is, Larry, if you go up, I'm only making thirty-eight myself, and I'm the manager, so it's two raises—

LARRY: Ray, I hate to make it tough for you, but my wife is driving me nuts. Now—

*Enter* JERRY MAXWELL *and* WILLY HOGAN, *both twenty-three.* JERRY *has a black eye; both are slick dressers.*

JERRY *and* WILLY: Morning. Morning, Gus.

RAYMOND: Aren't you late, fellas?

JERRY (*glancing at his gold wristwatch*): I've got one minute to nine, Mr. Ryan.

WILLY: That's Hudson Tubes time, Mr. Ryan.

GUS: The stopwatch twins.

RAYMOND (*to* JERRY): You got a black eye?

JERRY: Yeah, we went to a dance in Jersey City last night.

WILLY: Ran into a wise guy in Jersey City, Mr. Ryan.

JERRY (*with his taunting grin; he is very happy with himself*):
Tried to take his girl away from us.

RAYMOND: Well, get on the ball. Mr. Eagle's—

*Enter* TOM KELLY. GUS *rises from the desk.* BERT *enters, stands
still.* RAYMOND *and* LARRY *stand watching.* KENNETH *stops
wrapping.* TOM *is stiff; he moves in a dream to the chair* GUS
*has left and sits rigidly. He is a slight, graying clerk in his
late forties.*

GUS (*to* RAYMOND): Go 'way, go 'head.

RAYMOND *comes up and around the desk to face* TOM, *who sits
there, staring ahead, immobile, his hands in his lap.*

RAYMOND: Tommy.

JERRY *and* WILLY *titter.*

GUS (*to them*): Shatap, goddam bums!

JERRY: Hey, don't call me—

GUS: Shatap, goddamit I break you goddam head!

*He has an axle in his hand, and* RAYMOND *and* LARRY *are pulling his arm down.* JIM *enters and goes directly to him. All
are crying, "Gus! Cut it out! Put it down!"*

JERRY: What'd we do? What'd I say?

GUS: Watch out! Just watch out you make fun of this man! I
break you head, both of you!

*Silence. He goes to* TOM, *who has not moved since arriving.*

Tommy. Tommy, you hear Gus? Tommy?

TOM *is transfixed.*

RAYMOND: Mr. Eagle is coming today, Tommy.

GUS (*to all*): Go 'head, go to work, go to work!

*They all move;* JERRY *and* WILLY *go out.*

RAYMOND: Can you hear me, Tom? Mr. Eagle is coming to look things over today, Tom.

JIM: Little shot of whiskey might bring him to.

GUS: Bert! (*He reaches into his pocket.*) Here, go downstairs bring a shot. Tell him for Tommy. (*He sees what is in his hand.*) I only got ten cents.

RAYMOND: Here.

*He reaches into his pocket as* JIM, KENNETH, *and* LARRY *all reach into their own pockets.*

BERT (taking a coin from RAYMOND): Okay, I'll be right up. (*He hurries out.*)

RAYMOND: Well, this is it, Gus. I gave him his final warning.

GUS (*he is worried*): All right, go 'way, go 'way.

AGNES *enters.*

AGNES: Is he—?

RAYMOND: You heard me, Agnes. I told him on Saturday, didn't I? (*He starts past her.*)

AGNES: But Ray, look how nice and clean he came in today. His hair is all combed, and he's much neater.

RAYMOND: I did my best, Agnes. (*He goes out.*)

GUS (*staring into* TOMMY's *dead eyes*): Ach. He don't see nothin', Agnes.

AGNES (*looking into* TOMMY's *face*): And he's supposed to be saving for his daughter's confirmation dress! Oh, Tommy. I'd better cool his face. (*She goes into the toilet.*)

KENNETH (*to* LARRY): Ah, you can't blame the poor feller; sixteen years of his life in this place.

LARRY: You said it.

KENNETH: There's a good deal of monotony connected with the life, isn't it?

LARRY: You ain't kiddin'.

KENNETH: Oh, there must be a terrible lot of Monday mornings in sixteen years. And no philosophical idea at all, y'know, to pass the time?

GUS (*to* KENNETH): When you gonna shut up?

*Agnes comes from the toilet with a wet cloth. They watch as she washes* TOM's *face.*

KENNETH: Larry, you suppose we could get these windows washed sometime? I've often thought if we could see a bit of the sky now and again it would help matters now and again.

LARRY: They've never been washed since I've been here.

KENNETH: I'd do it myself if I thought they wouldn't all be laughin' at me for a greenhorn. (*He looks out through the open window, which only opens out a few inches.*) With all this glass we might observe the clouds and the various signs of approaching storms. And there might even be a bird now and again.

AGNES: Look at that—he doesn't even move. And he's been try-ing so hard! Nobody gives him credit, but he does try hard. (*To* LARRY:) See how nice and clean he comes in now?

JIM *enters, carrying parts.*

JIM: Did you try blowing in his ear?

GUS: Blow in his ear?

JIM: Yeah, the Indians used to do that. Here, wait a minute.

*He comes over, takes a deep breath, and blows into* TOM's *ear. A faint smile begins to appear on* TOM's *face, but, as* JIM *runs out of breath, it fades.*

KENNETH: Well, I guess he's not an Indian.

JIM: That's the truth, y'know. Out West, whenever there'd be a drunken Indian, they used to blow in his ear.

*Enter* BERT, *carefully carrying a shotglass of whiskey.*

GUS: Here, gimme that. (*He takes it.*)

BERT (*licking his fingers*): Boy, that stuff is strong.

GUS: Tommy? (*He holds the glass in front of* TOM's *nose.*) Whiskey. (TOM *doesn't move.*) Mr. Eagle is coming today, Tommy.

JIM: Leave it on the desk. He might wake up to it.

BERT: How's he manage to make it here, I wonder.

AGNES: Oh, he's awake. Somewhere inside, y'know. He just can't show it, somehow. It's not really like being drunk, even.

KENNETH: Well, it's pretty close, though, Agnes.

AGNES *resumes wetting* TOM's *brow.*

LARRY: Is that a fact, Jim, about blowing in a guy's ear?

JIM: Oh, sure. Indians always done that. (*He goes to the order book, leafs through.*)

KENNETH: What did yiz all have against the Indians?

JIM: The Indians? Oh, we didn't have nothin' against the Indians. Just law and order, that's all. Talk about heat, though. It was so hot out there we—

JIM *exits with an order as* FRANK *enters.*

FRANK: All right, I'll go to Brooklyn.

GUS: Where you running? I got nothing packed yet.

*Enter* JERRY, *who puts goods on the table.*

FRANK: Well, you beefed that I want to go Bronx, so I'm tellin' you now I'll go to Brooklyn.

GUS: You all fixed up in Brooklyn?

FRANK: Yeah, I just made a call.

AGNES (*laughing*): Oh, you're all so terrible! (*She goes out.*)

JERRY: How you doin', Kenny? You gittin' any?

KENNETH: Is that all two fine young fellas like you is got on your minds?

JERRY: Yeah, that's all. What's on your mind?

FRANK *is loading himself with packages.*

GUS (*of* TOMMY): What am I gonna do with him, Larry? The old man's comin'.

LARRY: Tell you the truth, Gus, I'm sick and tired of worrying about him, y'know? Let him take care of himself.

GUS *goes to* LARRY, *concerned, and they speak quietly.*

GUS: What's the matter with you these days?

LARRY: Two years I'm asking for a lousy five-dollar raise. Meantime my brother's into me for fifty bucks for his wife's special shoes; my sister's got me for sixty-five to have her kid's teeth fixed. So I buy a car, and they're all on my back —how'd I dare buy a car! Whose money is it? Y'know, Gus? I mean—

GUS: Yeah, but an Auburn Larry—

LARRY (*getting hot*): I happen to like the valves! What's so unusual about that?

*Enter* WILLY *and* JERRY *with goods.*

WILLY (*to* JERRY): Here! Ask Frank. (*To* FRANK:) Who played shortstop for Pittsburgh in nineteen-twenty-four?

FRANK: Pittsburgh? Honus Wagner, wasn't it?

WILLY (*to* JERRY): What I tell ya?

JERRY: How could it be Honus Wagner? Honus Wagner—

RAYMOND *enters with a* MECHANIC, *and* WILLY *and* JERRY *exit, arguing.* FRANK *goes out with his packages.* GUS *returns to his desk.*

RAYMOND: Larry, you want to help this man? He's got a part here.

LARRY *simply turns, silent, with a hurt and angry look. The mechanic goes to him, holds out the part; but* LARRY *does not take it, merely inspects it, for it is greasy, as is the man.*

RAYMOND (*going to the desk, where* GUS *is now seated at work beside* TOM KELLY): Did he move at all, Gus?

GUS: He's feeling much better, I can see. Go, go 'way, Raymond.

RAYMOND *worriedly stands there.*

LARRY (*to* MECHANIC): Where you from?

MECHANIC: I'm mechanic over General Truck.

LARRY: What's that off?

MECHANIC (*as* BERT *stops to watch, and* KENNETH *stops packing to observe*): That's the thing—I don't know. It's a very old coal truck, see, and I thought it was a Mack, because it says Mack on the radiator, see? But I went over to Mack, and they says there's no part like that on any Mack in their whole history, see?

LARRY: Is there any name on the engine?

MECHANIC: I'm tellin' you; on the engine it says American-La-France—must be a replacement engine.

LARRY: That's not off a LaFrance.

MECHANIC: I know! I went over to America-LaFrance, but they says they never seen nothin' like that in their whole life since the year one.

RAYMOND *joins them.*

LARRY: What is it, off the manifold?

MECHANIC: Well, it ain't exactly off the manifold. It like sticks out, see, except it don't stick out, it's like stuck in there—I mean it's like in a little hole there on top of the head, except it ain't exactly a hole, it's a thing that comes up in like a bump, see, and then it goes down. Two days I'm walkin' the streets with this, my boss is goin' crazy.

LARRY: Well, go find out what it is, and if we got it we'll sell it to you.

RAYMOND: Don't you have any idea, Larry?

LARRY: I might, Ray, but I'm not getting paid for being an encyclopedia. There's ten thousand obsolete parts upstairs—it was never my job to keep all that in my head. If the old man wants that service, let him pay somebody to do it.

RAYMOND: Ah, Larry, the guy's here with the part.

LARRY: The guy is always here with the part, Ray. Let him hire somebody to take an inventory up there and see what it costs him.

RAYMOND (*taking the part off the table*): Well, I'll see what I can find up there.

LARRY: You won't find it, Ray. Put it down.

RAYMOND *does, and* LARRY, *blinking with hurt, turns to the* MECHANIC.

What is that truck, about nineteen-twenty-two?

MECHANIC: That truck? (*He shifts onto his right foot in thought.*)

LARRY: Nineteen-twenty?

MECHANIC (*in a higher voice, shifting to the left foot*): That truck?

LARRY: Well, it's at least nineteen-twenty, isn't it?

MECHANIC: Oh, it's at least. I brung over a couple a friends of mine, and one of them is an old man and he says when he was a boy already that truck was an old truck, and he's an old, old man, that guy.

LARRY *takes the part now and sets it on the packing bench. Now even* GUS *gets up to watch as he stares at the part. There is a hush.* RAYMOND *goes out.* LARRY *turns the part a little and stares at it again. Now he sips his coffee.*

I understand this company's got a lot of old parts from the olden days, heh?

LARRY: We may have one left, if it's what I think it is, but you'll have to pay for it.

MECHANIC: Oh, I know; that's why my boss says try all the other places first, because he says youse guys charge. But looks to me like we're stuck.

LARRY: Bert. (*He stares in thought.*) Get the key to the third floor from Miss Molloy. Go up there, and when you open the door you'll see those Model-T mufflers stacked up.

BERT: Okay.

LARRY: You ever been up there?

BERT: No, but I always wanted to go.

LARRY: Well, go past the mufflers and you'll see a lot of bins going up to the ceiling. They're full of Marmon valves and ignition stuff.

BERT: Yeah?

LARRY: Go past them, and you'll come to a little corridor, see?

BERT: Yeah?

LARRY: At the end of the corridor is a pile of crates—I think there's some Maxwell differentials in there.

BERT: Yeah?

LARRY: Climb over the crates, but don't keep goin', see. Stand on top of the crates and turn right. Then bend down, and there's a bin—No, I tell you, get off the crates, and you can reach behind them, but to the right, and reach into that bin. There's a lot of Locomobile headnuts in there, but way back—you gotta stick your hand way in, see, and you'll find one of these.

BERT: Geez, Larry, how do you remember all that?

*AGNES rushes in.*

AGNES: Eagle's here! Eagle's here!

LARRY (*to the* MECHANIC): Go out front and wait at the counter, will ya?

*The* MECHANIC *nods and leaves.* LARRY *indicates the glass on the desk.*

Better put that whiskey away, Gus.

GUS (*alarmed now*): What should we do with him?

*LARRY goes to* TOM, *peeved, and speaks in his ear.*

LARRY: Tommy. Tommy!

AGNES: Larry, why don't you put him up on the third floor? He got a dozen warnings already. Eagle's disgusted—

GUS: Maybe he's sick. I never seen him like this.

*JIM enters with goods.*

JIM: Eagle's here.

LARRY: Let's try to walk him around. Come on.

*GUS looks for a place to hide the whiskey, then drinks it.*

GUS: All right, Tommy, come on, get up.

*They hoist him up to his feet, then let him go. He starts to sag; they catch him.*

I don't think he feel so good.

LARRY: Come on, walk him. (*To* AGNES.) Watch out for Eagle.

*She stands looking off and praying silently.*

Let's go, Tom.

*They try to walk* TOM, *but he doesn't lift his feet.*

AGNES (*trembling, watching* TOMMY): He's so kindhearted, y'see? That's his whole trouble—he's too kindhearted.

LARRY (*angering, but restrained, shaking* TOM): For God's sake, Tom, come on! Eagle's here! (*He shakes* TOM *more violently.*) Come on! What the hell is the matter with you, you want to lose your job? Goddamit, you a baby or something?

AGNES: Sssh!

*They all turn to the left. In the distance is heard the clacking of heel taps on a concrete floor.*

GUS: Put him down, Larry!

*They seat* TOM *before the desk.* AGNES *swipes back his mussed hair.* GUS *sets his right hand on top of an invoice on the desk.*

Here, put him like he's writing. Where's my pencil? Who's got pencil?

LARRY, KENNETH, AGNES *search themselves for a pencil.*

KENNETH: Here's a crayon.

GUS: Goddam, who take my pencil! Bert! Where's that Bert! He always take my pencil!

BERT *enters, carrying a heavy axle.*

BERT: Hey, Eagle's here!

GUS: Goddam you, why you take my pencil?

BERT: I haven't got your pencil. This is mine.

GUS *grabs the pencil out of* BERT'S *shirt pocket and sticks it upright into* TOM'S *hand. They have set him up to look as if he is writing. They step away.* TOM *starts sagging toward one side.*

AGNES (*in a loud whisper*): Here he comes!

*She goes to the order spike and pretends she is examining it.* LARRY *meanwhile rushes to* TOM, *sets him upright, then walks away, pretending to busy himself. But* TOM *starts falling off the chair again, and* BERT *rushes and props him up.*

*The sound of the heel taps is on us now, and* BERT *starts talk-*

*ing to* TOM, *meantime supporting him with one hand on his shoulder.*

BERT (*overloudly*): Tommy, the reason I ask, see, is because on Friday I filled an order for the same amount of coils for Scranton, see, and it just seems they wouldn't be ordering the same exact amount again.

*During his speech* EAGLE *has entered—a good-looking man in his late forties, wearing palm beach trousers, a shirt and tie, sleeves neatly folded up, a new towel over one arm. He walks across the shipping room, not exactly looking at anyone, but clearly observing everything. He goes into the toilet, past* AGNES, *who turns.*

AGNES: Good morning, Mr. Eagle.

EAGLE (*nodding*): Morning. (*He goes into the toilet.*)

KENNETH (*indicating the toilet*): Keep it up, keep it up now!

BERT (*loudly*): Ah—another thing that's bothering me, Tommy, is those rear-end gears for Riverhead. I can't find any invoice for Riverhead. I can't find any invoice for gears to Riverhead. (*He is getting desperate, looks to the others, but they only urge him on.*) So what happened to the invoice? That's the thing we're all wondering about, Tommy. What happened to that invoice? You see, Tom? That invoice—it was blue, I remember, blue with a little red around the edges—

KENNETH (*loudly*): That's right there, Bert, it was a blue invoice —and it had numbers on it—

*Suddenly* TOM *stands, swaying a little, blinking. There is a moment's silence.*

TOM: No, no, Glenn Wright was shortstop for Pittsburgh, not Honus Wagner.

EAGLE *emerges from the toilet.* BERT *goes to the order spike.*

LARRY: Morning, sir. (*He goes out.*)

TOM: (*half bewildered, shifting from foot to foot*): Who was talking about Pittsburgh? (*He turns about and almost collides with* EAGLE.) Morning, Mr. Eagle.

EAGLE (*as he passes* TOM *he lets his look linger on his face*): Morning, Kelly.

EAGLE *crosses the shipping room and goes out.* AGNES, KENNETH, *and* GUS *wait an instant.* JIM *enters, sees* TOM *is up.*

JIM: Attaboy, Tommy, knew you'd make it.

TOM: Glenn Wright was shortstop. Who asked about that?

GUS (*nodding sternly his approbation to* BERT): Very good, Bert, you done good.

BERT (*wiping his forehead*): Boy!

TOM: Who was talking about Pittsburgh?

AGNES *is heard weeping. They turn.*

Agnes? (*He goes to her.*) What's the matter, Ag?

AGNES: Oh, Tommy, why do you do that?

PATRICIA (*calling from offstage left*): Aggie? Your switchboard's ringing.

AGNES: Oh, Tommy! (*Weeping, she hurries out.*)

TOM (*to the others*): What happened? What is she cryin' for?

GUS (*indicating the desk*): Why don't you go to work, Tommy? You got lotta parcel post this morning.

TOM *always has a defensive smile. He shifts from foot to foot as he talks, as though he were always standing on a hot stove. He turns to the desk, sees* KENNETH. *He wants to normalize everything.*

TOM: Kenny! I didn't even see ya!

KENNETH: Morning, Tommy. Good to see you up and about.

TOM (*with a put-on brogue*): Jasus, me bye, y'r hair is fallin' like the dew of the evenin'.

KENNETH (*self-consciously wiping his hair*): Oh, Tommy, now—

TOM: Kenny, bye, y'r gittin' an awful long face to wash!

KENNETH (*gently cuffing him*): Oh, now, stop that talk!

TOM (*backing toward his desk*): Why, ya donkey, ya. I bet they had to back you off the boat!

KENNETH (*with mock anger*): Oh, don't you be callin' me a donkey now!

*Enter* RAYMOND.

RAYMOND: Tom? (*He is very earnest, even deadly.*)

TOM (*instantly perceiving his own guilt*): Oh, mornin', Ray, how's the twins? (*He gasps little chuckles as he sits at his desk, feeling about for a pencil.*)

RAYMOND *goes up close to the desk and leans over, as the others watch—pretending not to.*

RAYMOND (*quietly*): Eagle wants to see you.

TOM (*with foreboding, looking up into* RAYMOND's *face*): Eagle? I got a lot of parcel post this morning, Ray. (*He automatically presses down his hair.*)

RAYMOND: He's in his office waiting for you now, Tom.

TOM: Oh, sure. It's just that there's a lot of parcel post on Monday . . .

*He feels for his tie as he rises, and walks out.* RAYMOND *starts out after him, but* GUS *intercedes.*

GUS (*going up to* RAYMOND): What Eagle wants?

RAYMOND: I warned him, Gus, I warned him a dozen times.

GUS: He's no gonna fire him.

RAYMOND: Look, it's all over, Gus, so there's nothing—

GUS: He gonna fire Tommy?

RAYMOND: Now don't raise your voice.

GUS: Sixteen year Tommy work here! He got daughter gonna be in church confirmation!

RAYMOND: Now listen, I been nursing him along for—

GUS: Then you fire me! You fire Tommy, you fire me!

RAYMOND: Gus!

*With a stride* GUS *goes to the hook, takes his shirt down, thrusts himself into it.*

GUS: Goddam son-of-a-bitch.

RAYMOND: Now don't be crazy, Gus.

GUS: I show who crazy! Tommy Kelly he gonna fire!

*He grabs his bowler off the hook. Enter* AGNES, *agitated.*

AGNES: Gus! Go to the phone!

GUS (*not noticing her, and with bowler on, to* RAYMOND): Come on, he gonna fire me now, son-of-a-bitch!

*He starts out, shirttails flying, and* AGNES *stops him.*

AGNES (*indicating the phone*): Gus, your neighbor's—

GUS (*trying to disengage himself*): No, he gonna fire me now. He fire Tommy Kelly, he fire me!

AGNES: Lilly, Gus! Your neighbor wants to talk to you. Go, go to the phone.

GUS *halts, looks at* AGNES.

GUS: What, Lilly?

AGNES: Something's happened. Go, go to the phone.

GUS: Lilly? (*Perplexed, he goes to the phone.*) Hallo. Yeah, Gus. Ha?

*He listens, stunned. His hand, of itself, goes to his hatbrim as though to doff the hat, but it stays there.* JIM *enters, comes to a halt, sensing the attention, and watches* GUS.

When? When it happen? (*He listens, and then mumbles:*) Ya. Thank you. I come home right away.

*He hangs up.* JIM *comes forward to him questioningly. To* JIM, *perplexed:*

My Lilly. Die.

JIM: Oh? Hm!

LARRY *enters.* GUS *dumbly turns to him.*

GUS (*to* LARRY): Die. My Lilly.

LARRY: Oh, that's tough, Gus.

RAYMOND: You better go home. (*Pause.*) Go ahead, Gus. Go home.

GUS *stands blinking.* RAYMOND *takes his jacket from the hook and helps him on with it.* AGNES *starts to push his shirttails into his pants.*

GUS: We shouldn't've go to Staten Island, Jim. Maybe she don't feel good yesterday. Ts, I was in Staten Island, maybe she was sick.

TOMMY KELLY *enters, goes directly to his desk, sits, his back to the others. Pause. To* TOM:

He fire you, Tommy?

TOM (*holding tears back*): No, Gus, I'm all right.

GUS (*going up next to him*): Give you another chance?

TOM (*he is speaking with his head lowered*): Yeah. It's all right. Gus, I'm going to be all right from now on.

GUS: Sure. Be a man, Tommy. Don't be no drunken bum. Be a man. You hear? Don't let nobody walk on top you. Be man.

TOM: I'm gonna be all right, Gus.

GUS (*nodding*): One more time you come in drunk I gonna show you something.

AGNES *sobs. He turns to her.*

What for you cry all the time?

*He goes past her and out.* AGNES *then goes. A silence.*

RAYMOND (*breaking the silence*): What do you say, fellas, let's get going, heh?

*He claps his hands and walks out as all move about their work. Soon all are gone but* TOMMY KELLY, *slumped at his desk;* KENNETH, *wrapping; and* BERT, *picking an order from the hook. Now* KENNETH *faces* BERT *suddenly.*

KENNETH (*he has taken his feeling from the departing* GUS, *and turns now to* BERT): Bert? How would you feel about washing these windows—you and I—once and for all? Let a little of God's light in the place?

BERT (*excitedly, happily*): Would you?

KENNETH: Well, I would if you would.

BERT: Okay, come on! Let's do a little every day; couple of months it'll all be clean! Gee! Look at the sun!

KENNETH: Hey, look down there!
See the old man sitting in a chair?
And roses all over the fence!
Oh, that's a lovely back yard!

*A rag in hand,* BERT *mounts the table; they make one slow swipe of the window before them and instantly all the windows around the stage burst into the yellow light of summer that floods into the room.*

BERT: Boy, they've got a tree!
And all those cats!

KENNETH: It'll be nice to watch the seasons pass.
'That pretty up there now, a real summer sky
And a little white cloud goin' over?
I can just see autumn comin' in
And the leaves falling on the gray days.
You've got to have a sky to look at!

*Gradually, as they speak, all light hardens to that of winter, finally.*

BERT (*turning to* KENNETH): Kenny, were you ever fired from a job?

KENNETH: Oh, sure; two-three times.

BERT: Did you feel bad?

KENNETH: The first time, maybe. But you have to get used to that, Bert, I'll bet you never went hungry in your life, did you?

BERT: No, I never did. Did you?

KENNETH: Oh, many and many a time. You get used to that too, though.

BERT (*turning and looking out*): That tree is turning red.

KENNETH: It must be spectacular out in the country now.

BERT: How does the cold get through these walls?
Feel it, it's almost a wind!

KENNETH: Don't cats walk dainty in the snow!

BERT: Gee, you'd never know it was the same place—
How clean it is when it's white!
Gus doesn't say much any more, y'know?

KENNETH: Well, he's showin' his age. Gus is old.
When do you buy your ticket for the train?

BERT: I did. I've got it.

KENNETH: Oh, then you're off soon!
You'll confound all the professors, I'll bet!

*He sings softly.*

"The minstrel boy to the war has gone . . ."

BERT *moves a few feet away; thus he is alone.* KENNETH *remains at the window, looking out, polishing, and singing softly.*

BERT: There's something so terrible here!

There always was, and I don't know what.
Gus, and Agnes, and Tommy and Larry, Jim and Patricia—
Why does it make me so sad to see them every morning?
It's like the subway;
Every day I see the same people getting on
And the same people getting off,
And all that happens is that they get older. God!
Sometimes it scares me; like all of us in the world
Were riding back and forth across a great big room,
From wall to wall and back again,
And no end ever! Just no end!

*He turns to* KENNETH, *but not quite looking at him, and with a deeper anxiety.*

Didn't you ever want to be anything, Kenneth?

KENNETH: I've never been able to keep my mind on it, Bert . . .
I shouldn't've cut a hole in me shoe.
Now the snow's slushin' in, and me feet's all wet.

BERT: If you studied, Kenneth, if you put your mind to something great, I know you'd be able to learn anything, because you're clever, you're much smarter than I am!

KENNETH: You've got something steady in your mind, Bert;
Something far away and steady.
I never could hold my mind on a far-away thing . . .

*His tone changes as though he were addressing a group of men; his manner is rougher, angrier, less careful of proprieties.*

She's not giving me the heat I'm entitled to.
Eleven dollars a week room and board,
And all she puts in the bag is a lousy pork sandwich,
The same every day and no surprises.
Is that right? Is that right now?
How's a man to live,
Freezing all day in this palace of dust
And night comes with one window and a bed
And the streets full of strangers
And not one of them's read a book through,

Or seen a poem from beginning to end
Or knows a song worth singing.
Oh, this is an ice-cold city, Mother,
And Roosevelt's not makin' it warmer, somehow.

*He sits on the table, holding his head.*

And here's another grand Monday!

*They are gradually appearing in natural light now, but it is a cold wintry light which has gradually supplanted the hot light of summer.* BERT *goes to the hook for a sweater.*

Jesus, me head'll murder me. I never had the headache till this year.

BERT (*delicately*): You're not taking up drinking, are you?

KENNETH (*he doesn't reply. Suddenly, as though to retrieve something slipping by, he gets to his feet, and roars out*):

"The Ship of State," by Walt Whitman!
"O Captain! my Captain! our fearful trip is done!
The ship has weathered every wrack,
The prize we sought is won . . ."

Now what in the world comes after that?

BERT: I don't know that poem.

KENNETH: Dammit all! I don't remember the bloody poems any more the way I did! It's the drinkin' does it, I think. I've got to stop the drinkin'!

BERT: Well, why do you drink, Kenny, if it makes you feel—

KENNETH: Good God, Bert, you can't always be doin' what you're better off to do! There's all kinds of unexpected turns, y'know, and things not workin' out the way they ought! What in hell *is* the next stanza of that poem? "The prize we sought is won . . ." God, I'd never believe I could forget that poem! I'm thinkin', Bert, y'know—maybe I ought to go onto the Civil Service. The only trouble is there's no jobs open except for the guard in the insane asylum. And that'd be a nervous place to work, I think.

BERT: It might be interesting, though.

KENNETH: I suppose it might. They tell me it's only the more intelligent people goes mad, y'know. But it's sixteen hundred a year, Bert, and I've a feelin' I'd never dare leave it, y'know? And I'm not ready for me last job yet, I think. I don't want nothin' to be the last, yet. Still and all . . .

RAYMOND *enters, going to toilet. He wears a blue button-up sweater.*

RAYMOND: Morning, boys. (*He impales a batch of orders on the desk.*)

KENNETH (*in a routine way*): Morning, Mr. Ryan. Have a nice New Year's, did you?

RAYMOND: Good enough (*To* BERT, *seeing the book on the table.*) Still reading that book?

BERT: Oh, I'm almost finished now.

RAYMOND *nods, continues on.* BERT *jumps off the table.*

Mr. Ryan? Can I see you a minute? (*He goes to* RAYMOND.) I wondered if you hired anybody yet, to take my place.

RAYMOND (*pleasantly surprised*): Why? Don't you have enough money to go?

BERT: No, I'm going. I just thought maybe I could help you break in the new boy. I won't be leaving till after lunch tomorrow.

RAYMOND (*with resentment, even an edge of sarcasm*): We'll break him in all right. Why don't you just get on to your own work? There's a lot of excelsior laying around the freight elevator.

RAYMOND *turns and goes into the toilet. For an instant* BERT *is left staring after him. Then he turns to* KENNETH, *perplexed.*

BERT: Is he sore at me?

KENNETH (*deprecatingly*): Ah, why would he be sore at you?

*He starts busying himself at the table, avoiding* BERT's *eyes.* BERT *moves toward him, halts.*

BERT: I hope you're not, are you?

KENNETH (*with an evasive air*): Me? Ha! Why, Bert, you've got the heartfelt good wishes of everybody in the place for your goin'-away!

*But he turns away to busy himself at the table—and on his line* LARRY *has entered with a container of coffee and a cigarette.*

BERT: Morning, Larry. (*He goes to the book, takes an order.*)

LARRY (*leaning against the table*): Jesus, it'd be just about perfect in here for penguins.

BERT *passes him.*

You actually leaving tomorrow?

BERT (*eagerly*): I guess so, yeah.

LARRY (*with a certain embarrassed envy*): Got all the dough, heh?

BERT: Well, for the first year anyway. (*He grins in embarrassment.*) You mind if I thank you?

LARRY: What for?

BERT: I don't know—just for teaching me everything. I'd have been fired the first month without you, Larry.

LARRY (*with some wonder, respect*): Got all your dough, heh?

BERT: Well, that's all I've been doing is saving.

*Enter* TOM KELLY. *He is bright, clean, sober.*

TOM: Morning!

KENNETH (*with an empty kind of heartiness*): Why, here comes Tommy Kelly!

TOM (*passing to hang up his coat and hat*): Ah, y're gettin' an awful long face to wash, Kenny, me bye.

KENNETH: Oh, cut it out with me face, Tommy. I'm as sick of it as you are.

TOM: Go on, ya donkey ya, they backed you off the boat.

KENNETH: Why, I'll tear you limb from limb, Tom Kelly!

*He mocks a fury, and* TOM *laughs as he is swung about. And then, with a quick hug and a laugh:*

Oh, Tommy, you're the first man I ever heard of done it. How'd you do it, Tom?

TOM: Will power, Kenny. (*He walks to his desk, sits.*) Just made up my mind, that's all.

KENNETH: Y'know the whole world is talking about you, Tom— the way you mixed all the drinks at the Christmas party and never weakened? Y'know, when I heard it was you going to mix the drinks I was prepared to light a candle for you.

TOM: I just wanted to see if I could do it, that's all. When I done that—mixin' the drinks for three hours, and givin' them away —I realized I made it. You don't look so hot to me, you know that?

KENNETH (*with a sigh*): Oh, I'm all right. It's the sight of Monday, that's all, is got me down.

TOM: You better get yourself a little will power, Kenny. I think you're gettin' a fine taste for the hard stuff.

KENNETH: Ah, no, I'll never be a drunk, Tommy.

TOM: You're a drunk now.

KENNETH: Oh, don't say that, please!

TOM: I'm tellin' you, I can see it comin' on you.

KENNETH (*deeply disturbed*): You can't either. Don't say that, Tommy!

AGNES *enters.*

AGNES: Morning! (*She wears sheets of brown paper for leggings.*)

KENNETH: Winter's surely here when Agnes is wearin' her leggins.

AGNES (*with her laughter*): Don't they look awful? But that draft under the switchboard is enough to kill ya.

LARRY: This place is just right for penguins.

AGNES: Haven't you got a heavier sweater, Bert? I'm surprised at your mother.

BERT: Oh, it's warm; she knitted it.

KENNETH: Bert's got the idea. Get yourself an education.

TOM: College guys are sellin' ties all over Macy's. Accountancy, Bert, that's my advice to you. You don't even have to go to college for it either.

BERT: Yeah, but I don't want to be an accountant.

TOM (*with a superior grin*): You don't want to be an accountant?

LARRY: What's so hot about an accountant?

TOM: Well, try runnin' a business without one. That's what you should've done, Larry. If you'd a took accountancy, you'd a—

LARRY: You know, Tommy, I'm beginning to like you better drunk?

TOMMY *laughs, beyond criticism.*

I mean it. Before, we only had to pick you up all the time; now you got opinions about everything.

TOM: Well, if I happen to know something, why shouldn't I say—

*Enter* RAYMOND *from the toilet.*

RAYMOND: What do you say we get on the ball early today, fellas? Eagle's coming today. Bert, how about gettin' those carburetor crates open, will ya?

BERT: I was just going to do that.

*BERT and RAYMOND are starting out, and AGNES is moving to
go, when GUS and JIM enter. Both of them are on the verge
of staggering. GUS has a bright new suit and checked overcoat, a new bowler, and new shoes. He is carrying upright a
pair of Ford fenders, still in their brown paper wrappings—
they stand about seven feet in height. JIM aids him in carefully resting the fenders against the wall.*

*KENNETH, AGNES, and LARRY watch in silence.*

*PATRICIA enters and watches. She is wearing leggins.*

*WILLY and JERRY enter in overcoats, all jazzed up.*

WILLY: Morning!

JERRY: Morn—

*Both break off and slowly remove their coats as they note
the scene and the mood. GUS, now that the fenders are safely
stacked, turns.*

GUS (*dimly*): Who's got a hanger?

KENNETH: Hanger? You mean a coat-hanger, Gus?

GUS: Coat-hanger.

JERRY: Here! Here's mine!

*He gives a wire hanger to GUS. GUS is aided by JIM in remov-
ing his overcoat, and they both hang it on the hanger, then
on a hook. Both give it a brush or two, and GUS goes to his
chair, sits. He raises his eyes to them all.*

GUS: So what everybody is looking at?

*BERT, WILLY, JERRY go to work, gradually going out with
orders. JIM also takes orders off the hook, and the pattern of
going-and-coming emerges. PATRICIA goes to the toilet. TOM
KELLY works at the desk.*

LARRY (*half-kidding, but in a careful tone*): What are you all
dressed up about?

*GUS simply glowers in his fumes and thoughts. RAYMOND goes
over to JIM.*

RAYMOND: What's he all dressed up for?

JIM: Oh, don't talk to me about him, Ray, I'm sick and tired of him. Spent all Saturday buyin' new clothes to go to the cemetery; then all the way the hell over to Long Island City to get these damned fenders for that old wreck of a Ford he's got. Never got to the cemetery, never got the fenders on—and we been walkin' around all weekend carryin' them damn things.

RAYMOND: Eagle'll be here this morning. See if you can get him upstairs. I don't want him to see him crocked again.

JIM: I'd just let him sit there, Ray, if I was you. I ain't goin' to touch him. You know what he went and done? Took all his insurance money outa the bank Saturday. Walkin' around with all that cash in his pocket—I tell ya, I ain't been to sleep since Friday night. 'Cause you can't let him loose with all that money and so low in his mind, y'know . . .

GUS: Irishman!

*All turn to him. He takes a wad out of his pocket, peels one bill off.*

Here. Buy new pair shoes.

KENNETH: Ah, thank you, no, Gus, I couldn't take that.

RAYMOND: Gus, Eagle's coming this morning; why don't you—

GUS (*stuffing a bill into* KENNETH'S *pocket*): Go buy pair shoes.

RAYMOND: Gus, he's going to be here right away; why don't you—

GUS: I don't give one goddam for Eagle! Why he don't make one more toilet?

RAYMOND: What?

BERT *enters with goods.*

GUS: Toilet! That's right? Have one toilet for so many people? That's very bad, Raymond. That's no nice. (*Offering* BERT *a bill*): Here, boy, go—buy book, buy candy.

LARRY *goes to* GUS *before he gives the bill, puts an arm around him, and walks away from the group.*

LARRY: Come on, Gussy, let me take you upstairs.

GUS: I don't care Eagle sees me, I got my money now, goddam. Oh, Larry, Larry, twenty-two year I workin' here.

LARRY: Why don't you give me the money, Gus? I'll put in the bank for you.

GUS: What for I put in bank? I'm sixty-eight years old, Larry. I got no children, nothing. What for I put in bank? (*Suddenly, reminded, he turns back to* RAYMOND, *pointing at the floor scale.*) Why them goddam mice nobody does nothing?

RAYMOND (*alarmed by* GUS's *incipient anger*): Gus, I want you to go upstairs!

PATRICIA *enters from toilet.*

GUS (*at the scale*): Twenty-two years them goddam mice! That's very bad, Raymond, so much mice! (*He starts rocking the scale.*) Look at them goddam mice!

PATRICIA *screams as mice come running out from under the scale. A mêlée of shouts begins, everyone dodging mice or swinging brooms and boxes at them.* RAYMOND *is pulling* GUS *away from the scale, yelling at him to stop it.* AGNES *rushes in and, seeing the mice, screams and rushes out.* JERRY *and* WILLY *rush in and join in chasing the mice, laughing.* PATRICIA, *wearing leggins, is helped onto the packing table by* LARRY, *and* GUS *shouts up at her.*

Come with me Atlantic City, Patricia! (*He pulls out the wad.*) Five thousand dollars I got for my wife!

PATRICIA: You rotten thing, you! You dirty rotten thing, Gus!

GUS: I make you happy, Patricia! I make you—

*Suddenly his hand goes to his head; he is dizzy.* LARRY *goes to him, takes one look.*

LARRY: Come, come on. (*He walks* GUS *into the toilet.*)

PATRICIA (*out of the momentary silence*): Oh, that louse! Did you see what he did, that louse? (*She gets down off the table, and, glancing angrily toward the toilet, she goes out.*)

RAYMOND: All right, fellas, what do you say, heh? Let's get going.

*Work proceeds—the going and coming.*

TOM (*as* RAYMOND *passes him*): I tried talking to him a couple of times, Ray, but he's got no will power! There's nothing you can do if there's no will power, y'know?

RAYMOND: Brother! It's a circus around here. Every Monday morning! I never saw anything like . . .

*He is gone.* KENNETH *is packing.* TOM *works at his desk.* JIM *comes and, leaving goods on the packing table, goes to the toilet, peeks in, then goes out, studying an order.* BERT *enters with goods.*

KENNETH: There's one thing you have to say for the Civil Service; it seals the fate and locks the door. A man needn't wonder what he'll do with his life any more.

*JERRY enters with goods.*

BERT (*glancing at the toilet door*): Gee, I never would've thought Gus liked his wife, would you?

*TOM, studying a letter, goes out.*

JERRY (*looking up and out the window*): Jesus!

BERT (*not attending to* JERRY): I thought he always hated his wife—

JERRY: Jesus, boy!

KENNETH (*to* JERRY): What're you doin'? What's—?

JERRY: Look at the girls up in there. One, two, three, four windows—full a girls, look at them! Them two is naked!

*WILLY enters with goods.*

KENNETH: Oh, my God!

WILLY (*rushing to the windows*): Where? Where?

KENNETH: Well, what're you gawkin' at them for!

GUS *and* LARRY *enter from the toilet.*

JERRY: There's another one down there! Look at her on the bed! What a beast!

WILLY (*overjoyed*): It's a cathouse! Gus! A whole cathouse moved in!

WILLY *and* JERRY *embrace and dance around wildly;* GUS *stands with* LARRY, *staring out, as does* BERT.

KENNETH: Aren't you ashamed of yourself!!

TOM *enters with his letter.*

TOM: Hey, fellas, Eagle's here.

JERRY (*pointing out*): There's a new cathouse, Tommy!

TOM *goes and looks out the windows.*

KENNETH: Oh, that's a terrible thing to be lookin' at, Tommy!

AGNES *enters;* KENNETH *instantly goes to her to get her out.*

Oh, Agnes, you'd best not be comin' back here any more now—

AGNES: What? What's the matter?

JERRY *has opened a window, and he and* WILLY *whistle sharply through their fingers.* AGNES *looks out.*

KENNETH: Don't, Agnes, don't look at that!

AGNES: Well, for heaven's sake! What are all those women doing there?

GUS: That's whorehouse, Aggie.

KENNETH: Gus, for God's sake! (*He walks away in pain.*)

AGNES: What are they sitting on the beds like that for?

TOM: The sun is pretty warm this morning—probably trying to get a little tan.

AGNES: Oh, my heavens. Oh, Bert, it's good you're leaving! (*She turns to them.*) You're not all going, are you?

GUS *starts to laugh, then* TOM, *then* JERRY *and* WILLY, *then* LARRY, *and she is unstrung and laughing herself, but shocked.*

Oh, my heavens!

*She is gone, as* JIM *enters with goods.*

KENNETH: All right, now, clear off, all of you. I can't be workin' with a lot of sex maniacs blockin' off me table!

GUS: Look, Jim!

JIM *looks out.*

JIM: Oh, nice.

JERRY: How about it, fellas? Let's all go lunchtime! What do you say, Kenny? I'll pay for you!

GUS *goes to the desk, drags the chair over to the window.*

KENNETH: I'd sooner roll meself around in the horse manure of the gutter!

JERRY: I betcha you wouldn't even know what to do!

KENNETH (*bristling, fists shut*): I'll show you what I do! I'll show you right now!

*Enter* RAYMOND, *furious.*

RAYMOND: What the hell is this? What's goin ʔ on here?

GUS (*sitting in his chair, facing the windows*): Whorehouse.

RAYMOND *looks out the windows.*

KENNETH: You'd better pass a word to Mr. Eagle about this, Raymond, or the corporation's done for. Poor Agnes, she's all mortified, y'know.

RAYMOND: Oh, my God! (*To all:*) All right, break it up, come on, break it up, Eagle's here.

WILLY, JERRY, BERT, *and* JIM *disperse, leaving with orders.* TOMMY *returns to the desk.*

What're you going to do, Gus? You going to sit there?

GUS *doesn't answer; sits staring out thoughtfully.*

What's going on with you? Gus! Eagle's here! All right, cook in your own juice. Sit there. (*He glances out the windows.*) Brother, I needed this now! (*He goes out angrily.*)

LARRY: Give me the money, Gus, come on. I'll hold it for you.

GUS (*an enormous sadness is on him*): Go way.

*Enter* PATRICIA. *She glances at* LARRY *and* GUS, *then looks out the windows.*

KENNETH (*wrapping*): Ah, Patricia, don't look out there. It's disgraceful.

TOM: It's only a lot of naked women.

KENNETH: Oh, Tommy, now! In front of a girl!

PATRICIA (*to* KENNETH): What's the matter? Didn't you ever see that before? (*She sees* GUS *sitting there.*) Look at Kong, will ya? (*She laughs.*) Rememberin' the old days, heh, Kong?

LARRY *is walking toward an exit at left.*

GUS: Oh, shatap!

PATRICIA (*catching up with* LARRY *at the edge of the stage, quietly*): What's Ray sayin' about you sellin' the Auburn?

LARRY: Yeah, I'm kinda fed up with it. It's out of my class anyway.

PATRICIA: That's too bad. I was just gettin' to enjoy it.

LARRY (*very doubtfully*): Yeah?

PATRICIA: What're you mad at me for?

LARRY: Why should I be mad?

PATRICIA: You're married, what're you—?

LARRY: Let me worry about that, will you?

PATRICIA: Well, I gotta worry about it too, don't I?

LARRY: Since when do you worry about anything, Pat?

PATRICIA: Well, what did you expect me to do? How did I know you were serious?

*GUS goes to his coat, searches in a pocket.*

LARRY: What did you think I was telling you all the time?

PATRICIA: Yeah, but Larry, anybody could say those kinda things.

LARRY: I know, Pat. But I never did. (*With a cool, hurt smile.*) You know, kid, you better start believing people when they tell you something. Or else you're liable to end up in there. (*He points out the windows.*)

PATRICIA (*with quiet fury*): You take that back!

*He walks away; she goes after him.*

You're going to take that back, Larry!

*EAGLE enters, nods to LARRY and PATRICIA.*

EAGLE: Morning.

PATRICIA (*with a mercurial change to sunny charm*): Good morning, Mr. Eagle!

*LARRY is gone, and she exits. EAGLE crosses, noticing GUS who is standing beside his coat, drinking out of a pint whiskey bottle.*

EAGLE: Morning, Gus.

GUS (*lowering the bottle*): Good morning.

*EAGLE exits into the toilet.*

TOM (*to GUS*): You gone nuts?

*GUS returns, holding the bottle, to his chair, where he sits, looking out the window. He is growing sodden and mean. BERT enters with goods.*

KENNETH (*sotto voce*): Eagle's in there, and look at him. He'll get the back of it now for sure.

TOM (*going to* GUS): Gimme the bottle, Gus!

GUS: I goin' go someplace, Tommy. I goin' go cemetery. I wasn't one time in cemetery. I go see my Lilly. My Lilly die, I was in Staten Island. All alone she was in the house. Ts!

*JERRY enters with goods, sees him, and laughs.*

BERT: Gus, why don't you give Tommy the bottle?

GUS: Twenty-two years I work here.

KENNETH (*to* JERRY, *who is staring out the window*): Will you quit hangin' around me table, please?

JERRY: Can't I look out the window?

*WILLY enters with goods.*

WILLY: How's all the little pussies?

KENNETH: Now cut that out!

*They laugh at him.*

TOM (*sotto voce*): Eagle's in there!

KENNETH: Is that all yiz know of the world—filthy women and dirty jokes and the ignorance drippin' off your faces?

*EAGLE enters from the toilet.*

There's got to be somethin' done about this, Mr. Eagle. It's an awful humiliation for the women here.

*He points, and EAGLE looks.*

I mean to say, it's a terrible disorganizing sight starin' a man in the face eight hours a day, sir.

EAGLE: Shouldn't have washed the windows, I guess. (*He glances down at* GUS *and his bottle and walks out.*)

KENNETH: Shouldn't have washed the windows, he says!

*They are laughing;* GUS *is tipping the bottle up.* JIM *enters with goods.*

JERRY: What a donkey that guy is!

> KENNETH *lunges for* JERRY *and grabs him by the tie, one fist ready.*

KENNETH: I'll donkey you!

> JERRY *starts a swing at him, and* BERT *and* TOM *rush to separate them as* RAYMOND *enters.*

RAYMOND: Hey! Hey!

JERRY (*as they part*): All right, donkey, I'll see you later.

KENNETH: You'll see me later, all right—with one eye closed!

RAYMOND: Cut it out!

> KENNETH, *muttering, returns to work at his table.* JERRY *rips an order off the hook and goes out.* WILLY *takes an order.* BERT *goes out with an order.* RAYMOND *has been looking down at* GUS, *who is sitting with the bottle.*

You going to work, Gus? Or you going to do that?

> GUS *gets up and goes to his coat, takes it off the hanger.*

What're you doing?

GUS: Come on, Jim, we go someplace. Here—put on you coat.

RAYMOND: Where you going? It's half-past nine in the morning.

> *Enter* AGNES.

AGNES: What's all the noise here? (*She breaks off, seeing* GUS *dressing.*)

GUS: That's when I wanna go—half-past nine. (*He hands* JIM *his coat.*) Here. Put on. Cold outside.

JIM (*quietly*): Maybe I better go with him, Ray. He's got all his money in—

> BERT *enters with goods.*

RAYMOND (*reasonably, deeply concerned*): Gus, now look; where you gonna go now? Why don't you lie down upstairs?

GUS (*swaying, to* BERT): Twenty-two years I was here.

BERT: I know, Gus.

LARRY *enters, watches.*

GUS: I was here before you was born I was here.

BERT: I know.

GUS: Them mice was here before you was born.

BERT *nods uncomfortably, full of sadness.*

When Mr. Eagle was in high school I was already here. When there was Winton Six I was here. When was Minerva car I was here. When was Stanley Steamer I was here, and Stearns Knight, and Marmon was good car; I was here all them times. I was here first day Raymond come; he was young boy; work hard be manager. When Agnes still think she was gonna get married I was here. When was Loco-mobile, and Model K Ford and Model N Ford—all them different Fords, and Franklin was good car, Jordan car, Reo car, Pierce Arrow, Cleveland car—all them was good cars. All them times I was here.

BERT: I know.

GUS: You don't know nothing. Come on, Jim.

*He goes and gets a fender.* JIM *gets the other.*

Button up you coat, cold outside. Tommy? Take care everything good.

*He walks out with* JIM *behind him, each carrying a fender upright.* RAYMOND *turns and goes out, then* LARRY. AGNES *goes into the toilet. The lights lower as this movement takes place, until* BERT *is alone in light, still staring at the point where* GUS *left.*

BERT: I don't understand;
     I don't know anything:
     How is it me that gets out?
     I don't know half the poems Kenneth does,
     Or a quarter of what Larry knows about an engine.

I don't understand how they come every morning,
Every morning and every morning,
And no end in sight.
That's the thing—there's no end!
Oh, there ought to be a statue in the park—
"To All the Ones That Stay."
One to Larry, to Agnes, Tom Kelly, Gus . . .

Gee, it's peculiar to leave a place—forever!
Still, I always hated coming here;
The same dried-up jokes, the dust;
Especially in spring, walking in from the sunshine,
Or any Monday morning in the hot days.

*In the darkness men appear and gather around the packing
table, eating lunch out of bags; we see them as ghostly
figures, silent.*

God, it's so peculiar to leave a place!
I know I'll remember them as long as I live,
As long as I live they'll never die,
And still I know that in a month or two
They'll forget my name, and mix me up
With another boy who worked here once,
And went. Gee, it's a mystery!

*As full light rises* BERT *moves into the group, begins eating
from a bag.*

JERRY (*looking out the window*): You know what's a funny
thing? It's a funny thing how you get used to that.

WILLY: Tommy, what would you say Cobb's average was for
lifetime?

TOM: Cobb? Lifetime?

*He thinks. Pause.* KENNETH *sings.*

KENNETH: "The minstrel boy to the war has gone—

PATRICIA *enters, crossing to toilet—*

In the ranks of death you will find him."

PATRICIA: Is that an Irish song?

KENNETH: All Irish here, and none of yiz knows an Irish song!

*She laughs, exits into the toilet.*

TOM: I'd say three-eighty lifetime for Ty Cobb. (*To* LARRY.) You're foolish sellin' that car with all the work you put in it.

LARRY: Well, it was one of those crazy ideas. Funny how you get an idea, and then suddenly you wake up and you look at it and it's like—dead or something. I can't afford a car.

*AGNES enters, going toward the toilet.*

AGNES: I think it's even colder today than yesterday.

*RAYMOND enters.*

RAYMOND: It's five after one, fellas; what do you say?

*They begin to get up as JIM enters in his overcoat and hat.*

KENNETH: Well! The old soldier returns!

RAYMOND: Where's Gus, Jim?

*AGNES has opened the toilet door as PATRICIA emerges.*

AGNES: Oh! You scared me. I didn't know you were in there!

JIM (*removing his coat*): He died, Ray.

RAYMOND: What?

*The news halts everyone—but one by one—in midair, as it were.*

LARRY: He what?

AGNES: What'd you say?

JIM: Gus died.

KENNETH: Gus died!

BERT: Gus?

AGNES (*going to* JIM): Oh, good heavens. When? What happened?

LARRY: What'd you have an accident?

JIM: No, we—we went home and got the fenders on all right, and he wanted to go over and start at the bottom, and go right up Third Avenue and hit the bars on both sides. And we got up to about Fourteenth Street, in around there, and we kinda lost track of the car someplace. I have to go back there tonight, see if I can find—

AGNES: Well, what happened?

JIM: Well, these girls got in the cab, y'know, and we seen a lot of places and all that—we was to some real high-class places, forty cents for a cup of coffee and all that; and then he put me in another cab, and we rode around a while; and then he got another cab to follow us. Case one of our cabs got a flat, see? He just didn't want to be held up for a minute, Gus didn't.

LARRY: Where were you going?

JIM: Oh, just all over. And we stopped for a light, y'know, and I thought I'd go up and see how he was gettin' along, y'know, and I open his cab door, and—the girl was fast asleep, see—and he—was dead. Right there in the seat. It was just gettin' to be morning.

AGNES: Oh, poor Gus!

JIM: I tell ya, Agnes, he didn't look too good to me since she died, the old lady. I never knowed it. He—liked that woman.

RAYMOND: Where's his money?

JIM: Oh—(*With a wasting wave of the hand.*)—it's gone, Ray. We was stoppin' off every couple minutes so he call long distance. I didn't even know it, he had a brother someplace in California. Called him half a dozen times. And there was somebody he was talkin' to in Texas someplace, somebody that was in the Navy with him. He was tryin' to call all the guys that was in the submarine with him, and he was callin' all over hell and gone—and givin' big tips, and he bought a new suit, and give the cab driver a wristwatch and all like that. I think he got himself too sweated. Y'know it got pretty cold last night, and he was all sweated up. I kept tellin' him, I says, "Gus," I says, "you're gettin' yourself all sweated, y'know, and it's a cold night," I says; and all he kept sayin' to me all night he says, "Jim," he says, "I'm gonna do it right, Jim." That's all he says practically all night. "I'm gonna do it right," he says. "I'm gonna do it right." (*Pause.* JIM *shakes his head.*) Oh, when I open that cab door I knowed it right away. I takes one look at him and I knowed it.

*There is a moment of silence, and* AGNES *turns and goes into the toilet.*

Oh, poor Agnes, I bet she's gonna cry now.

JIM *goes to the order hook, takes an order off, and, putting a cigar into his mouth, he goes out, studying the order.* RAYMOND *crosses and goes out; then* PATRICIA *goes.* WILLY *and* JERRY *exit in different directions with orders in their hands;* KENNETH *begins wrapping.* TOM *goes to his desk and sits, clasps his hands, and for a moment he prays.*

BERT *goes and gets his jacket. He slowly puts it on.*

*Enter* FRANK, *the truckdriver.*

FRANK: Anything for West Bronx, Tommy?

TOM: There's some stuff for Sullivan's there.

FRANK: Okay. (*He pokes through the packages, picks some.*)

KENNETH: Gus died.

FRANK: No kiddin'!

KENNETH: Ya, last night.

FRANK: What do you know. Hm. (*He goes on picking packages out.*) Is this all for West Bronx, Tom?

TOM: I guess so for now.

FRANK (*to* KENNETH): Died.

KENNETH: Yes, Jim was with him. Last night.

FRANK: Jesus. (*Pause. He stares, shakes his head.*) I'll take Brooklyn when I get back, Tommy.

*He goes out, loaded with packages.* BERT *is buttoning his overcoat.* AGNES *comes out of the toilet.*

BERT: Agnes?

AGNES (*seeing the coat on, the book in his hand*): Oh, you're leaving, Bert!

BERT: Yeah.

AGNES: Well. You're leaving.

BERT (*expectantly*): Yeah.

*PATRICIA enters.*

PATRICIA: Agnes? Your switchboard's ringing.

*JERRY enters with goods.*

AGNES: Okay!

*PATRICIA goes out.*

Well, good luck. I hope you pass everything.

BERT: Thanks, Aggie.

*She walks across and out, wiping a hair across her forehead.* WILLY *enters with goods as* JERRY *goes out.* JIM *enters with goods.*

*BERT seems about to say good-by to each of them, but they are engrossed and he doesn't quite want to start a scene with them; but now* JIM *is putting his goods on the table, so* BERT *goes over to him.*

I'm leaving, Jim, so—uh—

JIM: Oh, leavin'? Heh! Well, that's—

TOM (*from his place at the desk, offering an order to* JIM): Jim? See if these transmissions came in yet, will ya? This guy's been ordering them all month.

JIM: Sure, Tom.

JIM *goes out past* BERT, *studying his order.* BERT *glances at* KENNETH, *who is busy wrapping. He goes to* TOM, *who is working at the desk.*

BERT: Well, so long, Tommy.

TOM (*turning*): Oh, you goin', heh?

BERT: Yeah, I'm leavin' right now.

TOM: Well, keep up the will power, y'know. That's what does it.

BERT: Yeah. I—uh—I wanted to—

RAYMOND *enters.*

RAYMOND (*handing* TOM *an order*): Tommy, make this a special, will you? The guy's truck broke down in Peekskill. Send it out special today.

TOM: Right.

RAYMOND *turns to go out, sees* BERT, *who seems to expect some moment from him.*

RAYMOND: Oh! 'By, Bert.

BERT: So long, Raymond, I—

RAYMOND *is already on his way, and he is gone.* JIM *enters with goods.* BERT *goes over to* KENNETH *and touches his back.* KENNETH *turns to him.* JIM *goes out as* WILLY *enters with goods—*JERRY *too, and this work goes on without halt.*

Well, good-by, Kenny.

KENNETH (*he is embarrassed as he turns to* BERT): Well, it's our last look, I suppose, isn't it?

BERT: No, I'll come back sometime. I'll visit you.

KENNETH: Oh, not likely; it'll all be out of mind as soon as you turn the corner. I'll probably not be here anyway.

BERT: You made up your mind for Civil Service?

KENNETH: Well, you've got to keep movin', and—I'll move there, I guess. I done a shockin' thing last night, Bert; I knocked over a bar.

BERT: Knocked it over?

KENNETH: It's disgraceful, what I done. I'm standin' there, havin' a decent conversation, that's all, and before I know it I start rockin' the damned thing, and it toppled over and broke every glass in the place, and the beer spoutin' out of the pipes all over the floor. They took all me money; I'll be six weeks payin' them back. I'm for the Civil Service, I think; I'll get back to regular there I think.

BERT: Well—good luck, Kenny. (*Blushing.*) I hope you'll remember the poems again.

KENNETH (*as though they were unimportant*): No, they're gone, Bert. There's too much to do in this country for that kinda stuff.

WILLY *enters with goods.*

TOM: Hey, Willy, get this right away; it's a special for Peekskill.

WILLY: Okay.

WILLY *takes the order and goes, and when* BERT *turns back to* KENNETH *he is wrapping again. So* BERT *moves away from the table.* JERRY *enters, leaves; and* JIM *enters, drops goods on the table, and leaves.* LARRY *enters with a container of coffee, goes to the order hook, and checks through the orders.* BERT *goes to him.*

BERT: I'm goin', Larry.

LARRY (*over his shoulder*): Take it easy, kid.

PATRICIA *enters and crosses past* BERT, *looking out through the windows.* TOM *gets up and bumbles through a pile of goods on the table, checking against an order in his hand. It is as though* BERT *wished it could stop for a moment, and as each person enters he looks expectantly, but nothing much happens. And so he gradually moves—almost* is *moved— toward an exit, and with his book in his hand he leaves.*

*Now* KENNETH *turns and looks about, sees* BERT *is gone. He resumes his work and softly sings.*

KENNETH: "The minstrel boy to the war has gone!" Tommy, I'll be needin' more crayon before the day is out.

TOM (*without turning from the desk*): I'll get some for you.

KENNETH (*looking at a crayon, peeling it down to a nub*): Oh, the damn mice. But they've got to live too, I suppose. (*He marks a package and softly sings.*)

"... in the ranks of death you will find him.
His father's sword he has girded on,
And his wild harp slung behind him."

CURTAIN

# The Chairs

## A Tragic Farce

by Eugène Ionesco

Translated by
Donald M. Allen

OLD MAN, *aged 95*

OLD WOMAN, *aged 94*

THE ORATOR, *aged 45 to 50*

*And many other characters*

*Scene: Circular walls with a recess upstage center. A large, very sparsely furnished room. To the right, going upstage from the proscenium, three doors. Then a window with a stool in front of it; then another door. In the center of the back wall of the recess, a large double door, and two other doors facing each other and bracketing the main door: these last two doors, or at least one of them, are almost hidden from the audience. To the left, going upstage from the proscenium, there are three doors, a window with a stool in front of it, opposite the window on the right, then a blackboard and a dais. See the plan below. Downstage are two chairs, side by side. A gas lamp hangs from the ceiling.*

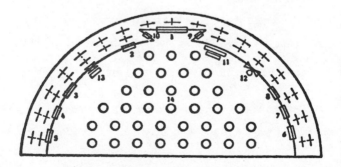

1: *Main double door.*
2, 3, 4, 5: *Side doors on the right.*
6, 7, 8: *Side doors on the left.*
9, 10: *Two doors hidden in the recess.*

> *11: Dais and blackboard.*
> *12, 13: Windows, with stools, left and right.*
> *14: Empty chairs.*
> *XXX Corridor, in wings.*

*The curtain rises. Half-light. The* OLD MAN *is up on the stool, leaning out the window on the left. The* OLD WOMAN *lights the gas lamp. Green light. She goes over to the* OLD MAN *and takes him by the sleeve.*

OLD WOMAN: Come my darling, close the window. There's a bad smell from that stagnant water, and besides the mosquitoes are coming in.

OLD MAN: Leave me alone!

OLD WOMAN: Come, come, my darling, come sit down. You shouldn't lean out, you might fall into the water. You know what happened to François I. You must be careful.

OLD MAN: Still more examples from history! Sweetheart, I'm tired of French history. I want to see—the boats on the water making blots in the sunlight.

OLD WOMAN: You can't see them, there's no sunlight, it's night-time, my darling.

OLD MAN: There are still shadows. (*He leans out very far.*)

OLD WOMAN (*pulling him in with all her strength*): Oh! . . . you're frightening me, my darling . . . come sit down, you won't be able to see them come, anyway. There's no use trying. It's dark . . .

*The* OLD MAN *reluctantly lets himself be pulled in.*

OLD MAN: I wanted to see—you know how much I love to see the water.

OLD WOMAN: How can you, my darling? . . . It makes me dizzy. Ah! this house, this island, I can't get used to it. Water all around us . . . water under the windows, stretching as far as the horizon.

*The* OLD WOMAN *drags the* OLD MAN *down and they move towards the two chairs downstage; the* OLD MAN *seats himself quite naturally on the lap of the* OLD WOMAN.

OLD MAN: It's six o'clock in the evening . . . it is dark already. It wasn't like this before. Surely you remember, there was still daylight at nine o'clock in the evening, at ten o'clock, at midnight.

OLD WOMAN: Come to think of it, that's very true. What a remarkable memory you have!

OLD MAN: Things have certainly changed.

OLD WOMAN: Why is that, do you think?

OLD MAN: I don't know, Semiramis, sweetheart . . . Perhaps it's because the further one goes, the deeper one sinks. It's because the earth keeps turning around, around, around, around . . .

OLD WOMAN: Around, around, my little pet. (*Silence.*) Ah! yes, you've certainly a fine intellect. You are very gifted, my darling. You could have been head president, head king, or even head doctor, or head general, if you had wanted to, if only you'd had a little ambition in life . . .

OLD MAN: What good would that have done us? We'd not have lived any better . . . and besides, we have a position here. I am a general, in any case, of the house, since I am the general factotum.

OLD WOMAN (*caressing the* OLD MAN *as one caresses a child*): My darling, my pet.

OLD MAN: I'm very bored.

OLD WOMAN: You were more cheerful when you were looking at the water . . . Let's amuse ourselves by making believe, the way you did the other evening.

OLD MAN: Make believe yourself, it's your turn.

OLD WOMAN: It's your turn.

OLD MAN: Your turn.

OLD WOMAN: Your turn.

OLD MAN: Your turn.

OLD WOMAN: Your turn.

OLD MAN: Drink your tea, Semiramis.

*Of course there is no tea.*

OLD WOMAN: Come on now, imitate the month of February.

OLD MAN: I don't like the months of the year.

OLD WOMAN: Those are the only ones we have, up till now. Come on, just to please me . . .

OLD MAN: All right, here's the month of February. (*He scratches his head like Stan Laurel.*)

OLD WOMAN (*laughing, applauding*): That's just right. Thank you, thank you, you're as cute as can be, my darling. (*She hugs him.*) Oh, you are so gifted, you could have been at least a head general, if you had wanted to . . .

OLD MAN: I am a general, general factotum. (*Silence.*)

OLD WOMAN: Tell me the story, you know *the* story: "Then at last we arrived . . ."

OLD MAN: Again? . . . I'm sick of it . . . "Then at last we arrived"? That again . . . you always ask for the same thing! . . . "Then at last we arrived . . ." But it's monotonous . . . For all of the seventy-five years that we've been married, every single evening, absolutely every blessed evening, you've made me tell the same story, you've made me imitate the same people, the same months . . . always the same . . . let's talk about something else . . .

OLD WOMAN: My darling, I'm not tired of it . . . it's your life, it fascinates me.

OLD MAN: You know it by heart.

OLD WOMAN: It's as if suddenly I'd forgotten everything . . . it's as though my mind were a clean slate every evening . . . Yes, my darling, I do it on purpose, I take a dose of salts . . . I become new again, for you, my darling, every evening . . . Come on, begin again, please.

OLD MAN: Well, if you want me to.

OLD WOMAN: Come on then, tell your story . . . It's also mine; what is yours is mine! Then at last we arrived . . .

OLD MAN: Then at last we arrived . . . my sweetheart . . .

OLD WOMAN: Then at last we arrived . . . my darling . . .

OLD MAN: Then at last we arrived at a big fence. We were soaked through, frozen to the bone, for hours, for days, for nights, for weeks . . .

OLD WOMAN: For months . . .

OLD MAN: . . . In the rain . . . Our ears, our feet, our knees, our noses, our teeth were chattering . . . that was eighty years ago . . . They wouldn't let us in . . . they might at least have opened the gate of the garden . . . (*Silence*.)

OLD WOMAN: In the garden the grass was wet.

OLD MAN: There was a path which led to a little square and in the center, a village church . . . Where was this village? Do you recall?

OLD WOMAN: No, my darling, I've forgotten.

OLD MAN: How did we reach it? Where is the road? This place was called Paris, I think . . .

OLD WOMAN: Paris never existed, my little one.

OLD MAN: That city must have existed because it collapsed . . . It was the city of light, but it has been extinguished, extinguished, for four hundred thousand years . . . Nothing remains of it today, except a song.

OLD WOMAN: A real song? That's odd. What song?

OLD MAN: A lullaby, an allegory: "Paris will always be Paris."

OLD WOMAN: And the way to it was through the garden? Was it far?

OLD MAN (*dreaming, lost*): The song? . . . the rain? . . .

OLD WOMAN: You are very gifted. If you had had a little ambition in life you could have been head king, head journalist, head comedian, head general . . . All that's gone down the drain, alas . . , down the old black drain . . . down the old drain, I tell you. (*Silence.*)

OLD MAN: Then at last we arrived . . .

OLD WOMAN: Ah! yes, go on . . . tell me . . .

OLD MAN (*while the* OLD WOMAN *begins to laugh softly, senilely, then progressively in great bursts, the* OLD MAN *laughs, too, as he continues*): Then at last we arrived, we laughed till we cried, the story was so idiotic . . . the idiot arrived full speed, bare-bellied, the idiot was pot-bellied . . . he arrived with a trunk chock full of rice; the rice spilled out on the ground . . . the idiot on the ground too, belly to ground . . . then at last we laughed, we laughed, we laughed, the idiotic belly, bare with rice on the ground, the trunk, the story of sick from rice belly to ground, bare-bellied, all with rice, at last we laughed, the idiot at last arrived all bare, we laughed . . .

OLD WOMAN (*laughing*): At last we laughed like idiots, at last arrived all bare, we laughed, the trunk, the trunk full of rice, the rice on the belly, on the ground . . .

OLD MAN AND OLD WOMAN (*laughing together*): At last we laughed. Ah! . . . laughed . . . arrived . . . arrived . . . Ah! . . . Ah! . . . rived . . . arrived . . . arrived . . . the idiotic bare belly . . . arrived with the rice . . . arrived with the rice . . . (*This is all we hear.*) At last we . . . bare-bellied . . . arrived . . . the trunk . . . (*Then the* OLD MAN *and* OLD WOMAN *calm down little by little.*) We lau . . . Ah! . . . aughed . . . Ah! . . . arrived . . . Ah! . . . arrived . . . aughed . . . aughed.

OLD WOMAN: So that's the way it was, your wonderful Paris.

OLD MAN: Who could put it better?

OLD WOMAN: Oh! my darling, you are so really fine. Oh! so really, you know, so really, so really, you could have been anything in life, a lot more than general factotum.

OLD MAN: Let's be modest . . . we should be content with the little . . .

OLD WOMAN: Perhaps you've spoiled your career?

OLD MAN (*weeping suddenly*): I've spoiled it? I've spilled it? Ah! where are you, Mamma, Mamma, where are you, Mamma? . . . hi, hi, hi, I'm an orphan. (*He moans.*) . . . an orphan, dworfan.

OLD WOMAN: Here I am, what are you afraid of?

OLD MAN: No, Semiramis, my sweetheart, you're not my mamma . . . orphan, dworfan, who will protect me?

OLD WOMAN: But I'm here, my darling!

OLD MAN: It's not the same thing . . . I want my mamma, na, you, you're not my mamma, you . . .

OLD WOMAN (*caressing him*): You're breaking my heart, don't cry, my little one.

OLD MAN: Hi, hi, let me go, hi, hi, I'm all spoiled, I'm wet all over, my career is spilled, it's spoiled.

OLD WOMAN: Calm down.

OLD MAN (*sobbing, his mouth wide open like a baby*): I'm an orphan . . . dworfan.

OLD WOMAN (*trying to console him by cajoling him*): My orphan, my darling, you're breaking my heart, my orphan.
*She rocks the* OLD MAN *who is sitting on her knees again.*

OLD MAN (*sobbing*): Hi, hi, hi! My mamma! Where is my mamma? I don't have a mamma anymore.

OLD WOMAN: I am your wife, I'm the one who is your mamma now.

OLD MAN (*giving in a little*): That's not true, I'm an orphan, hi, hi.

OLD WOMAN (*still rocking him*): My pet, my orphan, dworfan, worfan, morphan, orphan.

OLD MAN (*still sulky, but giving in more and more*): No . . . I don't wan't; I don't wa-a-a-ant.

OLD WOMAN (*crooning*): Orphan-ly, orhpan-lay, orphan-lo, orphan-loo.

OLD MAN: No-o-o . . . No-o-o.

OLD WOMAN (*same business*): Li lon lala, li lon la lay, orphan-ly, orphan-lay, relee-relay, orphan-li-relee-rela . . .

OLD MAN: Hi, hi, hi, hi. (*He sniffles, calming down little by little.*) Where is she? My mamma.

OLD WOMAN: In heavenly paradise . . . she hears you, she sees you, among the flowers; don't cry anymore, you will only make me weep!

OLD MAN: That's not even true-ue . . . she can't see me . . . she can't hear me. I'm an orphan, on earth, you're not my mamma . . .

OLD WOMAN (*he is almost calm*): Now, come on, calm down, don't get so upset . . . you have great qualities, my little general . . . dry your tears; the guests are sure to come this evening and they mustn't see you this way . . . all is not lost, all is not spoiled, you'll tell them everything, you will explain, you have a message . . . you always say you are going to deliver it . . . you must live, you have to struggle for your message . . .

OLD MAN: I have a message, that's God's truth, I struggle, a mission, I have something to say, a message to communicate to humanity, to mankind . . .

OLD WOMAN: To mankind, my darling, your message! . . .

OLD MAN: That's true, yes, it's true . . .

OLD WOMAN (*she wipes the* OLD MAN's *nose, dries his tears*): That's it . . . you're a man, a soldier, a general factotum . . .

OLD MAN (*he gets off the* OLD WOMAN's *lap and walks with short, agitated steps*): I'm not like other people, I have an ideal in life. I am perhaps gifted, as you say, I have some talent, but things aren't easy for me. I've served well in my capacity as general factotum, I've always been in command of the situation, honorably, that should be enough . . .

OLD WOMAN: Not for you, you're not like other people, you are much greater, and moreover you'd have done much better if you had got along with other people, like other people do. You've quarreled with all your friends, with all the directors, with all the generals, with your own brother.

OLD MAN: It's not my fault, Semiramis, you know very well what he said.

OLD WOMAN: What did he say?

OLD MAN: He said: "My friends, I've got a flea. I'm going to pay you a visit in the hope of leaving my flea with you."

OLD WOMAN: People say things like that, my dear. You shouldn't have paid any attention to it. But with Carel, why were you so angry with him. Was it his fault too?

OLD MAN: You're going to make me angry, you're going to make me angry. Na. Of course it was his fault. He came one evening, he said: "I know just the word that fits you. I'm not going to say it, I'll just think it." And he laughed like a fool.

OLD WOMAN: But he had a warm heart, my darling. In this life, you've got to be less sensitive.

OLD MAN: I don't care for jokes like that.

OLD WOMAN: You could have been head admiral, head cabinet-maker, head orchestra conductor.

*Long silence. They remain immobile for a time, completely rigid on their chairs.*

OLD MAN (*as in a dream*): At the end of the garden there was . . . there was . . . there was . . . there was . . . was what, my dear?

OLD WOMAN: The city of Paris!

OLD MAN: At the end, at the end of the end of the city of Paris, there was, there was, was what?

OLD WOMAN: My darling, was what, my darling, was who?

OLD MAN: The place and the weather were beautiful . . .

OLD WOMAN: The weather was so beautiful, are you sure?

OLD MAN: I don't recall the place . . .

OLD WOMAN: Don't tax your mind then . . .

OLD MAN: It's too far away, I can no longer . . . recall it . . . where was this?

OLD WOMAN: But what?

OLD MAN: What I . . . what I . . . where was this? And who?

OLD WOMAN: No matter where it is—I will follow you anywhere, I'll follow you, my darling.

OLD MAN: Ah! I have so much difficulty expressing myself . . . but I must tell it all.

OLD WOMAN: It's a sacred duty. You've no right to keep your message from the world. You must reveal it to mankind, they're waiting for it . . . the universe waits only for you.

OLD MAN: Yes, yes, I will speak.

OLD WOMAN: Have you really decided? You must.

OLD MAN: Drink your tea.

OLD WOMAN: You could have been head orator, if you'd had more will power in life . . . I'm proud, I'm happy that you have at last decided to speak to every country, to Europe, to every continent!

OLD MAN: Unfortunately, I have so much difficulty expressing myself, it isn't easy for me.

OLD WOMAN: It's easy once you begin, like life and death . . . it's enough to have your mind made up. It's in speaking that ideas come to us, words, and then we, in our own words, we find perhaps everything, the city too, the garden, and then we are orphans no longer.

OLD MAN: It's not I who's going to speak, I've hired a professional orator, he'll speak in my name, you'll see.

OLD WOMAN: Then, it really is for this evening? And have you invited everyone, all the characters, all the property owners, and all the intellectuals?

OLD MAN: Yes, all the owners and all the intellectuals. (*Silence.*)

OLD WOMAN: The janitors? the bishops? the chemists? the tin-smiths? the violinists? the delegates? the presidents? the police? the merchants? the buildings? the pen holders? the chromosomes?

OLD MAN: Yes, yes, and the post-office employees, the innkeepers, and the artists, everybody who is a little intellectual, a little proprietary!

OLD WOMAN: And the bankers?

OLD MAN: Yes, invited.

OLD WOMAN: The proletarians? the functionaries? the militaries? the revolutionaries? the reactionaries? the alienists and their alienated?

OLD MAN: Of course, all of them, all of them, all of them, since actually everyone is either intellectual or proprietary.

OLD WOMAN: Don't get upset, my darling, I don't mean to annoy you, you are so very absent-minded, like all great geniuses. This meeting is important, they must all be here this evening. Can you count on them? Have they promised?

OLD MAN: Drink your tea, Semiramis. (*Silence*).

OLD WOMAN: The papacy, the papayas, and the papers?

OLD MAN: I've invited them. (*Silence.*) I'm going to communicate the message to them . . . All my life, I've felt that I was suffocating; and now, they will know all, thanks to you and to the Orator, you are the only ones who have understood me.

OLD WOMAN: I'm so proud of you . . .

OLD MAN: The meeting will take place in a few minutes.

OLD WOMAN: It's true then, they're going to come, this evening?
You won't feel like crying any more, the intellectuals and
the proprietors will take the place of papas and mammas?
(*Silence.*) Couldn't you put off this meeting? It won't be
too tiring for us?

*More violent agitation. For several moments the* OLD MAN *has
been turning around the* OLD WOMAN *with the short, hesitant
steps of an old man or of a child. He takes a step or two
towards one of the doors, then returns and walks around her
again.*

OLD MAN: You really think this might tire us?

OLD WOMAN: You have a slight cold.

OLD MAN: How can I call it off?

OLD WOMAN: Invite them for another evening. You could telephone.

OLD MAN: No, my God, I can't do that, it's too late. They've
probably already embarked!

OLD WOMAN: You should have been more careful.

*We hear the sound of a boat gliding through the water.*

OLD MAN: I think someone is coming already . . .

*The gliding sound of a boat is heard more clearly . . . . .*

Yes, they're coming! . . .

*The* OLD WOMAN *gets up also and walks with a hobble.*

OLD WOMAN: Perhaps it's the Orator.

OLD MAN: He won't come so soon. This must be somebody else.

*We hear the doorbell ring.*

Ah!

OLD WOMAN: Ah!

*Nervously, the* OLD MAN *and the* OLD WOMAN *move towards the concealed door in the recess to the right. As they move upstage, they say:*

OLD MAN: Come on . . .

OLD WOMAN: My hair must look a sight . . . wait a moment . . .

*She arranges her hair and her dress as she hobbles along, pulling up her thick red stockings.*

OLD MAN: You should have gotten ready before . . . you had plenty of time.

OLD WOMAN: I'm so badly dressed . . . I'm wearing an old gown and it's all rumpled . . .

OLD MAN: All you had to do was to press it . . . hurry up! You're making our guests wait.

*The* OLD MAN, *followed by the* OLD WOMAN *still grumbling, reaches the door in the recess; we don't see them for a moment; we hear them open the door, then close it again after having shown someone in.*

VOICE OF OLD MAN: Good evening, madam, won't you please come in. We're delighted to see you. This is my wife.

VOICE OF OLD WOMAN: Good evening, madam, I am very happy to make your acquaintance. Take care, don't ruin your hat. You might take out the hatpin, that will be more comfortable. Oh! no, no one will sit on it.

VOICE OF OLD MAN: Put your fur down there. Let me help you. No, nothing will happen to it.

VOICE OF OLD WOMAN: Oh! what a pretty suit . . . and such darling colors in your blouse . . . Won't you have some cookies . . . Oh, you're not fat at all . . . no . . . plump . . . Just leave your umbrella there.

VOICE OF OLD MAN: Follow me, please.

OLD MAN (*back view*): I have only a modest position . . .

*The* OLD MAN *and* OLD WOMAN *re-enter together, leaving space between them for their guest. She is invisible. The* OLD MAN *and* OLD WOMAN *advance, downstage, facing the audience and speaking to the invisible* LADY, *who walks between them.*

OLD MAN (*to the invisible* LADY): You've had good weather?

OLD WOMAN (*to the* LADY): You're not too tired? . . . Yes, a little.

OLD MAN (*to the* LADY): At the edge of the water . . .

OLD WOMAN (*to the* LADY): It's kind of you to say so.

OLD MAN (*to the* LADY): Let me get you a chair.

    OLD MAN *goes to the left, he exits by door No. 6.*

OLD WOMAN (*to the* LADY): Take this one, for the moment, please. (*She indicates one of the two chairs and seats herself on the other, to the right of the invisible* LADY.) It seems rather warm in here, doesn't it? (*She smiles at the* LADY.) What a charming fan you have! My husband . . .

    *The* OLD MAN *re-enters through door No. 7, carrying a chair.*

. . . gave me one very like it, that must have been seventy-three years ago . . . and I still have it . . .

    *The* OLD MAN *places the chair to the left of the invisible* LADY.

. . . it was for my birthday! . . .

    *The* OLD MAN *sits on the chair that he has just brought onstage, so that the invisible* LADY *is between the old couple. The* OLD MAN *turns his face towards the* LADY, *smiles at her, nods his head, softly rubs his hands together, with the air of following what she says. The* OLD WOMAN *does the same business.*

OLD MAN: No, madam, life is never cheap.

OLD WOMAN (*to the* LADY): You are so right . . .

    *The* LADY *speaks.*

As you say, it is about time all that changed . . . (*Changing*

*her tone.*) Perhaps my husband can do something about it
. . . he's going to tell you about it.

OLD MAN (*to the* OLD WOMAN): Hush, hush, Semiramis, the time
hasn't come to talk about that yet. (*To the* LADY.) Excuse
me, madam, for having aroused your curiosity.

*The* LADY *reacts.*

Dear madam, don't insist . . .

*The* OLD MAN *and* OLD WOMAN *smile. They even laugh. They
appear to be very amused by the story the invisible* LADY
*tells them. A pause, a moment of silence in the conversation.
Their faces lose all expression.*

OLD MAN (*to the invisible* LADY): Yes, you're quite right . . .

OLD WOMAN: Yes, yes, yes . . . Oh! surely not.

OLD MAN: Yes, yes, yes. Not at all.

OLD WOMAN: Yes?

OLD MAN: No!?

OLD WOMAN: It's certainly true.

OLD MAN (*laughing*): It isn't possible.

OLD WOMAN (*laughing*): Oh! well. (*To the* OLD MAN.) She's
charming.

OLD MAN (*to the* OLD WOMAN): Madam has made a conquest.
(*To the invisible* LADY.) My congratulations! . . .

OLD WOMAN (*to the invisible* LADY): You're not like the young
people today . . .

OLD MAN (*bending over painfully in order to recover an invisible
object that the invisible* LADY *has dropped*): Let me . . . don't
disturb yourself . . . I'll get it . . . Oh! you're quicker than
I . . . (*He straightens up again.*)

OLD WOMAN (*to the* OLD MAN): She's younger than you!

OLD MAN (*to the invisible* LADY): Old age is a heavy burden. I can only wish you an eternal youth.

OLD WOMAN (*to the invisible* LADY): He's sincere, he speaks from the heart. (*To the* OLD MAN.) My darling!

*Several moments of silence. The* OLD MAN *and* OLD WOMAN, *heads turned in profile, look at the invisible* LADY, *smiling politely; they then turn their heads towards the audience, then look again at the invisible* LADY, *answering her smile with their smiles, and her questions with their replies.*

OLD WOMAN: It's very kind of you to take such an interest in us.

OLD MAN: We live a retired life.

OLD WOMAN: My husband's not really misanthropic, he just loves solitude.

OLD MAN: We have the radio, I get in some fishing, and then there's fairly regular boat service.

OLD WOMAN: On Sundays there are two boats in the morning, one in the evening, not to mention privately chartered trips.

OLD MAN (*to the invisible* LADY): When the weather's clear, there is a moon.

OLD WOMAN (*to the invisible* LADY): He's always concerned with his duties as general factotum . . . they keep him busy . . . On the other hand, at his age, he might very well take it easy.

OLD MAN (*to the invisible* LADY): I'll have plenty of time to take it easy in my grave.

OLD WOMAN (*to the* OLD MAN): Don't say that, my little darling . . . (*To the invisible* LADY.) Our family, what's left of it, my husband's friends, still came to see us, from time to time, ten years ago . . .

OLD MAN (*to the invisible* LADY): In the winter, a good book, beside the radiator, and the memories of a lifetime.

OLD WOMAN (*to the invisible* LADY): A modest life but a full one . . . he devotes two hours every day to work on his message.

*The doorbell rings. After a short pause, we hear the noise of a boat leaving.*

OLD WOMAN (*to the* OLD MAN): Someone has come. Go quickly.

OLD MAN (*to the invisible* LADY): Please excuse me, madam. Just a moment! (*To the* OLD WOMAN.) Hurry and bring some chairs!

*Loud ringing of the doorbell.*

OLD MAN (*hastening, all bent over, towards door No. 2 to the right, while the* OLD WOMAN *goes towards the concealed door on the left, hurrying with difficulty, hobbling along*): It must be someone important. (*He hurries, opens door No. 2, and the invisible* COLONEL *enters. Perhaps it would be useful for us to hear discreetly several trumpet notes, several phrases, like "Hail the Chief." When he opens the door and see the invisible* COLONEL, *the* OLD MAN *stiffens into a respectful position of attention.*) Ah! . . . Colonel! (*He lifts his hand vaguely towards his forehead, so as to roughly sketch a salute.*) Good evening, my dear Colonel . . . This is a very great honor for me . . . I . . . I . . . I was not expecting it . . . although . . . indeed . . . in short, I am most proud to welcome you, a hero of your eminence, into my humble dwelling . . . (*He presses the invisible hand that the invisible* COLONEL *gives him, bending forward ceremoniously, then straightening up again.*) Without false modesty, nevertheless, I permit myself to confess to you that I do not feel unworthy of the honor of your visit! Proud, yes . . . unworthy, no! . . .

*The* OLD WOMAN *appears with a chair, entering from the right.*

OLD WOMAN: Oh! What a handsome uniform! What beautiful medals! Who is it, my darling?

OLD MAN (*to the* OLD WOMAN): Can't you see that it's the Colonel?

OLD WOMAN (*to the* OLD MAN): Ah!

OLD MAN (*to the* OLD WOMAN): Count his stripes! (*To the* COLONEL.) This is my wife, Semiramis. (*To the* OLD WOMAN.) Come here so that I can introduce you to the Colonel. (*The* OLD WOMAN *approaches, dragging the chair by one hand, and makes a curtsey, without letting go of the chair. To the* COLONEL.) My wife. (*To the* OLD WOMAN.) The Colonel.

OLD WOMAN: How do you do, Colonel. Welcome. You're an old comrade of my husband's, he's a general . . .

OLD MAN (*annoyed*): factotum, factotum . . .

*The invisible* COLONEL *kisses the hand of the* OLD WOMAN. *This is apparent from the gesture she makes as she raises her hand toward his lips. Overcome with emotion, the* OLD WOMAN *lets go of the chair.*

OLD WOMAN: Oh! He's most polite . . . you can see that he's really superior, a superior being! . . . (*She takes hold of the chair again. To the* COLONEL.) This chair is for you . . .

OLD MAN (*to the invisible* COLONEL): This way, if you please . . . (*They move downstage, the* OLD WOMAN *dragging the chair. To the* COLONEL.) Yes, one guest has come already. We're expecting a great many more people! . . .

*The* OLD WOMAN *places the chair to the right.*

OLD WOMAN (*to the* COLONEL): Sit here, please.
*The* OLD MAN *introduces the two invisible guests to each other.*

OLD MAN: A young lady we know . . .

OLD WOMAN: A very dear friend . . .

OLD MAN (*same business*): The Colonel . . . a famous soldier.

OLD WOMAN (*indicating the chair she has just brought in to the* COLONEL): Do take this chair . . .

OLD MAN (*to the* OLD WOMAN): No, no, can't you see that the Colonel wishes to sit beside the Lady! . . .

*The* COLONEL *seats himself invisibly on the third chair from the left; the invisible* LADY *is supposedly sitting on the second chair; seated next to each other they engage in an inaudible conversation; the* OLD WOMAN *and* OLD MAN *continue to stand behind their chairs, on both sides of their invisible guests; the* OLD MAN *to the left of the* LADY, *the* OLD WOMAN *to the right of the* COLONEL.

OLD WOMAN (*listening to the conversation of the two guests*): Oh! Oh! That's going too far.

OLD MAN (*same business*): Perhaps. (*The* OLD MAN *and the* OLD WOMAN *make signs to each other over the heads of their guests while they follow the inaudible conversation which takes a turn that seems to displease them. Abruptly.*) Yes, Colonel, they are not here yet, but they'll be here. And the Orator will speak in my behalf, he will explain the meaning of my message . . . Take care, Colonel, this Lady's husband may arrive at any moment.

OLD WOMAN (*to the* OLD MAN): Who is this gentleman?

OLD MAN (*to the* OLD WOMAN): I've told you, it's the Colonel.

*Some embarrassing things take place, invisibly.*

OLD WOMAN (*to the* OLD MAN): I knew it. I knew it.

OLD MAN: Then why are you asking?

OLD WOMAN: For my information. Colonel, no cigarette butts on the floor!

OLD MAN (*to* COLONEL): Colonel, Colonel, it's slipped my mind—in the last war did you win or lose?

OLD WOMAN (*to the invisible* LADY): But my dear, don't let it happen!

OLD MAN: Look at me, look at me, do I look like a bad soldier? One time, Colonel, under fire . . .

OLD WOMAN: He's going too far! It's embarrassing! (*She seizes the invisible sleeve of the* COLONEL.) Listen to him! My darling, why don't you stop him!

OLD MAN (*continuing quickly*): And all on my own, I killed 209
of them; we called them that because they jumped so high to
escape, however there weren't so many of them as there were
flies; of course it is less amusing, Colonel, but thanks to my
strength of character, I have . . . Oh! no, I must, please.

OLD WOMAN (*to* COLONEL): My husband never lies; it may be true
that we are old, nevertheless we're respectable.

OLD MAN (*violently, to the* COLONEL): A hero must be a gentleman too, if he hopes to be a complete hero!

OLD WOMAN (*to the* COLONEL): I've known you for many years,
but I'd never have believed you were capable of this. (*To
the* LADY, *while we hear the sound of boats*.) I'd never have
believed him capable of this. We have our dignity, our self-
respect.

OLD MAN (*in a quavering voice*): I'm still capable of bearing arms.
(*Doorbell rings*.) Excuse me, I must go to the door. (*He
stumbles and knocks over the chair of the invisible* LADY.)
Oh! pardon.

OLD WOMAN (*rushing forward*): You didn't hurt yourself? (*The
OLD MAN and OLD WOMAN help the invisible LADY onto her
feet*.) You've got all dirty, there's some dust. (*She helps
brush the* LADY.)

*The doorbell rings again.*

OLD MAN: Forgive me, forgive me. (*To the* OLD WOMAN.) Go
bring a chair.

OLD WOMAN (*to the two invisible guests*): Excuse me for a moment.

*While the OLD MAN goes to open door No. 3, the OLD WOMAN
exits through door No. 5 to look for a chair, and she re-
enters by door No. 8.*

OLD MAN (*moving towards the door*): He was trying to get my
goat. I'm almost angry. (*He opens the door*.) Oh! madam,
you're here! I can scarcely believe my eyes, and yet, never-

theless . . . I didn't really dare to hope . . . really it's . . . Oh!
madam, madam . . . I have thought about you, all my life, all
my life, madam, they always called you La Belle . . . it's your
husband . . . someone told me, certainly . . . you haven't
changed a bit . . . Oh! yes, yes, your nose *has* grown longer,
maybe it's a little swollen . . . I didn't notice it when I first
saw you, but I see it now . . . a lot longer . . . ah! how unfortunate! You certainly didn't do it on purpose . . . how
did it happen? . . . little by little . . . excuse me, sir and dear
friend, you'll permit me to call you "dear friend," I knew
your wife long before you . . . she was the same, but with a
completely different nose . . . I congratulate you, sir, you
seem to love each other very much.

*The* OLD WOMAN *re-enters through door No. 8 with a chair.*
Semiramis, two guests have arrived, we need one more
chair . . .

*The* OLD WOMAN *puts the chair behind the four others, then
exits by door No. 8 and re-enters by door No. 5, after a few
moments, with another chair that she places beside the
one she has just brought in. By this time, the* OLD MAN *and
the two guests have moved near the* OLD WOMAN.

Come this way, please, more guests have arrived. I'm going
to introduce you . . . now then, madam . . . Oh! Belle, Belle,
Miss Belle, that's what they used to call you . . . now you're
all bent over . . . Oh! sir, she is still Belle to me, even so;
under her glasses, she still has pretty eyes; her hair is white,
but under the white one can see brown, and blue, I'm sure
of that . . . come nearer, nearer . . . what is this, sir, a gift,
for my wife? (*To the* OLD WOMAN, *who has just come on
with the chair.*) Semiramis, this is Belle, you know, Belle . . .
(*To the* COLONEL *and the invisible* LADY.) This is Miss, pardon, Mrs. Belle, don't smile . . . and her husband . . . (*To
the* OLD WOMAN.) A childhood friend, I've often spoken of
her to you . . . and her husband. (*Again to the* COLONEL *and
to the invisible* LADY.) And her husband . . .

OLD WOMAN (*making a little curtsey*): He certainly makes good introductions. He has fine manners. Good evening, madam, good evening, sir. (*She indicates the two first guests to the newly arrived couple.*) Our friends, yes . . .

OLD MAN (*to the* OLD WOMAN): He's brought you a present. (*The* OLD WOMAN *takes the present.*)

OLD WOMAN: Is it a flower, sir? or a cradle? a pear tree? or a crow?

OLD MAN (*to the* OLD WOMAN): No, no, can't you see that it's a painting?

OLD WOMAN: Oh! how pretty! Thank you, sir . . . (*To the invisible* LADY.) Would you like to see it, dear friend?

OLD MAN (*to the invisible* COLONEL): Would you like to see it?

OLD WOMAN (*to* BELLE's *husband*): Doctor, Doctor, I feel squeamish, I have hot flashes, I feel sick, I've aches and pains, I haven't any feeling in my feet, I've caught cold in my eyes, I've a cold in my fingers, I'm suffering from liver trouble, Doctor, Doctor! . . .

OLD MAN (*to the* OLD WOMAN): This gentleman is not a doctor, he's a photo-engraver.

OLD WOMAN (*to the first invisible* LADY): If you've finished looking at it, you might hang it up. (*To the* OLD MAN.) That doesn't matter, he's charming even so, he's dazzling. (*To the* PHOTO-ENGRAVER.) Without meaning to flatter you . . .

*The* OLD MAN *and the* OLD WOMAN *now move behind the chairs, close to each other, almost touching, but back to back; they talk: the* OLD MAN *to* BELLE, *the* OLD WOMAN *to the* PHOTO-ENGRAVER; *from time to time their replies, as shown by the way they turn their heads, are addressed to one or the other of the two first guests.*

OLD MAN (*to* BELLE): I am very touched . . . You're still the same, in spite of everything . . . I've loved you, a hundred years ago . . . But there's been such a change . . . No, you haven't changed a bit . . . I loved you, I love you . . .

OLD WOMAN (*to the* PHOTO-ENGRAVER): Oh! Sir, sir, sir . . .

OLD MAN (*to the* COLONEL): I'm in complete agreement with you on that point.

OLD WOMAN (*to the* PHOTO-ENGRAVER): Oh! certainly, sir, certainly, sir, certainly . . . (*To the first* LADY.) Thanks for hanging it up . . . Forgive me if I've inconvenienced you. *The light grows stronger. It should grow stronger and stronger as the invisible guests continue to arrive.*

OLD MAN (*almost whimpering to* BELLE): Where are the snows of yesteryear?

OLD WOMAN (*to the* PHOTO-ENGRAVER): Oh! Sir, sir, sir . . . Oh! sir . . .

OLD MAN (*pointing out the first* LADY *to* BELLE): She's a young friend . . . she's very sweet . . .

OLD WOMAN (*pointing the* COLONEL *out to the* PHOTO-ENGRAVER): Yes, he's a mounted staff colonel . . . a comrade of my husband . . . a subaltern, my husband's a general . . .

OLD MAN (*to* BELLE): Your ears were not always so pointed! . . . My Belle, do you remember?

OLD WOMAN (*to the* PHOTO-ENGRAVER, *simpering grotesquely; she develops this manner more and more in this scene; she shows her thick red stockings, raises her many petticoats, shows an underskirt full of holes, exposes her old breast; then, her hands on her hips, throws her head back, makes little erotic cries, projects her pelvis, her legs spread apart; she laughs like an old prostitute; this business, entirely different from her manner heretofore as well as from that she will have subsequently, and which must reveal the hidden personality of the* OLD WOMAN, *ceases abruptly*): So you think I'm too old for that, do you?

OLD MAN (*to* BELLE, *very romantically*): When we were young, the moon was a living star. Ah! yes, yes, if only we had dared, but we were only children. Wouldn't you like to recapture those bygone days . . . is it still possible? Is it still possible? Ah! no, no, it is no longer possible. Those days have flown away as fast as a train. Time has left the marks of his wheels on our skin. Do you believe surgeons can perform miracles? (*To the* COLONEL.) I am a soldier, and you too, we soldiers are always young, the generals are like gods . . . (*To* BELLE.) It ought to be that way . . . Alas! Alas! We have lost everything. We could have been so happy, I'm sure of it, we could have been, we could have been; perhaps the flowers are budding again beneath the snow! . . .

OLD WOMAN (*to* PHOTO-ENGRAVER): Flatterer! Rascal! Ah! Ah! I look younger than my years? You're a little savage! You're exciting.

OLD MAN (*to* BELLE): Will you be my Isolde and let me be your Tristan? Beauty is more than skin deep, it's in the heart . . . Do you understand? We could have had the pleasure of sharing, joy, beauty, eternity . . . an eternity . . . Why didn't we dare? We weren't brave enough . . . Everything is lost, lost, lost.

OLD WOMAN (*to* PHOTO-ENGRAVER): Oh no, Oh! no, Oh! la la, you give me the shivers. You too, are you ticklish? To tickle or be tickled? I'm a little embarrassed . . . (*She laughs.*) Do you like my petticoat? Or do you like this skirt better?

OLD MAN (*to* BELLE): A general factotum has a poor life!

OLD WOMAN (*turning her head towards the first invisible* LADY): In order to make crepes de Chine? A leaf of beef, an hour of flour, a little gastric sugar. (*To the* PHOTO-ENGRAVER.) You've got clever fingers, ah . . . all the sa-a-a-me! . . . Oh-oh-oh-oh.

OLD MAN (*to* BELLE): My worthy helpmeet, Semiramis, has taken the place of my mother. (*He turns towards the* COLONEL.) Colonel, as I've often observed to you, one must take the truth as one finds it. (*He turns back towards* BELLE.)

OLD WOMAN (*to* PHOTO-ENGRAVER): Do you really really believe that one could have children at any age? Any age children?

OLD MAN (*to* BELLE): It's this alone that has saved me: the inner life, peace of mind, austerity, my scientific investigations, philosophy, my message . . .

OLD WOMAN (*to* PHOTO-ENGRAVER): I've never yet betrayed my husband, the general . . . not so hard, you're going to make me fall . . . I'm only his poor mamma! (*She sobs.*) A great, great (*She pushes him back.*) great . . . mamma. My conscience causes these tears to flow. For me the branch of the apple tree is broken. Try to find somebody else. I no longer want to gather rosebuds . . .

OLD MAN (*to* BELLE): . . . All the preoccupations of a superior order . . .

*The* OLD MAN *and* OLD WOMAN *lead* BELLE *and the* PHOTO-ENGRAVER *up alongside the two other invisible guests, and seat them.*

OLD MAN *and* OLD WOMAN (*to the* PHOTO-ENGRAVER *and* BELLE): Sit down, please sit down.

*The* OLD MAN *and* OLD WOMAN *sit down too, he to the left, she to the right, with the four empty chairs between them. A long mute scene, punctuated at intervals with "no," "yes," "yes." The* OLD MAN *and* OLD WOMAN *listen to the conversation of the invisible guests.*

OLD WOMAN (*to the* PHOTO-ENGRAVER): We had one son . . . of course, he's still alive . . . he's gone away . . . it's a common story . . . or, rather, unusual . . . he abandoned his parents . . . he had a heart of gold . . . that was a long time ago . . . We loved him so much . . . he slammed the door . . . My husband and I tried to hold him back with all our might . . . he was seven years old, the age of reason, I called after him: "My son, my child, my son, my child." . . . He didn't even look back . . .

OLD MAN: Alas, no . . . no, we've never had a child . . . I'd hoped for a son . . . Semiramis, too . . . we did everything . . . and my poor Semiramis is so maternal, too. Perhaps it was better that way . . . As for me I was an ungrateful son myself . . . Ah! . . . grief, regret, remorse, that's all we have . . . that's all we have left . . .

OLD WOMAN: He said to me: "You kill birds! Why do you kill birds?" . . . But we don't kill birds . . . we've never harmed so much as a fly . . . His eyes were full of big tears. He wouldn't let us dry them. He wouldn't let me come near him. He said: "Yes, you kill all the birds, all the birds." . . . He showed us his little fists . . . "You're lying, you've betrayed me! The streets are full of dead birds, of dying baby birds." It's the song of the birds! . . . "No, it's their death rattle. The sky is red with blood." . . . No, my child, it's blue. He cried again: "You've betrayed me, I adored you, I believed you to be good . . . the streets are full of dead birds, you've torn out their eyes . . . Papa, mamma, you're wicked! . . . I refuse to stay with you." . . . I threw myself at his feet . . . His father was weeping. We couldn't hold him back. As he went we could still hear him calling: "It's you who are responsible" . . . What does that mean, "responsible?"

OLD MAN: I let my mother die all alone in a ditch. She called after me, moaning feebly: "My little child, my beloved son, don't leave me to die all alone . . . Stay with me. I don't have much time left." Don't worry, Mamma, I told her, I'll be back in a moment . . . I was in a hurry . . . I was going to the ball, to dance. I will be back in a minute. But when I returned, she was already dead, and they had buried her deep . . . I broke open the grave, I searched for her . . . I couldn't find her . . . I know, I know, sons, always, abandon their mothers, and they more or less kill their fathers . . . Life is like that . . . but I, I suffer from it . . . and the others, they don't . . .

OLD WOMAN: He cried: "Papa, Mamma, I'll never set eyes on you again."

OLD MAN: I suffer from it, yes, the others don't . . .

OLD WOMAN: Don't speak of him to my husband. He loved his parents so much. He never left them for a single moment.

He cared for them, coddled them . . . And they died in his arms, saying to him: "You have been a perfect son. God will be good to you."

OLD MAN: I can still see her stretched out in the ditch, she was holding lily of the valley in her hand, she cried: "Don't forget me, don't forget me" . . . her eyes were full of big tears, and she called me by my baby name: "Little Chick," she said, "Little Chick, don't leave me here all alone."

OLD WOMAN (*to the* PHOTO-ENGRAVER): He has never written to us. From time to time, a friend tells us that he's been seen here or there, that he is well, that he is a good husband . . .

OLD MAN (*to* BELLE): When I got back, she had been buried a long time. (*To the first invisible* LADY.) Oh, yes. Oh! yes, madam, we have a movie theatre in the house, a restaurant, bathrooms . . .

OLD WOMAN (*to the* COLONEL): Yes, Colonel, it is because he . . .

OLD MAN: Basically that's it.

*Desultory conversation, getting bogged down.*

OLD WOMAN: If only!

OLD MAN: Thus, I've not . . . I, it . . . certainly . . .

OLD WOMAN (*dislocated dialogue, exhaustion*): All in all.

OLD MAN: To ours and to theirs.

OLD WOMAN: So that.

OLD MAN: From me to him.

OLD WOMAN: Him, or her?

OLD MAN: Them.

OLD WOMAN: Curl-papers . . . After all.

OLD MAN: It's not that.

OLD WOMAN: Why?

OLD MAN: Yes.

OLD WOMAN: I.

OLD MAN: All in all.

OLD WOMAN: All in all.

OLD MAN (*to the first invisible* LADY): What was that, madam?

*A long silence, the* OLD MAN *and* OLD WOMAN *remain rigid on their chairs. Then the doorbell rings.*

OLD MAN (*with increasing nervousness*): Someone has come. People. Still more people.

OLD WOMAN: I thought I heard some boats.

OLD MAN: I'll go to the door. Go bring some chairs. Excuse me, gentlemen, ladies. (*He goes towards door No. 7.*)

OLD WOMAN (*to the invisible guests who have already arrived*): Get up for a moment, please. The Orator will be here soon. We must ready the room for the meeting. (*The* OLD WOMAN *arranges the chairs, turning their backs towards the audience.*) Lend me a hand, please. Thanks.

OLD MAN (*opening door No. 7*): Good evening, ladies, good evening, gentlemen. Please come in.

*The three or four invisible persons who have arrived are very tall, and the* OLD MAN *has to stand on his toes in order to shake hands with them. The* OLD WOMAN, *after placing the chairs as indicated above, goes over to the* OLD MAN.

OLD MAN (*making introductions*): My wife . . . Mr. . . . . Mrs. . . . my wife . . . Mr. . . . Mrs. . . . my wife . . .

OLD WOMAN: Who are all these people, my darling?

OLD MAN (*to* OLD WOMAN): Go find some chairs, dear.

OLD WOMAN: I can't do everything! . . .

*She exits, grumbling, by door No. 6 and re-enters by door No. 7, while the* OLD MAN, *with the newly arrived guests, moves downstage.*

OLD MAN: Don't drop your movie camera. (*More introductions.*) The Colonel . . . the Lady . . . Mrs. Belle . . . the Photo-engraver . . . These are the newspaper men, they have come to hear the Orator too, who should be here any minute now . . . Don't be impatient . . . You'll not be bored . . . all together now . . .

*The* OLD WOMAN *re-enters through door No. 7 with two chairs.*

Come along, bring the chairs more quickly . . . we're still short one.

*The* OLD WOMAN *goes to find another chair, still grumbling, exiting by door No. 3, and re-entering by door No. 8.*

OLD WOMAN: All right, and so . . . I'm doing as well as I can . . . I'm not a machine, you know . . . Who are all these people?

*She exits.*

OLD MAN: Sit down, sit down, the ladies with the ladies, and the gentlemen with the gentlemen, or vice versa, if you prefer . . . We don't have any more nice chairs . . . we have to make do with what we have . . . I'm sorry . . . take the one in the middle . . . does anyone need a fountain pen? Telephone Maillot, you'll get Monique . . . Claude is an angel. I don't have a radio . . . I take all the newspapers . . . that depends on a number of things; I manage these buildings, but I have no help . . . we have to economize . . . no interviews, please, for the moment . . . later, we'll see . . . you'll soon have a place to sit . . . what can she be doing?

*The* OLD WOMAN *enters by door No. 8 with a chair.*

Faster, Semiramis . . .

OLD WOMAN: I'm doing my best . . . Who are all these people?

OLD MAN: I'll explain it all to you later.

OLD WOMAN: And that woman? That woman, my darling?

OLD MAN: Don't get upset . . . (*To the* COLONEL.) Colonel, journalism is a profession too, like a fighting man's . . . (*To the* OLD WOMAN.) Take care of the ladies, my dear . . .

*The doorbell rings. The* OLD MAN *hurries towards door No. 8.*

Wait a moment . . . (*To the* OLD WOMAN.) Bring chairs!

OLD WOMAN: Gentlemen, ladies, excuse me . . .

*She exits by door No. 3, re-entering by door No. 2; the* OLD MAN *goes to open concealed door No. 9, and disappears at the moment the* OLD WOMAN *re-enters by door No. 2.*

OLD MAN (*out of sight*): Come in . . . come in . . . come in . . . come in . . . (*He reappears, leading in a number of invisible people, including one very small child he holds by the hand.*) One doesn't bring little children to a scientific lecture . . . the poor little thing is going to be bored . . . if he begins to cry or to peepee on the ladies' dresses, that'll be a fine state of affairs! (*He conducts them to stage center; the* OLD WOMAN *comes on with two chairs.*) I wish to introduce you to my wife, Semiramis; and these are their children.

OLD WOMAN: Ladies, gentlemen . . . Oh! aren't they sweet!

OLD MAN: That one is the smallest.

OLD WOMAN: Oh, he's so cute . . . so cute . . . so cute!

OLD MAN: Not enough chairs.

OLD WOMAN: Oh! dear, oh dear, oh dear . . .

*She exits, looking for another chair, using now door No. 2 as exit and door No. 3 on the right to re-enter.*

OLD MAN: Hold the little boy on your lap . . . The twins can sit together in the same chair. Be careful, they're not very strong . . . they go with the house, they belong to the landlord. Yes, my children, he'd make trouble for us, he's a bad man . . . he wants us to buy them from him, these worthless chairs.

*The* OLD WOMAN *returns as quickly as she can with a chair.*

You don't all know each other ... you're seeing each other
for the first time ... you knew each other by name ...
(*To the* OLD WOMAN.) Semiramis, help me make the introductions ...

OLD WOMAN:  Who are all these people? ... May I introduce
you, excuse me ... May I introduce you ... but who are
they?

OLD MAN:  May I introduce you ... Allow me to introduce you
... permit me to introduce you ... Mr., Mrs., Miss ...
Mr. ... Mrs. ... Mrs. ... Mr.

OLD WOMAN (*to* OLD MAN): Did you put on your sweater?
(*To the invisible guests.*) Mr., Mrs., Mr. ...

*Doorbell rings again.*

OLD MAN:  More people!

*Another ring of doorbell.*

OLD WOMAN:  More people!

*The doorbell rings again, then several more times, and more
times again; the* OLD MAN *is beside himself; the chairs,
turned towards the dais, with their backs to the audience,
form regular rows, each one longer as in a theatre; the* OLD
MAN *is winded, he mops his brow, goes from one door to
another, seats invisible people, while the* OLD WOMAN, *hobbling along, unable to move any faster, goes as rapidly as
she can, from one door to another, hunting for chairs and
carrying them in. There are now many invisible people on
stage; both the* OLD MAN *and* OLD WOMAN *take care not to
bump into people and to thread their way between the rows
of chairs. The movement could go like this: the* OLD MAN
*goes to door No. 4, the* OLD WOMAN *exits by door No. 3,
returns by door No. 2; the* OLD MAN *goes to open door No.
7, the* OLD WOMAN *exits by door No. 8, re-enters by door
No. 6 with chairs, etc., in this manner making their way
around the stage, using all the doors.*

OLD WOMAN: Beg pardon . . . excuse me . . . what . . . oh,
yes . . . beg pardon . . . excuse me . . .

OLD MAN: Gentlemen . . . come in . . . ladies . . . enter
. . . it is Mrs. . . . let me . . . yes . . .

OLD WOMAN (*with more chairs*): Oh dear . . . Oh dear . . .
there are too many . . . There really are too, too . . . too
many, oh dear, oh dear, oh dear . . .

*We hear from outside, louder and louder and approaching
nearer and nearer, the sounds of boats moving through the
water; all the noises come directly from the wings. The* OLD
WOMAN *and the* OLD MAN *continue the business outlined
above; they open the doors, they carry in chairs. The doorbell continues to ring.*

OLD MAN: This table is in our way. (*He moves a table, or
he sketches the business of moving it, without slowing down
his rhythm, aided by the* OLD WOMAN.) There's scarcely a
place left here, excuse us . . .

OLD WOMAN (*making a gesture of clearing the table, to the
OLD MAN*): Are you wearing your sweater?

*Doorbell rings.*

OLD MAN: More people! More chairs! More people! More
chairs! Come in, come in, ladies and gentlemen . . . Semiramis, faster . . . We'll give you a hand soon . . .

OLD WOMAN: Beg pardon . . . beg pardon . . . good evening,
Mrs. . . . Mrs. . . . Mr. . . . Mr. . . . yes, yes, the chairs . . .

*The doorbell rings louder and louder and we hear the
noises of boats striking the quay very close by, and more
and more frequently. The* OLD MAN *flounders among the
chairs; he has scarcely enough time to go from one door to
another, so rapidly do the ringings of the doorbell succeed
each other.*

OLD MAN: Yes, right away . . . are you wearing your sweater?
Yes, yes . . . immediately, patience, yes, yes . . . patience . . .

OLD WOMAN: Your sweater? My sweater? . . . Beg pardon, beg pardon.

OLD MAN: This way, ladies and gentlemen, I request you . . . I re you . . . pardon . . . quest . . . enter, enter . . . going to show . . . there, the seats . . . dear friend . . . not there . . . take care . . . you, my friend?

*Then a long moment without words. We hear waves, boats, the continuous ringing of the doorbell. The movement culminates in intensity at this point. The doors are now opening and shutting all together ceaselessly. Only the main door in the center of the recess remains closed. The OLD MAN and OLD WOMAN come and go, without saying a word, from one door to another; they appear to be gliding on roller skates. The OLD MAN receives the people, accompanies them, but doesn't take them very far, he only indicates seats to them after having taken one or two steps with them; he hasn't enough time. The OLD WOMAN carries in chairs. The OLD MAN and the OLD WOMAN meet each other and bump into each other, once or twice, without interrupting their rhythm. Then, the OLD MAN takes a position upstage center, and turns from left to right, from right to left, etc., towards all the doors and indicates the seats with his arms. His arms move very rapidly. Then, finally the OLD WOMAN stops, with a chair in one hand, which she places, takes up again, replaces, looks as though she, too, wants to go from one door to another, from right to left, from left to right, moving her head and neck very rapidly. This must not interrupt the rhythm; the OLD MAN and OLD WOMAN must still give the impression of not stopping, even while remaining almost in one place; their hands, their chests, their heads, their eyes are agitated, perhaps moving in little circles. Finally, there is a progressive slowing down of movement, at first slight: the ringings of the doorbell are less loud, less frequent; the doors open less and less rapidly; the gestures of the OLD MAN and OLD WOMAN slacken continuously. At the moment when the doors stop opening and closing altogether,*

*and the ringings cease to be heard, we have the impression
that the stage is packed with people.*

OLD MAN: I'm going to find a place for you . . . patience . . .
Semiramis, for the love of . . .

OLD WOMAN (*with a large gesture, her hands empty*): There
are no more chairs, my darling. (*Then, abruptly, she begins
to sell invisible programs in a full hall, with the doors
closed.*) Programs, get your programs here, the program of
the evening, buy your program!

OLD MAN: Relax, ladies and gentlemen, we'll take care of you
. . . Each in his turn, in the order of your arrival . . .
You'll have a seat. I'll take care of you.

OLD WOMAN: Buy your programs! Wait a moment, madam, I
cannot take care of everyone at the same time, I haven't
got thirty-three hands, you know, I'm not a cow . . . Mister,
please be kind enough to pass the program to the lady next
to you, thank you . . . my change, my change . . .

OLD MAN: I've told you that I'd find a place for you! Don't
get excited! Over here, it's over here, there take care . . . oh,
dear friend . . . dear friends . . .

OLD WOMAN: . . . Programs . . . get your grams . . . grams . . .

OLD MAN: Yes, my dear, she's over there, further down, she's
selling programs . . . no trade is unworthy . . . that's her . . .
do you see her? . . . you have a seat in the second row . . .
to the right . . . no, to the left . . . that's it! . . .

OLD WOMAN: . . . gram . . . gram . . . program . . . get your
program . . .

OLD MAN: What do you expect me to do? I'm doing my best!
(*To invisible seated people.*) Push over a little, if you will
please . . . there's still a little room, that will do for you,
won't it, Mrs. . . . come here. (*He mounts the dais, forced
by the pushing of the crowd.*) Ladies, gentlemen, please
excuse us, there are no more seats available . . .

OLD WOMAN (*who is now on the opposite side of the stage, across from the* OLD MAN, *between door No. 3 and the window*): Get your programs . . . who wants a program? Eskimo pies, caramels . . . fruit drops . . . (*Unable to move, the* OLD WOMAN, *hemmed in by the crowd, scatters her programs and candies anywhere, above the invisible heads.*) Here are some! There they are!

OLD MAN (*standing on the dais, very animated; he is jostled as he descends from the dais, remounts it, steps down again, hits someone in the face, is struck by an elbow, says*): Pardon . . . please excuse us . . . take care . . . (*Pushed, he staggers, has trouble regaining his equilibrium, clutches at shoulders.*)

OLD WOMAN: Why are there so many people? Programs, get your program here, Eskimo pies.

OLD MAN: Ladies, young ladies, gentlemen, a moment of silence, I beg you . . . silence . . . it's very important . . . those people who've no seats are asked to clear the aisles . . . that's it . . . don't stand between the chairs.

OLD WOMAN (*to the* OLD MAN, *almost screaming*): Who are all these people, my darling? What are they doing here?

OLD MAN: Clear the aisles, ladies and gentlemen. Those who do not have seats must, for the convenience of all, stand against the wall, there, along the right or the left . . . you'll be able to hear everything, you'll see everything, don't worry, you won't miss a thing, all seats are equally good!

*There is a great hullabaloo. Pushed by the crowd, the* OLD MAN *makes almost a complete turn around the stage and ends up at the window on the right, near to the stool. The* OLD WOMAN *makes the same movement in reverse, and ends up at the window on the left, near the stool there.*

OLD MAN (*making this movement*): Don't push, don't push.

OLD WOMAN (*same business*): Don't push, don't push.

OLD MAN (*same business*): Don't push, don't push.

OLD WOMAN (*same business*): Don't push, ladies and gentle-men, don't push.

OLD MAN (*same business*): Relax . . . take it easy . . . be quiet . . . what's going on here?

OLD WOMAN (*same business*): There's no need to act like savages, in any case.

*At last they reach their final positions. Each is near a win-dow. The* OLD MAN *to the left, by the window which is beside the dais. The* OLD WOMAN *on the right. They don't move from these positions until the end.*

OLD WOMAN (*calling to the* OLD MAN): My darling . . . I can't see you, anymore . . . where are you? Who are they? What do all these people want? Who is that man over there?

OLD MAN: Where are you? Where are you, Semiramis?

OLD WOMAN: My darling, where are you?

OLD MAN: Here, beside the window . . . Can you hear me?

OLD WOMAN: Yes, I hear your voice! . . . there are so many . . . but I can make out yours . . .

OLD MAN: And you, where are you?

OLD WOMAN: I'm beside the window too! . . . My dear, I'm frightened, there are too many people . . . we are very far from each other . . . at our age we have to be careful . . . we might get lost . . . We must stay close together, one never knows, my darling, my darling . . .

OLD MAN: Ah! . . . I just caught sight of you . . . Oh! . . . We'll find each other, never fear . . . I'm with friends. (*To the friends.*) I'm happy to shake your hands . . . But of course, I believe in progress, uninterrupted progress, with some jolts, nevertheless . . .

OLD WOMAN: That's fine, thanks . . . What foul weather! Yes, it's been nice! (*Aside.*) I'm afraid, even so . . . What am I doing here? . . . (*She screams.*) My darling, my dar-ling!

*The* OLD MAN *and* OLD WOMAN *individually speak to guests near them.*

OLD MAN: In order to prevent the exploitation of man by man, we need money, money, and still more money!

OLD WOMAN: My darling! (*Then, hemmed in by friends.*) Yes, my husband is here, he's organizing everything . . . over there . . . Oh! you'll never get there . . . you'd have to go across, he's with friends . . .

OLD MAN: Certainly not . . . as I've always said . . . pure logic does not exist . . . all we've got is an imitation.

OLD WOMAN: But you know, there are people who are happy. In the morning they eat breakfast on the plane, at noon they lunch in the pullman, and in the evening they dine aboard the liner. At night they sleep in the trucks that roll, roll, roll . . .

OLD MAN: Talk about the dignity of man! At least let's try to save face. Dignity is only skin deep.

OLD WOMAN: Don't slink away into the shadows . . . (*She bursts out laughing in conversation.*)

OLD MAN: Your compatriots ask of me.

OLD WOMAN: Certainly . . . tell me everything.

OLD MAN: I've invited you . . . in order to explain to you . . . that the individual and the person are one and the same.

OLD WOMAN: He has a borrowed look about him. He owes us a lot of money.

OLD MAN: I am not myself. I am another. I am the one in the other.

OLD WOMAN: My children, take care not to trust one another.

OLD MAN: Sometimes I awaken in the midst of absolute silence. It's a perfect circle. There's nothing lacking. But one must be careful, all the same. Its shape might disappear. There are holes through which it can escape.

OLD WOMAN: Ghosts, you know, phantoms, mere nothings . . . The duties my husband fulfills are very important, sublime.

OLD MAN: Excuse me . . . that's not at all my opinion! At the proper time, I'll communicate my views on this subject to you . . . I have nothing to say for the present! . . . We're waiting for the Orator, he'll tell you, he'll speak in my behalf, and explain everything that we hold most dear . . . he'll explain everything to you . . . when? . . . when the moment has come . . . the moment will come soon . . .

OLD WOMAN (*on her side to her friends*): The sooner, the better . . . That's understood . . . (*Aside.*) They're never going to leave us alone. Let them go, why don't they go? . . . My poor darling, where is he? I can't see him any more . . .

OLD MAN (*same business*): Don't be so impatient. You'll hear my message. In just a moment.

OLD WOMAN (*aside*): Ah! . . . I hear his voice! . . . (*To her friends.*) Do you know, my husband has never been understood. But at last his hour has come.

OLD MAN: Listen to me, I've had a rich experience of life. In all walks of life, at every level of thought . . . I'm not an egotist: humanity must profit by what I've learned.

OLD WOMAN: Ow! You stepped on my foot . . . I've got chilblains!

OLD MAN: I've perfected a real system. (*Aside.*) The Orator ought to be here. (*Aloud.*) I've suffered enormously.

OLD WOMAN: We have suffered so much. (*Aside.*) The Orator ought to be here. It's certainly time.

OLD MAN: Suffered much, learned much.

OLD WOMAN (*like an echo*): Suffered much, learned much.

OLD MAN: You'll see for yourselves, my system is perfect.

OLD WOMAN (*like an echo*): You'll see for yourselves, his system is perfect.

OLD MAN: If only my instructions are carried out.

OLD WOMAN (*echo*): If only his instructions are carried out.

OLD MAN: We'll save the world! . . .

OLD WOMAN (*echo*): Saving his own soul by saving the world! . . .

OLD MAN: One truth for all!

OLD WOMAN (*echo*): One truth for all!

OLD MAN: Follow me! . . .

OLD WOMAN (*echo*): Follow him! . . .

OLD MAN: For I have absolute certainty! . . .

OLD WOMAN (*echo*): He has absolute certainty!

OLD MAN: Never . . .

OLD WOMAN (*echo*): Ever and ever . . .

*Suddenly we hear noises in the wings, fanfares.*

OLD WOMAN: What's going on?

*The noises increase, then the main door opens wide, with a great crash; through the open door we see nothing but a very powerful light which floods onto the stage through the main door and the windows, which at the entrance of the* EMPEROR *are brightly lighted.*

OLD MAN: I don't know . . . I can scarcely believe . . . is it possible . . . but yes . . . but yes . . . incredible . . . and still it's true . . . yes . . . if . . . yes . . . it is the Emperor! His Majesty the Emperor!

*The light reaches its maximum intensity, through the open door and through the windows; but the light is cold, empty; more noises which cease abruptly.*

OLD MAN: Stand up! . . . It's His Majesty the Emperor! The Emperor in my house, in our house . . . Semiramis . . . do you realize what this means?

OLD WOMAN (*not understanding*): The Emperor . . . the Emperor? My darling! (*Then suddenly she understands.*) Ah, yes, the Emperor! Your Majesty! Your Majesty! (*She wildly makes countless grotesque curtsies.*) In our house! In our house!

OLD MAN (*weeping with emotion*): Your Majesty! . . . Oh! Your Majesty! . . . Your little, Your great Majesty! . . . Oh! what a sublime honor . . . it's all a marvelous dream.

OLD WOMAN (*like an echo*): A marvelous dream . . . arvelous . . .

OLD MAN (*to the invisible crowd*): Ladies, gentlemen, stand up, our beloved sovereign, the Emperor, is among us! Hurrah! Hurrah!

*He stands up on the stool; he stands on his toes in order to see the* EMPEROR; *the* OLD WOMAN *does the same on her side.*)

OLD WOMAN: Hurrah! Hurrah!

*Stamping of feet.*

OLD MAN: Your Majesty! . . . I'm over here! . . . Your Majesty! Can you hear me? Can you see me? Please tell His Majesty that I'm here! Your Majesty! Your Majesty!!! I'm here, your most faithful servant! . . .

OLD WOMAN (*still echoing*): Your most faithful servant, Your Majesty!

OLD MAN: Your servant, your slave, your dog, arf, arf, your dog, Your Majesty! . . .

OLD WOMAN (*barking loudly like a dog*): Arf . . . arf . . . arf . . .

OLD MAN (*wringing his hands*): Can you see me? . . . Answer, Sire! . . . Ah, I can see you, I've just caught sight of Your Majesty's august face . . . your divine forehead . . . I've seen you, yes, in spite of the screen of courtiers . . .

OLD WOMAN: In spite of the courtiers . . . we're here, Your Majesty!

OLD MAN: Your Majesty! Your Majesty! Ladies, gentlemen, don't

keep him—His Majesty standing . . . you see, Your Majesty,
I'm truly the only one who cares for you, for your health,
I'm the most faithful of all your subjects . . .

OLD WOMAN (*echoing*): Your Majesty's most faithful subjects!

OLD MAN: Let me through, now, ladies and gentlemen . . . how
can I make my way through such a crowd? . . . I must go to
present my most humble respects to His Majesty the
Emperor . . . let me pass . . .

OLD WOMAN (*echo*): Let him pass . . . let him pass . . . pass . . .
ass . . .

OLD MAN: Let me pass, please, let me pass. (*Desperate.*) Ah!
Will I ever be able to reach him?

OLD WOMAN (*echo*): Reach him . . . reach him . . .

OLD MAN: Nevertheless, my heart and my whole being are at his
feet, the crowd of courtiers surrounds him, ah! ah! they
want to prevent me from approaching him . . . They know
very well that . . . oh! I understand, I understand . . . Court
intrigues, I know all about it . . . They hope to separate me
from Your Majesty!

OLD WOMAN: Calm yourself, my darling . . . His Majesty sees
you, he's looking at you . . . His Majesty has given me a
wink . . . His Majesty is on our side! . . .

OLD MAN: They must give the Emperor the best seat . . . near the
dais . . . so that he can hear everything the Orator is going
to say.

OLD WOMAN (*hoisting herself up on the stool, on her toes, lifting
her chin as high as she can, in order to see better*): At last
they're taking care of the Emperor.

OLD MAN: Thank heaven for that! ( *To the* EMPEROR.) Sire . . .
Your Majesty may rely on him. It's my friend, it's my repre-
sentative who is at Your Majesty's side. (*On his toes, standing on the stool.*) Gentlemen, ladies, young ladies, little
children, I implore you.

OLD WOMAN (*echoing*): Plore . . . plore . . .

OLD MAN: . . . I want to see . . . move aside . . . I want . . . the celestial gaze, the noble face, the crown, the radiance of His Majesty . . . Sire, deign to turn your illustrious face in my direction, toward your humble servant . . . so humble . . . Oh! I caught sight of him clearly that time . . . I caught sight . . .

OLD WOMAN (*echo*): He caught sight that time . . . he caught sight . . . caught . . . sight . . .

OLD MAN: I'm at the height of joy . . . I've no more words to express my boundless gratitude . . . in my humble dwelling, Oh! Majesty! Oh! radiance! . . . here . . . here . . . in the dwelling where I am, true enough, a general . . . but within the hierarchy of your army, I'm only a simple general factotum . . .

OLD WOMAN (*echo*): General factotum . . .

OLD MAN: I'm proud of it . . . proud and humble, at the same time . . . as I should be . . . alas! certainly, I am a general, I might have been at the imperial court, I have only a little court here to take care of . . . Your Majesty . . . I . . . Your Majesty, I have difficulty expressing myself . . . I might have had . . . many things, not a few possessions if I'd known, if I'd wanted, if I . . . if we . . . Your Majesty, forgive my emotion . . .

OLD WOMAN: Speak in the third person!

OLD MAN (*sniveling*): May Your Majesty deign to forgive me! You are here at last . . . We had given up hope . . . you might not even have come . . . Oh! Savior, in my life, I have been humiliated . . .

OLD WOMAN (*echo, sobbing*): . . . miliated . . . miliated . . .

OLD MAN: I've suffered much in my life . . . I might have been something, if I could have been sure of the support of Your Majesty . . . I have no other support . . . if you hadn't come, everything would have been too late . . . you are, Sire, my last recourse . . .

OLD WOMAN (*echo*): Last recourse . . . Sire . . . ast recourse . . . ire . . . recourse . . .

OLD MAN: I've brought bad luck to my friends, to all those who have helped me . . . Lightning struck the hand which was held out toward me . . .

OLD WOMAN (*echo*): . . . hand that was held out . . . held out . . . out . . .

OLD MAN: They've always had good reasons for hating me, bad reasons for loving me . . .

OLD WOMAN: That's not true, my darling, not true. *I* love you, I'm your little mother . . .

OLD MAN: All my enemies have been rewarded and my friends have betrayed me . . .

OLD WOMAN (*echo*): Friends . . . betrayed . . . betrayed . . .

OLD MAN: They've treated me badly. They've persecuted me. If I complained, it was always they who were in the right . . . Sometimes I've tried to revenge myself . . . I was never able to, never able to revenge myself . . . I have too much pity . . . I refused to strike the enemy to the ground, I have always been too good.

OLD WOMAN (*echo*): He was too good, good, good, good, good . . .

OLD MAN: It is my pity that has defeated me.

OLD WOMAN (*echo*): My pity . . . pity . . . pity . . .

OLD MAN: But they never pitied me. I gave them a pin prick, and they repaid me with club blows, with knife blows, with cannon blows, they've crushed my bones . . .

OLD WOMAN (*echo*): . . . My bones . . . my bones . . . my bones . . .

OLD MAN: They've supplanted me, they've robbed me, they've assassinated me . . . I've been the collector of injustices, the lightning rod of catastrophes . . .

OLD WOMAN (*echo*): Lightning rod . . . catastrophe . . . lightning rod . . .

OLD MAN: In order to forget, Your Majesty, I wanted to go in for sports . . . for mountain climbing . . . they pulled my feet and made me slip . . . I wanted to climb stairways, they rotted the steps . . . I fell down . . . I wanted to travel, they refused me a passport . . . I wanted to cross the river, they burnt my bridges . . .

OLD WOMAN (*echo*): Burnt my bridges.

OLD MAN: I wanted to cross the Pyrenees, and there were no more Pyrenees.

OLD WOMAN (*echo*): No more Pyrenees . . . He could have been, he too, Your Majesty, like so many others, a head editor, a head actor, a head doctor, Your Majesty, a head king . . .

OLD MAN: Furthermore, no one has ever shown me due consideration . . . no one has ever sent me invitations . . . However, I, hear me, I say this to you, I alone could have saved humanity, who is so sick. Your Majesty realizes this as do I . . . or, at the least, I could have spared it the evils from which it has suffered so much this last quarter of a century, had I had the opportunity to communicate my message; I do not despair of saving it, there is still time, I have a plan . . . alas, I express myself with difficulty . . .

OLD WOMAN (*above the invisible heads*): The Orator will be here, he'll speak for you. His Majesty is here, thus you'll be heard, you've no reason to despair, you hold all the trumps, everything has changed, everything has changed . . .

OLD MAN: I hope Your Majesty will excuse me . . . I know you have many other worries . . . I've been humiliated . . . Ladies and gentlemen, move aside just a little bit, don't hide His Majesty's nose from me altogether, I want to see the diamonds of the imperial crown glittering . . . But if Your Majesty has deigned to come to our miserable home, it is because you have condescended to take into consideration my wretched self. What an extraordinary reward. Your Majesty, if corporeally I raise myself on my toes, this is not through pride, this is only in order to gaze upon you! . . . morally, I throw myself at your knees.

OLD WOMAN (*sobbing*): At your knees, Sire, we throw ourselves at your knees, at your feet, at your toes . . .

OLD MAN: I've had scabies. My employer fired me because I did not bow to his baby, to his horse. I've been kicked in the ass, but all this, Sire, no longer has any importance . . . since . . . since . . . Sir . . . Your Majesty . . . look . . . I am here . . . here . . .

OLD WOMAN (*echo*): Here . . . here . . . here . . . here . . . here . . . here . . .

OLD MAN: Since Your Majesty is here . . . since Your Majesty will take my message into consideration . . . But the Orator should be here . . . he's making His Majesty wait . . .

OLD WOMAN: If Your Majesty will forgive him. He's surely coming. He will be here in a moment. They've telephoned us.

OLD MAN: His Majesty is so kind. His Majesty wouldn't depart just like that, without having listened to everything, heard everything.

OLD WOMAN (*echo*): Heard everything . . . heard . . . listened to everything . . .

OLD MAN: It is he who will speak in my name . . . I, I cannot . . . I lack the talent . . . he has all the papers, all the documents . . .

OLD WOMAN (*echo*): He has all the documents . . .

OLD MAN: A little patience, Sire, I beg of you . . . he should be coming.

OLD WOMAN: He should be coming in a moment.

OLD MAN (*so that the* EMPEROR *will not grow impatient*): Your Majesty, hear me, a long time ago I had the revelation . . . I was forty years old . . . I say this also to you, ladies and gentlemen . . . one evening, after supper, as was our custom, before going to bed, I seated myself on my father's knees . . . my mustaches were longer than his and more pointed . . . I had more hair on my chest . . . my hair was graying already, but his was still brown . . . There were some guests, grownups, sitting at table, who began to laugh, laugh.

OLD WOMAN (*echo*): Laugh . . . laugh . . .

OLD MAN: I'm not joking, I told them, I love my papa very much. Someone replied: It is midnight, a child shouldn't stay up so late. If you don't go beddy-bye, then you're no longer a kid. But I'd still not have believed them if they hadn't addressed me as an adult.

OLD WOMAN (*echo*): An adult.

OLD MAN: Instead of as a child . . .

OLD WOMAN (*echo*): A child.

OLD MAN: Nevertheless, I thought to myself, I'm not married. Hence, I'm still a child. They married me off right then, expressly to prove the contrary to me . . . Fortunately, my wife has been both father and mother to me . . .

OLD WOMAN: The Orator should be here, Your Majesty . . .

OLD MAN: The Orator will come.

OLD WOMAN: He will come.

OLD MAN: He will come.

OLD WOMAN: He will come.

OLD MAN: He will come.

OLD WOMAN: He will come.

OLD MAN: He will come, he will come.

OLD WOMAN: He will come, he will come.

OLD MAN: He will come.

OLD WOMAN: He is coming.

OLD MAN: He is coming.

OLD WOMAN: He is coming, he is here.

OLD MAN: He is coming, he is here.

OLD WOMAN: He is coming, he is here.

OLD MAN AND OLD WOMAN: He is here . . .

OLD WOMAN: Here he is!

*Silence; all movement stops. Petrified, the two old people stare at door No. 5; this immobility lasts rather long—about thirty seconds; very slowly, very slowly the door opens wide, silently; then the* ORATOR *appears. He is a real person. He's a typical painter or poet of the nineteenth century; he wears a large black felt hat with a wide brim, loosely tied bow tie, artist's blouse, mustache and goatee, very histrionic in manner, conceited; just as the invisible people must be as real as possible, the* ORATOR *must appear unreal. He goes along the wall to the right, gliding, softly, to upstage center, in front of the main door, without turning his head to right or left; he passes close by the* OLD WOMAN *without appearing to notice her, not even when the* OLD WOMAN *touches his arm in order to assure herself that he exists. It is at this moment that the* OLD WOMAN *says: "Here he is!"*

OLD MAN: Here he is!

OLD WOMAN (*following the* ORATOR *with her eyes and continuing to stare at him*): It's really he, he exists. In flesh and blood.

OLD MAN (*following him with his eyes*): He exists. It's really he. This is not a dream!

OLD WOMAN: This is not a dream, I told you so.

*The* OLD MAN *clasps his hands, lifts his eyes to heaven; he exults silently. The* ORATOR, *having reached upstage center, lifts his hat, bends forward in silence, saluting the invisible* EMPEROR *with his hat with a Musketeer's flourish and somewhat like an automaton. At this moment.*

OLD MAN: Your Majesty . . . May I present to you, the Orator . . .

OLD WOMAN: It is he!

*Then the* ORATOR *puts his hat back on his head and mounts the dais from which he looks down on the invisible crowd on the stage and at the chairs; he freezes in a solemn pose.*

OLD MAN (*to the invisible crowd*): You may ask him for autographs.

*Automatically, silently, the* ORATOR *signs and distributes numberless autographs. The* OLD MAN *during this time lifts his eyes again to heaven, clasping his hands, and exultantly says.*

No man, in his lifetime, could hope for more . . .

OLD WOMAN (*echo*): No man could hope for more.

OLD MAN (*to the invisible crowd*): And now, with the permission of Your Majesty, I will address myself to all of you, ladies, young ladies, gentlemen, little children, dear colleagues, dear compatriots, Your Honor the President, dear comrades in arms . . .

OLD WOMAN (*echo*): And little children . . . dren . . . dren . . .

OLD MAN: I address myself to all of you, without distinction of age, sex, civil status, social rank, or business, to thank you, with all my heart.

OLD WOMAN (*echo*): To thank you . . .

OLD MAN: As well as the Orator . . . cordially, for having come in such large numbers . . . silence, gentlemen! . . .

OLD WOMAN (*echo*): . . . Silence, gentlemen . . .

OLD MAN: I address my thanks also to those who have made possible the meeting this evening, to the organizers . . .

OLD WOMAN: Bravo!

*Meanwhile, the* ORATOR *on the dais remains solemn, immobile, except for his hand, which signs autographs automatically.*

OLD MAN: To the owners of this building, to the architect, to the masons who were kind enough to erect these walls! . . .

OLD WOMAN (*echo*): . . . walls . . .

OLD MAN: To all those who've dug the foundations . . . Silence, ladies and gentlemen . . .

OLD WOMAN: . . . 'adies and gentlemen . . .

OLD MAN: Last but not least I address my warmest thanks to the cabinet-makers who have made these chairs on which you have been able to sit, to the master carpenter . . .

OLD WOMAN (*echo*): . . . penter . . .

OLD MAN: . . . Who made the armchair in which Your Majesty is sinking so softly, which does not prevent you, nevertheless, from maintaining a firm and manly attitude . . . Thanks again to all the technicians, machinists, electrocutioners . . .

OLD WOMAN (*echoing*): . . . cutioners . . . cutioners . . .

OLD MAN: . . . To the paper manufacturers and the printers, proofreaders, editors to whom we owe the programs, so charmingly decorated, to the universal solidarity of all men, thanks, thanks, to our country, to the State (*He turns toward where the* EMPEROR *is sitting.*) whose helm Your Majesty directs with the skill of a true pilot . . . thanks to the usher . . .

OLD WOMAN (*echo*): . . . usher . . . rusher . . .

OLD MAN (*pointing to the* OLD WOMAN): Hawker of Eskimo pies and programs . . .

OLD WOMAN (*echo*): . . . grams . . .

OLD MAN: . . . My wife, my helpmeet . . . Semiramis! . . .

OLD WOMAN (*echo*): . . . ife . . . meet . . . mis . . . (*Aside.*)
The darling, he never forgets to give me credit.

OLD MAN: Thanks to all those who have given me their precious
and expert, financial or moral support, thereby contributing
to the overwhelming success of this evening's gathering . . .
thanks again, thanks above all to our beloved sovereign, His
Majesty the Emperor . . .

OLD WOMAN (*echo*): . . . jesty the Emperor . . .

OLD MAN (*in a total silence*): . . . A little silence . . . Your
Majesty . . .

OLD WOMAN (*echo*): . . . jesty . . . jesty . . .

OLD MAN: Your Majesty, my wife and myself have nothing more
to ask of life. Our existence can come to an end in this
apotheosis . . . thanks be to heaven who has granted us such
long and peaceful years . . . My life has been filled to overflowing. My mission is accomplished. I will not have lived in
vain, since my message will be revealed to the world . . .
(*Gesture towards the* ORATOR, *who does not perceive it; the*
ORATOR *waves off requests for autographs, very dignified and
firm.*) To the world, or rather to what is left of it! (*Wide
gesture toward the invisible crowd.*) To you, ladies and gentlemen, and dear comrades, who are all that is left from
humanity, but with such leftovers one can still make a very
good soup . . . Orator, friend . . .

*The* ORATOR *looks in another direction.*

If I have been long unrecognized, underestimated by my
contemporaries, it is because it had to be . . .

*The* OLD WOMAN *sobs.*

What matters all that now when I am leaving to you, to you,
my dear Orator and friend

*The* ORATOR *rejects a new request for an autograph, then
takes an indifferent pose, looking in all directions.*

. . . the responsibility of radiating upon posterity the light of my mind . . . thus making known to the universe my philosophy. Neglect none of the details of my private life, some laughable, some painful or heartwarming, of my tastes, my amusing gluttony . . . tell everything . . . speak of my helpmeet . . .

*The* OLD WOMAN *redoubles her sobs.*

. . . of the way she prepared those marvelous little Turkish pies, of her potted rabbit à la Normandabbit . . . speak of Berry, my native province . . . I count on you, great master and Orator . . . as for me and my faithful helpmeet, after our long years of labor in behalf of the progress of humanity during which we fought the good fight, nothing remains for us but to withdraw . . . immediately, in order to make the supreme sacrifice which no one demands of us but which we will carry out even so . . .

OLD WOMAN (*sobbing*): Yes, yes, let's die in full glory . . . let's die in order to become a legend . . . At least, they'll name a street after us . . .

OLD MAN (*to* OLD WOMAN): O my faithful helpmeet! . . . you who have believed in me, unfailingly, during a whole century, who have never left me, never . . . alas, today, at this supreme moment, the crowd pitilessly separates us . . .

> Above all I had hoped
> that together we might lie
> with all our bones together
> within the selfsame skin
> within the same sepulchre
> and that the same worms
> might share our old flesh
> that we might rot together . . .

OLD WOMAN: . . . Rot together . . .

OLD MAN: Alas! . . . alas! . . .

OLD WOMAN: Alas! . . . alas! . . .

OLD MAN: . . . Our corpses will fall far from each other, and we will rot in an aquatic solitude . . . Don't pity us over much.

OLD WOMAN: What will be, will be!

OLD MAN: We shall not be forgotten. The eternal Emperor will remember us, always.

OLD WOMAN (*echo*): Always.

OLD MAN: We will leave some traces, for we are people and not cities.

OLD MAN AND OLD WOMAN (*together*): We will have a street named after us.

OLD MAN: Let us be united in time and in eternity, even if we are not together in space, as we were in adversity: let us die at the same moment . . . (*To the* ORATOR, *who is impassive, immobile.*) One last time . . . I place my trust in you . . . I count on you. You will tell all . . . bequeath my message . . . (*To the* EMPEROR.) If Your Majesty will excuse me . . . Farewell to all. Farewell, Semiramis.

OLD WOMAN: Farewell to all! . . . Farewell, my darling!

OLD MAN: Long live the Emperor!

*He throws confetti and paper streamers on the invisible* EMPEROR; *we hear fanfares; bright lights like fireworks.*

OLD WOMAN: Long live the Emperor!

*Confetti and streamers thrown in the direction of the* EM-PEROR, *then on the immobile and impassive* ORATOR, *and on the empty chairs.*

OLD MAN (*same business*): Long live the Emperor!

OLD WOMAN (*same business*): Long live the Emperor!
*The* OLD WOMAN *and* OLD MAN *at the same moment throw themselves out the windows, shouting "Long Live the Emperor." Sudden silence; no more fireworks; we hear an "Ah" from both sides of the stage, the sea-green noises of bodies falling into the water. The light coming through the main*

*door and the windows has disappeared; there remains only
a weak light as at the beginning of the play; the darkened
windows remain wide open, their curtains floating on the
wind.*

ORATOR (*he has remained immobile and impassive during the
scene of the double suicide, and now, after several moments,
he decides to speak. He faces the rows of empty chairs; he
makes the invisible crowd understand that he is deaf and
dumb; he makes the signs of a deafmute; desperate efforts
to make himself understood; then he coughs, groans, utters
the guttural sounds of a mute*): He, mme, mm, mm. Ju, gou,
hou, hou. Heu, heu, gu gou, gueue.

*Helpless, he lets his arms fall down alongside his body; sud-
denly, his face lights up, he has an idea, he turns toward
the blackboard, he takes a piece of chalk out of his pocket,
and writes, in large capitals:*

ANGELFOOD

*then:*

NNAA NNM NWNWNW V

*He turns around again, towards the invisible crowd on the
stage, and points with his finger to what he's written on the
blackboard.*

ORATOR: Mmm, Mmm, Gueue, Gou, Gu. Mmm, Mmm, Mmm,
Mmm.

*Then, not satisfied, with abrupt gestures he wipes out the
chalk letters, and replaces them with others, among which
we can make out, still in large capitals:*

ΛADIEU ΛDIEU ΛPΛ

*Again, the* ORATOR *turns around to face the crowd; he smiles,
questions, with an air of hoping that he's been understood,
of having said something; he indicates to the empty chairs
what he's just written. He remains immobile for a few
seconds, rather satisfied and a little solemn; but then, faced*

*with the absence of the hoped for reaction, little by little his smile disappears, his face darkens; he waits another moment; suddenly he bows petulantly, brusquely, descends from the dais; he goes toward the main door upstage center, gliding like a ghost; before exiting through this door, he bows ceremoniously again to the rows of empty chairs, to the invisible* EMPEROR. *The stage remains empty with only the chairs, the dais, the floor covered with streamers and confetti. The main door is wide open onto darkness.*

*We hear for the first time the human noises of the invisible crowd; these are bursts of laughter, murmurs, shh's, ironical coughs; weak at the beginning, these noises grow louder, then, again, progressively they become weaker. All this should last long enough for the audience—the real and visible audience—to leave with this ending firmly impressed on its mind. The curtain falls very slowly.*

CURTAIN *

*In the original production the curtain fell on the mumblings of the mute Orator. The blackboard was not used.*

# Other Grove Press Drama and Theater Paperbacks